WALTER H. SOKEL

The Writer in Extremis

Expressionism in Twentieth-Century German Literature

STANFORD UNIVERSITY PRESS
STANFORD, CALIFORNIA

Stanford University Press
Stanford, California
© 1959 by the Board of Trustees of the
Leland Stanford Junior University
Printed in the United States of America
Published with the assistance of the Ford Foundation
Original edition 1959
Reprinted 1968

The Writer in Extremis

Contents

Preface

THE FIRST VERSION OF THE PRESENT WORK WAS GREATLY AIDED BY THE sympathetic advice and encouragement of Professor André von Gronicka of Columbia University. Its final version owes its existence to the enthusiastic interest of Professor Fritz Stern of Columbia University and to the friendly, warm, and generous encouragement and excellent editorial suggestions of Mr. J. Christopher Herold of Stanford University Press. To both I wish to acknowledge my profound gratitude.

I also wish to acknowledge my gratitude to the Columbia University Council for Research in the Humanities for the generous award which made the completion of this work possible in a comparatively short time; to Professor James Gutmann of Columbia University for his friendly interest in the progress of this work from its original to its final version; to Professor Lionel Trilling of Columbia University for his warm praise of the original version of this book and his enthusiastic encouragement of further work on it; to Dr. Kurt Pinthus of Columbia University, who from his rich personal memories has furnished invaluable information on the movement of which he formed so central a part; to Dr. Hans Weil, formerly of the Johann Wolfgang von Goethe University in Frankfurt am Main, and Professor Edgar Lohner of New York University for conversations and discussions of cherished memory which stimulated the conception of several ideas developed in this work; and to Miss Aina Bergman for her faithful assistance in the preparation of the manuscript.

I also am indebted to the publishers who gave their kind permission to quote from the following works: T. S. Eliot, *Collected Poems 1909–1935*, copyright 1936, by Harcourt, Brace and Company, Inc.; *Selected Writings of Gerard de Nerval*, translated with a critical introduction by Geoffrey Wagner, published by Grove Press, Inc.; Thomas Mann, *Doctor Faustus*, translated by H. T. Lowe Porter, published by Alfred A. Knopf and Co.; *The Diaries of Franz Kafka 1910–1913*, edited by Max Brod, translated by Joseph Kresh, and *The Diaries of Franz Kafka, 1914–1923*, edited by Max Brod, translated by Martin Greenberg, with the co-operation of Hannah

Arendt, both published by Schocken Books, Inc., and to the editors of *The Germanic Review* and *Monatshefte* for their kind permission to incorporate portions of my articles "The Thorn of Socrates" and "The other Face of Expressionism" into this book.

W. H. S.

New York, March 31, 1959

The Writer in Extremis

Introduction

AROUND THE YEAR 1910 A FAR-REACHING REVOLUTION TOOK PLACE IN WESTERN
art and literature which was not unconnected to the contemporary revolutions in science. Between 1905 and 1910 Picasso and his associates developed
Cubism in painting while Apollinaire and Max Jacob started a "cubist"
poetry which Apollinaire later called Surrealism. In 1910 Marinetti wrote
his manifesto of Futurism. T. S. Eliot began his "Prufrock" in 1910, Joyce
his *Ulysses* in 1914. In 1913 Stravinsky's *Sacre du Printemps* threw its
Parisian audience into an uproar. Einstein's theory of special relativity had
appeared in 1905 and a few years earlier, in 1900, Freud published his *Interpretation of Dreams*. These men and others like them have revolutionized
our world and changed our concepts of the universe and of the self. World
War I with its aftermath was the political counterpart to this upheaval
which is only now settling into a new tradition—the modern tradition. Yet
shocking and upsetting as this "birth of the modern era" was for its contemporaries, it was not really new, but a culmination of developments
which characterized the whole nineteenth century and had its roots in even
earlier periods.

The term Expressionism designates one aspect of this modern revolution in art and literature, an aspect which between 1910 and 1925 came to
particular prominence in Germany. However, its principles transcend national boundaries and form an integral part of modern literature and art.
Expressionist principles inform O'Neill's *The Great God Brown;* Thorn-
ton Wilder's *Our Town* and *The Skin of Our Teeth;* the Nighttown episode in James Joyce's *Ulysses;* Elmer Rice's *The Adding Machine;* and a
number of works by Sean O'Casey, Tennessee Williams, Samuel Beckett,
Friedrich Dürrenmatt, and others. However, Expressionism also contains
many features that date it as a German phenomenon of the World War I
period.

As early as 1901 the term "Expressionism" was coined in France to
distinguish Matisse and other "Indépendents" from the preceding Impressionist painters. In Germany it was first applied to groups of painters in

Dresden, Berlin, and Munich who followed and developed the style of Van Gogh, Gauguin, and Munch. Soon the term also included the new poetry, drama, and narrative fiction, most of which was first published after 1910 by *avant-garde* periodicals like *Der Sturm, Die Aktion,* and *Die weissen Blätter,* and by progressive publishers like Kurt Wolff in Leipzig, who united many Expressionists in a series of books and pamphlets called *Der jüngste Tag (The Day of Judgment).* Yearbooks and anthologies likewise propagated Expressionism; most important among them was Kurt Pinthus' *Menschheitsdämmerung (Twilight of Mankind).* Its apocalyptic title was ambiguous because the German word *Dämmerung* can mean both "twilight" and "dawn." This particular ambiguity—reflecting extremes of pessimism and optimism—was to become a decisive characteristic of German Expressionism.

We must distinguish between Expressionism as a form of modern art and literature with forerunners in the Book of Revelation, Dante's *Inferno,* the paintings of Bosch, Grünewald, Rembrandt, Goya, and the poetry of Blake, and Expressionism as a peculiarly German phenomenon, which contains elements, notably the violent conflict between the generations, not to be found to the same extent in the experimental literature of other countries. The history of German literature since the 1770's has been marked by revolts of youthful poets and writers which aim not only at a new style in writing but at a new way of life as well. Expressionism is the last and most intense of these revolts. The crest of the Expressionist wave is always associated with the German revolutions of 1918 and 1919, and Expressionism was the target of Hitler's attacks upon "degenerate art" and "cultural bolshevism." On the other hand, the Nazis, members of the Expressionist generation themselves, transmuted the bizarre horror of Kafka's tales and Heym's visions into social reality. Hannah Arendt speaks of the "political expressionism" of totalitarian terror, and a Dutch investigator sees in Expressionist poetry "the shadow of nihilism" that was to thicken into the night of barbarism two decades later. Affinities between the Expressionist longing for the "total man" and the subsequent regime of the total state were pointed out as early as 1933. Günther Anders has accused Franz Kafka of subtle complicity in the creation of the totalitarian frame of mind, and Albert Camus has shed light on the connections between the sensibilities of literary "modernism" and the totalitarian imagination. The fact that Expressionism can be considered the antithesis (and principal cultural victim) of Nazism as well as its forerunner and kin indicates the complexity and inner range of this movement as well as its central position in the *Geistesgeschichte* of Central Europe. Thus Expressionism has a double interest for us. On the one hand, it is part of the great international movement of modernism in art and literature; on the other hand, it is a turbulent and vital chapter in the catastrophic history of modern Germany.

It follows from this double aspect of Expressionism that there could not be stylistic unity among the German Expressionists. Political Expressionists like Frank, Rubiner, and Toller put their message above everything else. Other Expressionists, such as Kafka, Trakl, Heym, Barlach, and Benn, put their art above everything else; they were true pioneers of modernist literature and made outstanding contributions to the international movement. Yet there were many Expressionists—Werfel, Otten, and Rubiner, for example—who hardly belonged to modernism. They merely injected revolutionary or ecstatic frenzy into basically conservative forms. Wolfgang Paulsen in his pioneering study on Expressionism, *Aktivismus und Expressionismus,* distinguished between political Activists and genuine Expressionists. But perhaps it would be even more appropriate to distinguish between Expressionists who contributed to the artistic success of the international modern movement (and there are Activists like Sternheim among them) and those who merely copied a few devices of modernism, but remained basically old-fashioned in their form.

Such very diverse foreign authors as Walt Whitman, Tolstoy, Dostoevski, Strindberg, and Rimbaud made the greatest impact on different Expressionists. However, poets like Werfel, deeply impressed with Walt Whitman's ecstatic humanitarianism, or Rubiner, worshiping Tolstoy's radical negation of esoteric art, hardly could have accepted Rimbaud's coldly "irresponsible" *Illuminations* which in turn deeply influenced the finest poets of early Expressionism, Heym and Trakl. Yet the example of Rimbaud shows that we cannot always draw a sharp line between artistic experiment and spiritual revolt. For the Expressionists, Rimbaud's experimental poetry merged with the legend of his life. Introduced to the Germans in 1907 in a mixture of mediocre translations and fabulous hagiography, Rimbaud became a symbol for the Expressionists. Although Rimbaud repudiated his poetry when he set out to Africa to become a trader, the Expressionists saw his art and life merged in a greater unity: existence as spiritual adventure and the violent rejection of the European establishment, first in its traditional poetry, then in its traditional way of life.

Beneath its stylistic diversity there is an underlying spiritual unity in Expressionism. Kurt Pinthus in the introduction to his anthology *Twilight of Mankind* calls the common element of Expressionist poets "the intensity and radicalism of feeling, world-view, expression, form." Titles like *Twilight of Mankind, Day of Judgment,* "World's End," "Demons of the

Cities," *Parricide,* and *Gas* reveal an apocalyptic extremity that gave Expressionism its distinctive note. Ludwig Meidner's paintings of tumbling cities and the Norwegian Munch's painting "The Cry," showing a scream of utter horror, correspond to Expressionist writing. Hermann Bahr, the Viennese critic, playwright, and essayist, singled out the shriek as the chief characteristic of Expressionism. Many Expressionists endeavored to give the same effect on the printed page that Munch achieved in his painting. Some writers expressed their feeling of gruesome urgency by monosyllabic outcries, furious hyperboles, and cannonades of exclamation points. Others, like Kafka with his calmly controlled nightmares or Kaiser with his dagger-thrust dialogues, expressed the same feeling with infinitely greater artistic effectiveness.

Expressionism as abstract form, as part of the modernist movement, and Expressionism as formless shriek arise from the same factor—subjectivism. This subjectivism in turn results from a peculiar social-cultural constellation endemic to Germany since the eighteenth century. Germany was the homeland both of "autonomous art," abstractness in the best sense, and of a tradition of rhetorical formlessness, abstractness in the worst sense. This double aspect of abstractness also underlies Expressionism, which is firmly rooted in certain German traditions even though it rebels against others. But abstractness also underlies the whole phenomenon of modernism.

The task of this study is to come to an understanding of Expressionism through an understanding of some of the philosophical assumptions underlying the practice of modern art and literature; the social situation in which these assumptions were first formulated; the primary formal tendency of Expressionism in relation to other modernist tendencies; and, above all, the social-personal problems or "the existential situation" of the Expressionists. Social and psychological factors must be considered in the history of literature as a dimension of the human spirit. The history of styles is not a history of chess moves in a vacuum. It is intimately related to the problems which creative men and women face and seek to circumvent or to solve. This is especially true in a movement like Expressionism in which, as we shall see, the creative artist's loss of certainty as to the justification of his art and his existence plays a prominent role.

Seeking to shed light on the complex and multi-faceted phenomenon of Expressionism, this study, it is hoped, will also contribute to a further understanding of the "modernist" artist and clarify some aspects of the social and cultural history of twentieth-century Germany.

PART ONE

The New Form

CHAPTER ONE

Pure Form
and Pure Formlessness

MODERN ART BREAKS WITH THE AGE-OLD ASSUMPTION FORMULATED BY ARISTOTLE that art is mimesis or the imitation of nature.[1] Of course, Aristotle's doctrine has been variously interpreted. For some it meant that art creates the illusion of life, to which end painters applied perspective and writers psychology. Others believed that art selects what is morally and aesthetically best in nature and man in order to educate the beholder and cause him to emulate great and noble models. Others again believed that art should dwell on the sordid and wretched in life to arouse an indignant public to reform. Instruction, the didactic in art, could easily be linked to mimesis, although they are not the same.

Opposed to mimesis, which is most appropriate to the plastic arts, is Plato's and Longinus' view that art originates in inspiration rather than in observation. The artist, particularly the poet, listens to his inner voice and vision and gives expression to what divinity has "breathed" into him. Truth here is not the sensory scene of nature, but something hidden to be revealed. As this kind of truth is spiritual, not tangible, the artist must find appropriate symbols for its revelation.

What then are the symbols that the poet uses to reveal his inner truth? How can he make the invisible apparent? The symbols are, of course, words—and shapes in the plastic arts; these words or shapes represent objects and parts of objects found in the natural world. If they are to express a spiritual reality they must be so combined as to allow the invisible spirit to shine through the visible material. The Book of Revelation, Dante's *Divine Comedy*, Bosch's paintings, show that the best way to do this is to

[1] In this discussion the term "modern" will not be used as synonymous with recent, but as designating certain qualities in recent art and literature which the public has found baffling, obscure, and radically divergent from the familiar European traditions of art and literature.

combine these natural objects in a meaningful and yet fantastic way. Dante uses metaphoric visualizations to present psychic and spiritual conditions. The twisted heads of the soothsayers in his *Inferno,* looking backward instead of forward; the oppressively heavy cloaks of the hypocrites gilded outside but leaden within; the shifting shapes of the thieves who cannot remain themselves but continuously exchange their shapes with serpents: all these are extended metaphors presenting in images the inner reality of the sin and, at the same time, the sinner's psychic condition.

In his use of metaphor Dante anticipates the fundamental method of Expressionism. However, Dante's fantastic images are included in a universal frame of reference, that of Catholic Christianity. Therefore, they are logically meaningful even if the frame of reference, the underlying doctrine, is not accepted intellectually. For the very existence of a universal scheme assumed by the author and understood (even if rejected) by the reader creates the context in which the fantastic image makes sense. The metamorphosis of the thief into a serpent is understandable if we know that the man is the soul of a sinner who suffers in hell for his crime on earth. The symbol belongs to a meaningful universe, a cosmos, and, therefore, to a meaningful universe of discourse. Dante interprets a doctrine. His interpretation is personal, but the doctrine is not.

The explicit or implicit existence of a cosmos separates Dante and all figurative Christian literature and art—and even the Romantics—from modernism and links them to mimesis. The metaphoric visualizations of modernism, on the other hand, are frequently suspended in a void like the two ladders in Rilke's fifth *Duino Elegy* which, suspended in space, are only supported by each other, a situation which beautifully symbolizes the attempt of modern art.

Both historically and epistemologically the theory of mimesis is connected with the belief in a cosmos. For Aristotle nature was a cosmos, i.e., it was form materialized in matter or matter shaped into form. God, pure Form, informs all of nature. In imitating nature the artist necessarily imitates forms since form is everywhere in nature. By the process of creation the artist performs what God performs by simply existing: he shapes matter into form. Literary Naturalism, even though it frequently rejects the belief in God, still accepts the existence of an external universe of which the self forms a part. Even the Romantics, though in many ways close to modernism, still believed in the ultimate union between man and nature. They still refused to accept the whole lesson of Kant, which spells inexorable estrangement between man and nature, a lesson that most moderns have learned by heart whether they have read Kant or not. The philosophical foundation of modernism, and indeed a good part of its program, are to be found in Kant.

Nature, for Kant, is not a given framework in which man has his place, but a construction which our mind imposes upon phenomena. Without the mind there would be no nature since there would be no quantitative formulations called laws of nature and, therefore, no ordered universe. It is we who connect phenomena through causality and relation. It is we who have to perceive phenomena in succession and call this subjective necessity time; it is we who have to perceive phenomena in location and call this subjective necessity space. But space and time are neither given facts nor empirical concepts. They constitute themselves in our perception. But they are not objective absolutes, existing outside ourselves. The source of phenomena is forever unknowable. The walls of our heads form external barriers between ourselves and the thing-in-itself.

The *Critique of Pure Reason* unmasks the world as the product of our mind and declares the supernatural unknowable. With these two blows Kant shatters the foundation for art as mimesis and art as revelation. For if nature as we know it does not exist outside our mind the imitation of nature becomes a rather dubious affair and subjectivism is fostered; if the supernatural is not accessible to man its revelation is impossible.[2] Thus the *Critique of Pure Reason* is more instrumental than is generally realized in bringing about the climate of modern art as well as that of modern science. Modern art abandons the illusion of three-dimensional space in favor of a freely constructed space, and deviation from the law of causality or probability does not prevent the artist from pursuing his particular design. Absolute art, i.e., art as utterly free creation or pure design, became theoretically conceivable after Kant's *Critique of Pure Reason*. But it was the *Critique of Judgment* which spelled out its momentous implications for art.

The artist's "arbitrary freedom to create according to his intentions" is the prime foundation of Kant's aesthetics. The artist's absolute sovereignty does not imply chaotic formlessness, but adherence to a form discovered or chosen by himself. Like Lessing and Herder, Kant expects genius to legislate its own laws. He emancipates the artist from all external shackles and nonartistic considerations. Faithfulness to nature, moral purpose, empirical truth, religious faith—all are considered irrelevant to art. The artist's self-chosen purpose and his freely imposed form for expressing his particular purpose are his only concerns. The work of art is a universe of its own. It is "another nature," not a copy of the sensory nor a revelation of a super-

---

[2] Cf. Kant's polemic against Swedenborg, who inspired the Romantics and French Symbolists, in *Träume eines Geistersehers*.

natural world. The artist is more than a discoverer of symbols and even a prophet of truth—he is the creator and legislator of a universe; and this universe of art is the only one in which man is completely free of the yoke of empirical necessity and the categorical imperative of moral law. Thus art assumed a far greater importance than it had possessed in earlier aesthetics. Both art as mimesis and art as revelation had been subservient to other realities, physical or spiritual, means to an end; for Kant art became an end in itself. And since it was the only realm in which man could be free it also became man's salvation. In art man became God, not by discovering or revealing Him, but by creating as a god creates. Art assumed the grandeur but also the burden of religion. Schiller, developing in his *Letters on the Aesthetic Education of Man* Kant's ideas with great acumen, celebrated the aesthetic state as the gate to the highest human perfection and so helped to originate that religion of art which we find in Wagner, French Symbolism, and modernism in general. But the two Kantian contributions most crucial for the development of modern aesthetics were the clear distinction between aesthetic and logical ideas and the concept of organism.

According to Kant, aesthetic ideas, i.e., the ideas forming a work of art, are very different from logical thought.

But, by an aesthetic idea I mean that representation of the imagination which induces much thought, yet without the possibility of any definite thought whatever, i.e., *concept*, being adequate to it, and which language, consequently, can never quite get on level terms with or render completely intelligible. It is easily seen that an aesthetic idea is the counterpart of a *rational idea,* which, conversely, is a concept to which no *intuition* (representation of the imagination) can be adequate.[3]

The fundamental importance of this passage for the understanding of modern art and literature can never be overstated. Anticipating I. A. Richards' distinction between scientific and emotive language, Kant here pronounces the divorce not only between art and logical discourse, but also between art and empirical experience, from which logic abstracts its concepts. This divorce underlies the practice of modern art and causes its baffling quality.

Logical concepts, as Kant had stated in his *Critique of Pure Reason,* are abstracted from empirical experience. The language of science, for instance, is simply the most precise and concise way of communicating meaningful statements about facts. It differs only in degree from everyday speech in so far as everyday speech aims to convey factual information. But, based as it is on the observation of external facts, the language of logic cannot

[3] Kant, *Critique of Aesthetic Judgment,* tr. by James Creed Meredith, pp. 175–76.

cope with inner experience. The basic principle of logic and empirical experience, which tells us that an object cannot be in more than one place at one time, does not apply to our feelings. Our emotional experience is more complex than our factual experience. In our inner life we can visualize objects existing in several different places and in several states or conditions simultaneously. Meeting a beggar, we might see in him the millionaire he once was or might have been, or the revolutionary leader he might be tomorrow. In our inner life we can love and hate the same object simultaneously or see the snake in the thief or a beautiful girl in a rose. Art is the language to express this metalogical reality.

If art is to do justice to its peculiar function, it has to use a language quite different from the language with which we convey factual information. It must be a language of connotations. In music this has always been recognized or at least tacitly assumed. But literature uses the same units of discourse as conceptual or factual language. Factual reports use the very words poetry uses although two distinct languages are involved. Kant defined the distinction between them and thus emancipated literature from the illusion that it must represent empirical or moral truth, and obey the rules of logical discourse, which were designed for a very different purpose.

Kant recognized the metaphor as "the aesthetic attribute" of language and contrasted it to the "logical attributes" of conceptual speech. The metaphor corresponds to the chord of music or the color shade of painting. It is the primary means of transforming literature from a language of logical ideas into a language of aesthetic ideas. Kant defines the function of "aesthetic attributes" the following way:

They do not, like *logical attributes*, represent what lies in our concepts . . . but rather something else—something that gives the imagination an incentive to spread its flight over a whole host of kindred ideas that provoke more thought than admits of expression in a verbal concept. They furnish an *aesthetic idea*, which serves the . . . rational idea as a substitute for logical presentation, but *with the proper function of animating the mind* by opening out for it limitless vistas of kindred ideas.[4]

Aesthetic discourse, according to this passage, differs from logical discourse above all in basic purpose. Its purpose is neither to inform nor to reform us, neither to teach nor to preach, not even to uplift us by the sight of pure

[4] Pp. 177–78. Last italics mine. I have made slight changes in Mr. Meredith's translation. I have rendered the German term "Vorstellung" by "idea," instead of using Mr. Meredith's term "representation," to make Kant's meaning clearer to the nonprofessional reader. My precedent has been the famous translation of Schopenhauer's work as *The World as Will and Idea* (rather than *The World as Will and Representation*). I also changed Meredith's "a prospect into a field of kindred representations stretching beyond its ken" into "limitless vistas of kindred ideas."

beauty. Its only purpose is to stimulate our inner life by producing unexpected associations. The aesthetic attribute broadens the range of our thoughts and feelings, quickens their flow, accelerates our psychic metabolism. It acts as a spiritual tonic.

With his concept of "the aesthetic attribute," Kant anticipates Mallarmé's distinction between the two aspects of words, "la parole immédiate" and "la parole essentielle." "La parole immédiate" is the word as an abstract concept, a practical sign to orient us in the business of living; by it we receive vital information and give it to others. "La parole essentielle" is the same word as an aesthetic phenomenon, an instrument to produce emotional effects and conjure up strange worlds, forgotten continents of our mind. It is more than a spiritual tonic; it is magic.

From Mallarmé's distinction it is only one step to Kafka's definition of art. "Art reveals a reality which surpasses our conceptual ability."[5] Thus the road from Kant's *Critique of Judgment* leads to the very heart of modernism. And indeed Kafka's tales seem to be written about the unknowable thing-in-itself and man's futile struggle to break out of the prison of his head into a reality that he can never know. We remember, too, that the reading of Kant's *Critique of Pure Reason* was the most shattering and decisive experience for Kafka's stylistic predecessor, the displaced Romantic Heinrich von Kleist.

The concept of organism was the common property of German Idealism; it was developed not only by Kant, but also by Goethe and Herder, and found a brilliant application to art in Schiller's *Letters on the Aesthetic Education of Man*. Schiller saw the work of art as similar to the organism. The functional relationship of all its parts, and not its theme or subject, expresses its meaning. The idea of a work of art cannot lie in any one of its parts, but only in the structure or form of the whole. The idea of a drama, for instance, is to be found, not in any of the speeches uttered by the characters, but in the relationship of speeches and events and in the final outcome of these events. None of the speeches in isolation expresses the dramatic idea. Indeed the essence of a work of art cannot be anything explicit, but only the invisible immaterial form. Schiller categorically resolves the question of rank between content and form in favor of form.

In a genuine work of art the content should effect nothing, but the form everything; since the whole man is acted upon by form alone, but only single faculties by content. However noble and comprehensive then the content may be, it is always confined in its influence upon the spirit, and true aesthetic freedom

---

[5] Quoted by Wilhelm Emrich, "Die poetische Wirklichkeitskritik Franz Kafkas," *Orbis Litterarum*, XI (1956), 215–28.

is to be expected only from form. Herein then consists the art-secret of the master that *by the form he abolishes the content.*[6]

Form is to abolish content! With this amazing formulation Schiller anticipates the program of non-objective art of the Expressionist painter Kandinsky, whose theories, set forth in his book *The Spiritual in Art* (1912), had enormous influence on the German Expressionist painters and authors as well as on the American Abstract Expressionists of our time. Kandinsky, of course, did not have Schiller in mind when he wrote his treatise; he refers to Wagner, Monet, Maeterlinck, and the art historian Worringer, whose *Abstraction and Empathy* (1908) was of great importance for the aesthetics of modern art. Yet Kandinsky's theory is basically a consistent elaboration of the implications of Schiller's phrase.

With these three concepts—the sovereign freedom of genius to find and apply its own laws, the separation of aesthetic from logical ideas, and the absorption of content in organic form—German Idealism established the groundwork for the modernist structure. Here we confront an apparent paradox. The German civilization, famous less for its sense of form than for the opposite, has given birth to the ideal of absolute form. We shall find the same paradox in Expressionism, where the greatest sense of formal abstraction exists side by side with the most chaotic formlessness. How can we account for this paradox?

The concept of abstractness, of course, applies to two different phenomena: stylization, on the one hand, and rhetorical lack of concreteness, on the other. Both are called abstract because both lack the full-bodied three-dimensional impression of life at which realistic art aims. To understand the two kinds of abstractness in German literature and thought and their relationship to each other, it will be helpful to consider the social texture in which both forms of abstractness arose. We shall then find that the apparent paradox actually represents two parallel attempts to deal with a single situation. The examination of the creative process in a social context may shed more light upon the forms and principles of art than any history of ideas or aesthetics considered in a vacuum.

We have encountered three basic principles of artistic creation: mimesis, revelation, and free creation or autonomous art. Each of these principles implies a special relationship between the artist and other men.

The theory of mimesis arose in the Greek city-state in which art had a central position. The sculptor chiseled the statues of the gods which the

---

[6] Schiller, *The Aesthetic Letters, Essays, and the Philosophical Letters*, tr. by J. Weiss, p. 106. I have made slight changes in the translation, substituting the term "content" for the term "subject" as the translation of the German term "Inhalt."

state worshiped. Without proper homage to the gods the city-state could not survive. The state needed the artist as desperately as the artist needed the state. The artist was an essential citizen. If we turn to literature we find the same situation. The dramatist imitated the actions of the ancient myths which formed the basis of the religious cults. His models, like the sculptor's, were the objects of communal worship and his drama was the occasion of a public festival. The poet, like the artist, performed a vital service to the community. As he could not dispense with society which provided him with its myths, society in turn could not dispense with him. Aristotle's theory of mimesis thus presupposes not only a cosmos, but also a stable, closely knit society in which art has a vital function.

Aristotelianism was cultivated by the Catholic Church of medieval Europe, which in many ways inherited the central religious role of the ancient city-state. The idea of mimesis was resuscitated in Catholic countries. However, it was not the Church but the court societies of Renaissance Italy and especially seventeenth-century France which caused it to flourish once more. Society had been transformed from the community of free citizens to "polite" or court society, but for the artist and poet the situation was not unlike that of ancient Greece. Through him polite society celebrated and glorified itself. Even as the Greek sculptor had idealized the athletes and maidens of his city into the gods and goddesses of religious worship, Racine idealized the gentlemen and ladies of the court into the mythical heroes and heroines of his tragedies. Molière's comedy, too, looked to society for its norms in order to satirize those who deviated from them. In seventeenth-century France, the poet—whether tragic or comic—exercised an indispensable function even though it was no longer cultic and religious. Society needed him, for without him its glory could not be completely manifest. It needed him as a flatterer and as an entertainer who made it laugh at those who were not properly part of it. Even when, a century later, society itself became the target of Voltaire's lashing wit, it still remained the model. Instead of its glory and splendor, its grossness, hypocrisy, and folly were inspected and held up to it as a mirror.[7] Indeed, in the eighteenth century the man of letters rose to unheard-of heights in Western Europe. The adversary of kings and nobles, feared and feasted by the aristocracy, the articulate consciousness of the rising bourgeoisie, he had never played so glorious a role as now.

In Germany, however, the situation was entirely different. Eighteenth-century Germany had no "society" in the sense in which France and Eng-

---

[7] The remarkable exception was Rousseau and, to some extent, already La Bruyère. Both, it is interesting to note, were socially inferior.

land had societies. It had no capital city and no central court where a cultured aristocracy gathered and a polished literary style could arise from polished conversation and courtly manners. The numerous courts of Germany were too petty to allow a "polite society" to develop, and the only monarchy powerful enough to do it was first ruled by a sergeant, then by an odd and billiant soldier-philosopher who, in his mature years, despised society and disdained the German language, then by a bigot, and finally by a pious nonentity. Germany's tragedy was that culture proved unable to attract the Prussian monarchy.

If rich enough to afford it—and almost all of them were ruthless and vain enough to pretend they could—the petty rulers of Germany vied with each other for the services of artists and musicians. Princes and bishops ordered paintings, sculptures, castles, gardens, operas, and concertos to glorify themselves. As the magnificent late flowering of Baroque and Rococo in Germany shows, for the nonliterary artist Germany was a thriving business. But the writer was left out. There was no demand for him and he had no audience.

The fact that most of the courts in his realm disdained to use the German language proved disastrous for the German man of letters. The man whom many of them admired, Frederick the Great, owned to his faulty and rudimentary knowledge of the German language and scorned German literature. The work of German philosophy most influential for the flowering of German literature, Leibniz's *Nouveaux Essais* (published 1765), was written in French, and Goethe felt it was his misfortune to have had to work in such a poor medium as the German language. The German man of letters was not needed by an aristocracy that either spoke and read only French or was too rustic and uncouth to appreciate belles-lettres.

The German writer not only had no polite society as his audience; what was even worse, society could not serve him as a model. He could not glorify the petty courts that rejected him and were, at any rate, unable to arouse the pride and enthusiasm with which the citizen of Western Europe identified himself with his monarch and his nation. With the exception of Prussia, these German principalities were too insignificant and too brazenly oppressive to inspire poets and writers with the incentive to idealize them. If the German writer looked at polite society at all it was with indignation, scorn, and resentment. Inwardly fortified by his strong religious feelings (fostered directly and indirectly through pietism), he felt far above "society" with its unbelievably petty intrigues and heartless egotisms. Excluded from or arrogantly patronized by it, he inwardly despised its conventions to which he outwardly conformed. Since he knew no other, he scorned "society" as such and rejected, wherever he dared, all convention as unnatural. Manners and polish—in short, form—were associated in his mind with the scented, hypocritical, ridiculously small-minded lackeys and climbers of the court. Associated with French speech, form was felt as foreign and un-German.

The German intellectual's hostility to conventions had, as Nietzsche diagnosed, a lasting and unfortunate effect on his relationship to artistic form, to style in general.

"Form" generally implies for us Germans some convention, disguise or hypocrisy, and if not hated, is at any rate not loved. We have an extraordinary fear of both the word convention and the thing. This fear drove the German from the French school; for he wished to become more natural and therefore more German. But he seems to have come to a false conclusion with his "therefore." . . . In the belief that he was returning to Nature, he merely followed caprice and comfort with the smallest possible amount of self-control.[8]

German formlessness, so aptly censured by Nietzsche, must be viewed in the light of German social traditions. Form, taste, lucidity, fluency and ease of style, subtlety, the sense of literary tact, and above all vividness and accuracy of observation are qualities not acquired in isolation. They depend on a lively and well-disciplined social life. Like the social dance, the primary skill of "polite society," these accomplishments are acquired by continuous practice in the arena of society, the court, and, later, the drawing room. The only salons to become famous in German cultural life were those of a few Jewish ladies whose families had only recently become members of the German community.

The Germans had no models to imitate. The vital interrelationship between aristocracy of birth and aristocracy of intellect never or rarely existed in Germany. There were no wits from whom the great writers could learn the art of pithy formulation, no brilliant patterns of conversation which could have sharpened their pens as well as their speech. There were no great or interesting characters to portray, no actions of great import to celebrate or to relate. The German intellectuals were self-made men of the spirit.

If the German writer did use court society as his theme, as Lessing used it in *Emilia Galotti* and Schiller in *Cabal and Love,* it was to castigate and condemn this society.[9] This explains the rise in late eighteenth-century

---

[8] Nietzsche, "The Use and Abuse of History," in *Thoughts Out of Season,* tr. by Adrian Collins, in *The Complete Works of Nietzsche,* ed. by Oscar Levy, V, 34-35.

[9] The classical German dramas of Goethe and Schiller, written at the court of Weimar, form a significant exception for reasons which will soon become apparent.

German literature of a powerful social drama in a seminaturalistic style that surpasses Diderot in audacity and radicalism and already forms a link to Ibsen and Strindberg. But a highly critical climate is less favorable to the development of robust realism in literature than a mildly ironical and basically affirmative atmosphere. Schiller's youthful dramas show that a largely negative attitude to society leads away from realistic observation to exaggeration, distortion, shrillness, and abstractness, qualities which reappear in Expressionism, in many ways the direct heir of Schiller's Storm and Stress.

The paucity of good novels and comedies in German literature is intimately linked to this absence of a calmly observant attitude toward social reality. In a climate hostile to polite society, comedy either changes into biting parody, of which German literature shows numerous excellent examples from Lenz and Büchner to Brecht, or drowns in pathos. Both possibilities are abundantly realized in Expressionism. The novel, too, is genetically connected with the comic spirit of detachment which is able to observe and smile without grimacing at the human foibles set against a solid background of social reality.[10] *Don Quixote*, prototype of the European novel, starts as a humorous tale and the eighteenth-century novel in England is not yet divorced from its comic origins.[11]

Unattached or hostile to high society, the German man of letters, unlike his British counterpart, had no other class of society to serve him as a substitute model for his work. His small-townish or rustic surroundings could not inspire him to mimesis, although, if he cared to, he could achieve a striking and stirring realism in the portrayal of petty-bourgeois life, as Goethe's Gretchen episodes show, because he felt isolated from them, too. His superior education set him apart from family and childhood friends. The princes, even though they had no use for German men of letters, could use educated bureaucrats in great numbers; and a bureaucrat's post as jurist, clergyman, or professor was the German writer's alternative to starvation. Consequently, there were many highly educated Germans whose education could do nothing for them except tie them to a dull official routine. Isolated from their uneducated fellow-townsmen, barred from the aristocracy, scattered over many sleepy little residences throughout a vast,

---

[10] Wolfgang Kayser points out that the grotesque arises in societies that have lost their firm standards and bearings.

[11] Samuel Richardson, of course, differs from the dominant tradition represented by Defoe, Fielding, Smollet, and Sterne because of his much closer connection to the emotional Protestantism of the middle classes. See Herbert Schöffler, *Protestantismus und Literatur* (Leipzig, 1922), pp. 163 ff. for a discussion of this problem.

disorganized realm, with no salons or coffeehouses in which to find their equals, the German intellectual had nothing to look to except himself and the vast unused knowledge in his mind. This was the existential situation, so memorably expressed in Goethe's *Werther,* of the men who in theory and practice overthrew the doctrine of mimesis.

Although he had nothing to imitate or serve him as his model, the German writer had an enormous reservoir of tense, dammed-up emotions to be expressed. His isolation, his fervent attachments to few friends, his strong religious feelings, and his lonely love of nature, which became his refuge, sought for means of expression, and his emotions at times burst out with explosive force. This explains the enormous vogue of Rousseauism in Germany where Rousseau was felt as a universal liberator. Rousseau gave the German writer the right and the courage to express himself without regard to external considerations such as taste, form, or the sensibilities of an audience. Rousseau's sharp division between society and nature shattered the implicit assumption of mimesis that society was a part—and the most important part—of nature imitated by the artist. To be sure, Rousseau believed in a reconstituted society. He condemned existing society as corrupted and perverted but did not dispense with all society. It was, however, not this side of Rousseau that appealed in Germany. It was not the *Social Contract,* but *La Nouvelle Héloïse, The Confessions,* and *Emile* that caused the enthusiasm of the Germans. *The Social Contract* was meaningless in a country that had not yet produced a national society and was, therefore, largely ignored by the German writers and thinkers. At any rate, Rousseau encouraged the German writer to express himself, his own nature, directly instead of observing and describing nature in others.

This tendency, which underlies the aesthetics of the Storm and Stress movement, is a primitive or naïve form of Expressionism. The writer imitates not an external model, but, as it were, himself. Either he lays bare his soul and composes the biography of his innermost self or he states his feelings directly, "sings as the bird," shouts out his joy, and screams out his pain in the moment or near the moment of experiencing them. In the first case the writer moves toward the exploration of his subconscious, his dream world, and the line, as Marcel Raymond has traced it, leads then from Rousseauism to Storm and Stress, Romanticism, Surrealism, and, we might add, the sophisticated and modernist version of Expressionism. In the second case the line leads from Storm and Stress to the folk-song school of Romanticism, the so-called Younger or Heidelberg Romantics, and finally to what we might call naïve or rhetorical Expressionism.

This kind of Expressionism is not modernist at all but simply a revived and extreme version of the Storm and Stress, made more extreme by the writers' situation which the Prussianization and industrialization of Germany in the Second *Reich* had immensely aggravated. The stylistic influences are partly the Storm and Stress writers themselves, especially the youthful Schiller who exerted a great influence on the young Expressionists. The characters in Paul Kornfeld's, Walter Hasenclever's, and Fritz von Unruh's dramas frequently sound like extreme variants of Karl and Franz Moor or Ferdinand Walter or Fiesco. But the expressionist *Ichdrama* also follows the tradition of Goethe's *Faust,* a work conceived and begun in the Storm and Stress. The Expressionists greatly esteemed Storm and Stress authors like Lenz and Klinger. Georg Büchner forms an interesting nineteenth-century link between the Storm and Stress and the drama of Wedekind, Johst, and Bert Brecht. Nietzsche was for the Expressionists what Rousseau had been for the Storm and Stress. But it was the declamatory and pseudo-Biblical Nietzsche of *Thus Spake Zarathustra* rather than the brilliant aphorist of *Beyond Good and Evil* who molded the style of the naïve Expressionists. The Storm and Stress had been more fortunate in possessing the actual Bible as inspiration instead of Nietzsche's immensely popular pseudobible. What Macpherson's *Ossian* and Percy's *Ballads* had been for the Storm and Stress, Walt Whitman was for the naïve Expressionists Werfel, Wegner, Rubiner, Iwan Goll (in his early stage), and the semi-modernist Ernst Stadler.

There are striking stylistic analogies between Storm and Stress and naïve Expressionism. The style of both movements tends to be jerky and hectic. It consists of abrupt exclamations and sentence fragments. Although vivid and striking, it threatens to become incoherent and distracted by random associations which confuse the reader and lead the author astray. The greatest danger of this formlessness is not its sincerity but its opposite—that while still believing himself sincere the author has in fact become rhetorical. The time lapsed between the feeling and the writing suffices to adulterate the feeling, if sincerity is the guiding criterion of creation. The lapse of time allows extraneous associations or unconscious censorship to slip in between the heart and the tip of the pen, and instead of the genuine emotion we get its hollow rhetorical counterfeit. The logical extreme of naïve Expressionism is the automatic writing practiced by many Surrealists. It offers sentences of arresting beauty in an ocean of plain boredom. (Stream-of-consciousness does not at all derive from naïve Expressionism, but from a systematic extension of scientific Naturalism.)

The mere look of the printed page of poems by the Expressionists Johannes Becher and Wilhelm Klemm spells aggression against the reader. Exclamation points, question marks, and dashes follow the one-word sentences in menacing crescendos. Here the Rousseauistic self is not merely screaming its agony without regard to the eardrums and polite manners of society, it attacks, pursues, threatens, and woos society. Its very bellowing and screaming is, like a tantrum forcing attention, a desperate attempt to relate to society, but on the terms of the self, not on the terms of the group.

The drama of the Storm and Stress, as well as the drama of Expressionism, abounds in bitter, intense, and often fatal family conflicts. At the height of the Storm and Stress movement, in 1775, three dramas were submitted for a prize. All three dealt with fratricide. The most famous drama of fratricidal conflict is Schiller's *The Robbers*. But in Storm and Stress the relationship between parents and children is almost as tense as that between siblings, as Schiller's *Cabal and Love,* Klinger's *The Twins,* Leisewitz's *Julius of Tarent,* and even the Gretchen episode in *Faust* reveal. In Expressionism, the revolt of sons against their fathers, frequently with patricidal outcome, is one of the major themes. This concentration on family tensions drastically exemplifies the deeply personal inspiration and the subjectivism common to both movements.

Naïve Expressionism is to the full-fledged Expressionism of Trakl, Kafka, or Barlach what the gaseous cloud is to the shining star: a state of incubation from which the finished work can issue forth. Between naïve and full-fledged Expressionism there prevails a relationship similar to that between Storm and Stress and the serene formal perfectionism implied in Kant's doctrine of autonomous art and expressed by Schiller in his classical period. The same subjectivism that gave rise to the Storm and Stress still appears in Kant's and Schiller's doctrine. The artist's sovereign disregard of society is the common element. In the pure abstraction of the modernist, as in the formless shriek of the naïve Expressionist, lies the same basic indifference to the world in its twofold aspect as model and as audience. As the naïve Expressionist is unconcerned about his offenses to public taste and morals, the true modernist is equally callous as to whether or not the public can understand him. Neither is inclined to compromise. They intentionally alienate their audience and put deliberate obstacles between the public and themselves. Kant, who destroyed the concept of an objectively existing world together with the concept of mimesis, remained all his life a fervent admirer of Rousseau; and in a sense

Kant completed Rousseau's half-finished work. Rousseau had abstracted society from the individual and extolled natural man ("naked man" will be a favorite of the Expressionists) in his purity. Kant abstracted even nature from man so that naked mind was left without either a social or a natural world surrounding it. Rousseau (as seen by his German admirers) had thought that man could live without society. Kant thought that man could live without a world. It is a difference in the degree of abstraction—the same kind of difference which we will find again within the Expressionist movement.

Violent self-expression or absolute art are only two possibilities open to the creative mind isolated from its environment. The third possibility is one of hope. The creative mind can seek to create the public for itself by educating the surrounding world. For the German man of letters in the late eighteenth century this implied a twofold mission: educating his countrymen and creating a German nation. To the German *Klassik*, into which Herder's, Goethe's, and Schiller's Storm and Stress evolved, Weimar offered a center from where a pedagogic-cultural mission could radiate throughout Germany. The court of Weimar had opened itself to the German intellect and the symbiosis of the two aristocracies of birth and mind could, for a little over a decade, inspire Germany's greatest writers. At this one moment of history, when Napoleon's hammer blows dissolved the Holy Roman Empire, Germany's vague First *Reich,* German Idealism hoped to educate the Germans into "a nation of humanity," a second Greece, a realm of aesthetic and spiritual perfection. Schiller's *Letters on the Aesthetic Education of Man,* Herder's *Letters Promoting Humanity,* and Goethe's *Wilhelm Meister* testify to the faith of Weimar. But a peculiarly unrealistic, abstract quality informed this hope—a quality that would have been absent if Weimar had been Berlin or Vienna. At any rate the example of the tiny duchy remained isolated; the great courts of the German realm refused to emulate it, and the first Weimar experiment, like its successor in our century, remained, in several senses of the word, Platonic. After Schiller's death in 1805, even Goethe, lone survivor of the dream of Weimar, ceased to believe in it.[12]

Although the spirit of Weimar failed to produce results in the political-social sphere of German life, it bequeathed a legacy of lofty didacticism and high moral seriousness to German literature, which frustrated the true fruition of Kant's and Schiller's radical aesthetics. The extremely original

[12] For a discussion of Goethe's progressive disillusionment see Johannes Hoffmeister, *Die Heimkehr des Geistes.*

and revolutionary insights of German Idealism were connected with elements which led in precisely the opposite direction. Schiller offers a striking example of this ambivalence in German Idealism. At the end of his *Letters,* Schiller smuggled the moral-didactic view back into his aesthetics from which he had so ruthlessly expunged it before. Although art was to be free of moralizing, it was still a means for the education of man to moral perfection. Art was to make man free so that he could choose the moral state. Thus Schiller attempted to reconcile and synthetize two radically opposed views of art, the moral-didactic and the purely aesthetic.

Schiller's influence combining with the ever continuing need of German writers to create an audience for themselves, to educate a nation which was of the past or the future but never of the present, made it difficult for Germans to practice art based on purely formal considerations. A tendency to sermonize hampered the progress of German literature toward absolute art. This tendency is especially marked in Expressionism and makes many Expressionist works seem dated and strangely old-fashioned despite experimental details. High moral seriousness drives Fritz von Unruh, for example, into a rhetorical directness that runs counter to the abstract conception of his work and, in addition, debases his language. His attempt to combine a moral-didactic with a purely aesthetic radicalism causes von Unruh, like many lesser Expressionists in Schiller's succession, to sin in two directions. He must sin against the concrete freshness of realism; but at the same time he sins against the austere consistency of "abstract" or "absolute" art. The union of missionary zeal and formal abstraction proved artistically debilitating to many Expressionists.

Schiller's own mature dramas were saved from becoming rhetorical abstractions by his acute sense of dramatic conflict, an asset arising from his brilliant antithetical turn of mind, which can be detected in the structure of his individual phrases. This tendency led Schiller into an interesting and aesthetically powerful kind of abstractness. It is a "French" quality in German style, and its greatest representatives, Schiller, Heine, and Nietzsche, were singularly drawn to French literature. (Schiller, for instance, was drawn to the French neoclassic drama of Racine.) This sharp antithetical and epigrammatic intellectuality also lives on in Thomas Mann's essayistic irony (which, to be sure, is found less in his essays than in his great narrative prose). It is a very important tendency to Expressionism, where it appears in the provocative and stimulating style of Heinrich Mann and the dialogues of Wedekind, Sternheim, Kaiser, and Toller.

Schiller's moral-didactic bent was encouraged by Goethe's Weimarian

ideal of education or *Bildung,* but also by Kant's secularized Protestantism, his *Critique of Practical Reason.* Both influences interfered with the
development of a literature of purely "aesthetic ideas." Coleridge, less en-
cumbered by didacticism than the Germans, was more instrumental in
developing both in theory and in practice the implications of Kant's liberation of the creative imagination. But it was Schopenhauer who took the
decisive step beyond Kant on the road toward absolute art. By demonstrat-
ing the incompatibility between human aspirations and human existence,
Schopenhauer completed the process Kant had begun.

CHAPTER TWO

Music and Existence

FOR SCHOPENHAUER THE THING-IN-ITSELF IS THE WILL, A BLIND, FURIOUS, PUR-
poseless striving, utterly meaningless to man. Nature is the disguise assumed by the Will. The variegated spectacle of forms and species which
the mind perceives in nature is not the ultimate Reality, but conceals its
terror from our eyes. The Will spawns forth and devours myriads of
individual existences in whose blind struggle for survival the blind Will
struggles with itself and continuously devours itself. The only escape from
this insanity is either Buddhist abnegation of the Will, nirvana, or (still
second best for Schopenhauer) the elevation and transfiguration of the
Will into Idea, an object of aesthetic contemplation. This is the task of
music. All the other arts represent the illusory world of nature; they are
mere ideas of ideas. But music, which represents nothing specific, reveals
to us absolute Reality, the furious, ceaseless energy behind all forms and
phenomena, the Will itself. Thus, through music, art becomes salvation.

Schopenhauer postulates a meaningless universe in which the gulf between man and nature, which Kant and, indeed, Hobbes and Hume had
opened, yawns wider than ever without being bridged either by the pan-
theistic mysticism of the Romantics or by the moral law of Kant and
Schiller. His view of the universe, which alienates human existence from
any possible purpose or meaning, is profoundly modern. Schopenhauer's
Will is in no way different from Melville's and Joyce's vision of God as
the maw of universal death. It anticipates the view of nature fostered by
Darwinism. It underlies much of Existentialism. Ultimate reality is without meaning for human existence. Therefore, the art which reveals reality
has to be free of the illusions of natural forms, conceptual content, or moral
purpose. It is an art without ideas, or rather an art in which ideas are
identical with form and do not lead outside the functional, self-sufficient
universe of the work to the illusory cosmos of empirical experience. It is
an art untranslatable into any terms of external experience. Such an art
is salvation for two reasons. It takes man out of the snare of practical concerns with which the Will fools him into doing its bidding, and it unmasks

the senseless struggle for existence which both logic and morality serve by seeking to regulate it instead of doing away with it and makes us behold the truth—the pulse-beat of the Will throbbing through Eternity. But in the very process of revealing the meaninglessness of Reality, music creates form and meaning. It captures the formless Will in man-made form. It raises Reality to an Idea. It asserts man against the Will by chaining the Will and thus becomes a supreme act of man. Music becomes man's salvation, as art had been earlier for Schiller and the Romantics, because it liberates man from delusion, initiates him into knowledge, and creates meaning in a meaningless universe. It is not a means to redemption; it is redemption itself. These are the implications of Schopenhauer's aesthetics which fascinated Wagner, Baudelaire, Mallarmé, and the French Symbolists in general, who developed them further into the foundations of modernism.[1]

Schopenhauer's aesthetics is the logical culmination of Kant's. Music, in its purest form, is nothing but aesthetic idea. Its form is its content and its content is inseparable from its formulation. This is, of course, also the fundamental concept of the *Klassik* of Goethe and Schiller and of the Romanticism of Schelling; it is essential to all of German Idealism. In Schopenhauer, however, it combines with the conviction of a meaningless, even absurd, universe. It is this peculiar combination of Idealism and nihilism that explains the fascination of Schopenhauer for the emerging modernist mentality. The chords of Schopenhauer's music signify withdrawal from the Will even while they portray the Will. Thematic variations, harmony, and counterpoint have no concern with practical reality in any sense. They do not portray nature; they do not exhort us to moral behavior; they do not transmit any information except their own formal structure. The disinterested, playful purpose of the artist, his sovereign freedom, alone determines the nature of his work.

Yet though utterly free of empirical "sense," music is not "contentless." It conveys emotions before the practical needs of life (that is, of the Will) have channeled and narrowed them into definite feelings and conceptualized thoughts, and so it reveals the naked Will, as it exists before assuming the disguises of individuation. Music reveals a universal longing without purpose and object, an emotional absolute, reality in its true and original state. With this radical twist that Schopenhauer gave to it, the aesthetics of German Idealism made its enormous impact upon France and led, either directly or through Wagner, to the rise of modernism.

[1] For the influence of Schopenhauer on the French Symbolists see Lehmann, *The Symbolist Aesthetics in France 1885–1895*, pp. 57–67.

Music replaced sculpture as the primary art of the West. Free composition of functional, self-sufficient universes replaced the imitation of natural forms as the primary purpose and consideration of all the arts. In painting this meant that not likeness to external subjects, landscapes or persons, for instance, but only the artist's intentions were to dictate his organization of colors and lines on the canvas. In literature it meant that the framework of a poem, drama, or narrative would no longer have to be consistent with any external standard; the images in a poem would no longer have to follow a plausible and logically coherent sequence; the actions of characters in dramas or novels would no longer have to be consistent with psychological plausibility; metaphors could be abstracted from their context and used arbitrarily or autonomously, exactly as color was to be used by Van Gogh and Gauguin to express directly the emotional values of the composition without regard to the spectator's expectations based on his empirical experience. The adoption of these principles of musical composition by the other arts is probably the single most dominant characteristic of all modernism.

Full modernism sets in only when the principle of musical composition no longer merely coexists with the older concerns of art—plausibility, logical coherence of ideas, accuracy of description and portrayal. Thomas Mann and Marcel Proust, though great symphonic composers, cannot be considered entirely modernistic because the symphonic structure of their novels exists side by side with those older and traditional criteria or considerations. They do not depart from the tradition of the character-portrait as radically as Joyce in *Finnegans Wake* or Kafka. It is the exclusiveness rather than the application of the musical principle which makes for modernism. Kandinsky calls on all the arts to become like music. Paul Valéry names architecture and music as the primary arts which all the others should emulate. And we note that architecture and music are the only arts in which representation of man or any natural object is almost impossible, almost all references to an external universe are banished, and the unit of the work, the individual chord, for instance, receives its meaning exclusively from its function in the whole.[2]

This musicalization is usually connected with the belief that there is no meaning in the universe outside man, and indeed not outside the self, and that by creating an artificial universe of formal relationships man

[2] The meaning of "function" in architecture refers to a utility in an external universe, to be sure; but so does music in so far as it may be written for a specific purpose, to meet the order of a patron, for instance, or to incite people to adopt a certain emotional attitude. This ulterior purpose does not alter the fact that these two arts are equally nonrepresentational and independent of an extra-artistic frame of reference.

creates the only meaning there is. Or it is based on the belief that there is a meaning outside man, but one extremely difficult to perceive and relate to. In this case the act of artistic creation or self-expression can clarify man's perception of meaning. Here again, art becomes the only road to meaning. Hatred of or indifference to nature and the "natural" characterize modernism. Modernism rejects the "given" and strains to transcend it. Yeats' "artifice of eternity" could serve as its motto.

The appeal of Schopenhauer's and Wagner's version of German Idealism coincided with a marked change in the social situation of the writer and the artist in post-Napoleonic Western Europe, especially France. The symbiosis of artist and society, from which the theory of mimesis had been born, no longer existed after the final victory of the *bourgeoisie*. The importation of German ideas into France and Western Europe in the nineteenth century was accompanied by a development in which the social position of the Western (and especially French) artist began to approximate that of the German man of letters. The serious artist became functionless in the newly emerging noncultic and nonaristocratic society. Bourgeois society was neither a politico-religious community like the ancient city-state nor a center of elegance and glory like the Renaissance and seventeenth-century courts. It had no need for celebration. It was disorganized and decentralized although the salons continued the tradition of the courts for a long time. All the decentralized bourgeois society wanted was entertainment as distraction from its exacting money-making tasks. The artist had three choices. He could turn manufacturer of articles of distracting entertainment as Dumas *père* did. He could also continue the satirical tradition set by Cervantes, Swift, and Voltaire, combine it with the scientific temper of the industrial *bourgeoisie*, and develop what later was to be called Naturalism. Balzac in the novel and Dumas *fils* in the drama combined entertainment with the serious, observant spirit of literary Naturalism. In Naturalism the theory of mimesis is triumphant once more, to be sure. But the artist's attitude toward society has changed. He stands apart and trains the sharp lens of his scientific and reforming mind upon the fissures and horrors society offers his view. There is no glorification or celebration. The Naturalist sees not the glory and sweetness of society, but its tyranny and evil. The doctrine of the inescapable and crushing omnipotence of milieu views society as a monstrous rather than a beneficent reality, exactly as nature after Schopenhauer and Darwin was seen not as a cosmos but as a monstrous jaw of eternal annihilation. Naturalism driven to the extremes of its own momentum prepared the death blows against mimesis from which it had sprung. It was Zola's friend Cézanne who went far beyond mimesis in painting, and the extreme Naturalism of the stream-of-consciousness technique ended in the musical structures of T. S. Eliot and Joyce.

The third choice of the artist in the bourgeois nineteenth century was to make his lack of function his fate, turn utterly free, *poète maudit*, and modernist. The asocial and antisocial character of the French Symbolists to whom Schopenhauer's philosophy and Wagner's music especially appealed is well known. But even before the advent of Symbolism, Gérard de Nerval, link between the Romanticism of E. T. A. Hoffmann, Baudelaire, and Surrealism, contemplates the "ivory tower" as a way of life. In one of the first passages in which this term occurs, the ivory tower, symbol of the artist's haughty withdrawal from the world, is seen to be a fate imposed upon the sensitive mind by the nature of the new society emerging after the Napoleonic wars.

We were then living in a strange period, such as usually succeeds revolutions or the decline of great reigns. It was no longer the gallant heroism of the Fronde, the elegant, dressed-up vice of the Regency, or the scepticism and insane orgies of the Directoire. It was an age in which activity, hesitation, and indolence were mixed up, together with dazzling Utopias, philosophies, and religious aspirations, vague enthusiasms, mild ideas of a Renaissance, weariness with past struggles, insecure optimisms—somewhat like the period of Peregrinus and Apuleius. . . . We had not reached the age of ambition, and the greedy scramble for honors and positions caused us to stay away from all spheres of activity. The only refuge left to us was the poet's ivory tower, which we climbed ever higher, to isolate ourselves from the mob.[3]

As Schopenhauer's philosophy and nineteenth-century science explode the idea of a meaningful natural cosmos, the idea of a meaningful social cosmos crumbles away simultaneously. Chaos, however, cannot be imitated by art. It can only be transcended, or recreated, in the artificial universe of surreality.

Schopenhauer's elevation of music implied that the task of art was to represent the world below the level of individuation, the world as Will and not as Idea. Nietzsche extolled the collective ecstasy of "the spirit of music" which liberates us from the tragedy of individuation and reunites us with the source of both creation and destruction, the all-devouring, all-creating Will. Far from deploring the blind destructiveness of the Will (as "bourgeois" Schopenhauer had still deplored it), Nietzsche rejoiced in the possibility of ecstatic union with it. Rimbaud, ten years younger than

[3] Nerval, *Sylvie* in *Selected Writings*, tr. by Geoffrey Wagner, p. 50.

Nietzsche, arrived one year earlier than the youthful German professor at a more violent form of Dionysianism. The poet had to destroy, or at least to derange, his individual "self," his "bourgeois" crust, to allow the buried reality of the world to erupt from him in visions and hallucinations. Rimbaud postulated not only the destruction of the self, but also the destruction of the world. He called for the "time of the assassins" who would destroy the social fabric as the poet had to destroy the customary fabric of discourse to become God and create a new universe from the ruins of the old, a universe purer and more perfect than Jehovah's, the tedious tyrant whom all respectable people, especially Rimbaud's narrow-minded, tyrannical mother, worshiped. In a more violent form Rimbaud anticipates Nietzsche's transvaluation of all values and the concept of the superman, the new Human God.

There are, however, several ways of achieving "musicalization" and creating the artificial universe of "surreality." One of these could be called Surrealism. It descends from Romanticism, Nerval, Baudelaire, and especially Rimbaud. It is subjective and creates surreality by means of dream images and hallucinations—at any rate, by means of visualization. Nietzsche's concept of the Dionysian is not far removed from it.

Opposed to Surrealism is another very important branch of modernism, which is closer to Mallarmé than to Rimbaud, closer to Bergson's serene recapture of timeless memory than to Nietzsche's time-forgetting ecstasy. Valéry, T. E. Hulme, Pound, Eliot, and Joyce represent it. Cubism, descending from Cézanne, is its equivalent in painting. I shall call this particular form of modernism "cubist," a term much more appropriate to serve as a common denominator than might appear at first. Cubism aims at "surreality" and musicalization primarily by intellectual means. It is more radically experimental than Surrealism, but at the same time much more objective. Its point of departure is an objective situation rather than the personal subconscious. It relies on the latter, too, but merely as one means among many others. It emphasizes the structural element rather than the striking visual detail. Literary "cubism" experiments with language rather than with imagery and metaphor.

Expressionism is a collective term which includes both forms of modernism. There are surrealist Expressionists, notably the poets Heym, Lichtenstein, Van Hoddis, but Trakl, Kafka, and several dramatists come close to it, too. There are also cubist Expressionists; the most pronouncedly cubist among them is Gottfried Benn. The poets of the *Sturm* circle, and the dramatists Wedekind, Sternheim, and Kaiser come close to it. Nevertheless, the most important formal tendency of Expressionism, Expressionism proper, is much closer to Surrealism than to Cubism. It is subjective, dreamlike, visionary rather than object-centered, intellectual, and linguistically experimental. What distinguishes it from Surrealism is its existential seriousness and consistency. Expressionism proper is the existential or protoexistentialist form of modernism.

All three schools of modernism tend toward the musicalization and functionalization of art, the abandonment of external frameworks, and the creation of self-contained artificial universes. They reject mimesis and portrait art for a mixture of free creation and revelation. All reject the traditional treatment of character in literature.

The musicalization of the symbol and the accompanying destruction of the traditional concept of character are the strongest common links between all modernisms, but especially between Surrealism and Expressionism. A brief discussion of the symbol and the significance of the profound changes it underwent in nineteenth- and twentieth-century poetry, drama, and narrative prose will lead us to the heart of the problem of modernism.

The symbol for Goethe united an individual character or phenomenon with a universal idea. It is a scene or personage in a work of art which exists as a full-fledged, a priori individual (in contrast to the allegorical) but represents, at the same time, a totality of similar cases and, therefore, a universal idea. Goethe insists that to be effective it must above all be complete and meaningful in and by itself. In fact, the universal truth embodied in the symbol can be poetically effective only when the symbol lives an autonomous and self-sufficient existence and makes a convincing impression of reality.[4]

Goethe's theory of the symbol preserves the principle of mimesis in its most illusionistic form (the work of art has to give the illusion of reproducing empirical reality). It strikingly parallels his concept of personality, the representative person in whom the claims of individual peculiarity or "character" and the claims of social conformity or the "universal" receive a perfect synthesis. Both symbol and personality show in different and yet closely related ways Goethe's persistent effort to save the individual together with the idea of cosmic and social order. *Bildung*, for which "forming or shaping education" might be the nearest equivalent in English, forms personality; but the term derives from the image-making activity (*bilden*) of the artist. The ideals of Greek sculpture (via "the shades

---

[4] The difference between symbol and allegory for Goethe is discussed extremely well by Johannes Hoffmeister in his introduction to his edition of Goethe's *Märchen*, pp. 8 ff. My discussion of Goethe's and Schelling's concept of the symbol is partly based on René Wellek, *A History of Modern Criticism: 1750–1950*, I, 210–11; II, 76.

of Winckelmann") underlie Goethe's concept of the symbol. A human figure shaped to perfection embodies a universal force, the divinity whom the statue represents.

In practice Goethe did not usually conform to his own theory. Especially in the works of his old age, he tended to stress the universal at the cost of the individual component of the symbol and thus moved toward allegory. The figure of Care in *Faust II* is a good example. This female figure is allegorical, not symbolic, because she is not presented to us as a concrete individual but as an obvious embodiment of a universal idea, the idea of care. Every reader immediately understands what she is. The Expressionist character, as we shall see, remains mysterious because he does not embody a universal idea, nor, of course, is he an individual. The allegorical is only possible if a universal frame of reference which author and reader have in common is taken for granted.

Schelling shows even more clearly than Goethe the close connection of the classic-romantic idea of the symbol to the art of ancient Greece. For Schelling the best examples of symbolism are the gods of Greek myths. They are sharply profiled individuals who represent universal forces of nature or universal aspects of mind. The symbol keeps the same role in Hegel's aesthetics. According to Hegel, art causes a universal idea to become transparent in an individual phenomenon. These views of the symbol then presuppose the coexistence of individuality and cosmic order and the possibility of an intimate relationship between them.

The great Realists of the nineteenth century, above all Flaubert and Ibsen, took a decisive step toward absolute art by making individual events, objects, or persons in their works symbolic not of universal forces or ideas, but of the aesthetic idea of the work itself. Although it still retains its self-evident "realistic" existence as an independent individual event or object or person, the symbol also becomes a function in the work. Any reader of Ibsen's *Wild Duck* and *Rosmersholm* must be aware of the important and peculiar role of symbolism in these model plays of European Realism, and this tendency becomes, of course, ever stronger in the works of Ibsen's old age. It is well known how the great modernists Joyce and Kafka admired the masters of nineteenth-century Realism, Ibsen and Flaubert. This admiration, as our discussion shall show, is not accidental. They developed to their logical extreme implications contained in the method of nineteenth-century Realism. For our present discussion I shall choose an example from Flaubert's *Madame Bovary*.

In *Madame Bovary*, a blind, disfigured beggar appears several times at the stagecoach which takes Emma Bovary home after her assignations with her lover, Leon. Later when Emma Bovary, having taken the poison, lies dying, she hears the beggar in the streets beneath her windows. This figure exists as a well-rounded and credible individual apart from the heroine's life. His appearances at the coach are logical because it is a good place for begging. His reappearance in Emma's town at the time of her death is also logically justified. The author has been at pains to provide a rational explanation for this coincidence. The druggist, M. Homais, had suggested to the beggar that he come to see him about a cure. Clutching at this straw of hope, the beggar groped his way to Yonville, Madame Bovary's and M. Homais's town, on the day Emma Bovary happened to be dying. The three-dimensional reality of the beggar is further strengthened by M. Homais's indignation at the "outmoded medieval conditions" of France which the existence of such a wretch points up. By emphasizing the various reactions of individuals to the beggar—M. Homais's political indignation, Emma's instinctive and aesthetic horror and melancholy, the coachman's callous brutality—Flaubert has produced in us a strong conviction of his character's factual reality. He has brought him into the perspective in which the artist's creation looks like a phenomenon of real life.

However, we also feel that the beggar appears in the novel for reasons other than the author's mimetic wish to portray social misery or to represent through the beggar the universal idea of human wretchedness. The hideous face emerging before Emma's eyes, the quavering voice haunting her in her death agony express something about her that the author could not express as succinctly and vividly in any other way.

The beggar is introduced into the story when Emma's romantic illusions about her love affair have not yet been shattered. The true face of this affair, its sordid wretchedness, has not yet become visible to her romantic mind. At this point in the novel the beggar appears, showing his frightful visage to the shocked and nauseated lady, and sings a ditty about a maiden's desire for love in May. The gruesome face being uncovered before her foreshadows the dreadful unveiling of the true face of her love. Together with the idiotically sentimental and lecherous song, it telescopes the essence of her life.

The beggar stands in a functional relationship to Emma Bovary's inner life. His appearances foreshadow, parallel, and underline the main idea of the work and the essence of the heroine's existence. Character has become symbol. But the symbol does not, like Goethe's or Hegel's, represent a universal idea; it reflects what Kant calls the aesthetic idea of the work. Flaubert's symbolic character embodies the idea of the plot. He affects the reader's emotions in a way that reinforces the emotional effects produced by the plot. The beggar, therefore, corresponds to Kant's concept of "the aesthetic attribute." The character is used like a metaphor. As the metaphor makes visual and thereby underlines the emotional meaning of a passage, the beggar in Flaubert's novel reinforces the emotional effect of the whole novel. He acts like a musical variation of the main theme.

Flaubert extends the role of the symbol even further. He makes it expressive of the inner states of his main character. The beggar's first appearance in the novel brings to the fore Emma's hidden feelings about her love affair and her life. She is not conscious of them at the time and the author carefully refrains from becoming explicit about it. But the beggar arouses a profound melancholy in her. This melancholy has no specified cause. It is not the beggar's appearance as such that causes it. She has just left her lover with high romance in her mind. But the repressed presentiment of her despair, which circumstances will lift up into her consciousness one day, have found an embodiment in the beggar's senseless existence and inane song. In the very work which represents the crowning achievement of nineteenth-century Realism, Flaubert anticipates a device essential to Expressionism. He expresses the main character's repressed feelings or repressed awareness by embodying them in another character; this symbolic character becomes then the objective correlative for inner states which the main character has concealed from himself. He makes what is unknown to the character, but significant about him and hidden within him, visible to the reader without directly informing him as traditional narrative was wont to do.

The two traditional methods of conveying information about a character's inner states had been the dramatic method, which discloses character and emotions through action and speech, and the narrative method, by which the author himself informs us about and comments on his character's emotions and thoughts. Homer shows us Achilles screaming and rolling about in the dust; Virgil tells us that Aeneas was sad and describes his thoughts for us. The advantage of the dramatic method is its vividness. The advantage of the narrative method is its analytical scope; it can inform us of emotions which the character has not allowed to become conscious to himself, of things about him which the character himself does not know, and above all of feelings which the character does know but does not dare to show to others and perhaps even to admit fully to himself. Authors dealing with sophisticated, inhibited, and inwardly divided characters, such as Henry James and Proust, masters of character analysis, rarely use the dramatic method. But the narrative method, too, has disadvantages. First of all, it may easily lack vividness and immediacy and become overburdened by its cerebral approach. This, according to Kandinsky, poses a serious problem for the modern writer. How can he do justice to the complex, inhibited, and ambivalent emotions of modern man without sacrificing vividness? The problem is especially acute in the drama, in which monologue had been the chief vehicle for the expression of a character's inner states. Realism, however, banished the monologue, and furthermore, the monologue is unable to express the character's subconscious. How can the dramatist let his audiences know, or rather sense, what lies in the recesses of a character's soul? Here Ibsen's symbolism as developed by Maeterlinck, and, as Kandinsky points out, Wagner's leitmotiv pointed the way to a new solution.

Wagner expresses the essence of a character or emotional situation by a sequence of musical notes designed to arouse definite emotional responses in the listener. The character is not analyzed as in the narrative method nor does he act or speak as in the dramatic method. He is contained in an aesthetic attribute, the musical theme which signals an emotional attitude to the audience. Thus, the leitmotiv becomes a symbol. But it is a symbol which, unlike the symbol of Goethe's definition, does not represent a universal idea, but serves as a function of expression in the work of art. Transferred to literature, the leitmotiv symbol may be a simile or metaphor, or the looks and gestures of a character (Thomas Mann's early use of the leitmotiv), or it may assume the shape of an independent character as partially it does in Flaubert. If this device is carried to an extreme point and extended to the entire composition of the work, it becomes Expressionism. Then the symbolic character ceases to be the portrait of a three-dimensional person and becomes nothing but a functional idea of the work. In this case, too, the symbol points beyond itself, to be sure; however, it points not outward to a world, a cosmos, but inward, back to the work of which it forms a part. The character becomes somewhat similar to a musical note which receives its meaning not by representing anything objective in the external world, but solely by functioning in a self-enclosed, artificial world, a composition.

In the first fully Expressionist drama ever written, August Strindberg's *To Damascus* (1898), a beggar also appears; but, unlike Flaubert's, this beggar does not resemble an actual person. His speeches, his looks, his whereabouts reveal analogies to the protagonist's existence which cannot possibly prevail between two different, empirically existing persons. Meeting the hero for the first time, he utters the hero's innermost thoughts. He tells of experiences exactly like those the hero himself has undergone. He bears a scar on his forehead that looks exactly like the scar on the hero's forehead. The hero had received his wound from his brother; the beggar

says he received his scar from "a close relative." In addition to these un-
canny resemblances, the beggar frequently appears in places and at times
where he could not possibly be if he were a character based on empirical
existence as Flaubert's beggar still is. In Strindberg's drama the hero's emotional situation determines the beggar's whereabouts, and his appearances
at the most unexpected times and places are never explained in terms of
empirical causality or plausibility and, therefore, baffle and mystify the
reader. Upon careful reading of the play, however, it becomes clear to us
that Strindberg's intention is not to mystify us, but to express a functional
relationship between the hero and the beggar. When the hero seeks to
drown his self-contempt and self-hatred in a defiant and misanthropic
pride, the beggar comes into view. The hero is told that he and the beggar
belong together, but the idea revolts him. When he first meets this strange
beggar he insults and reviles him. In the course of the drama he moves
into a state more and more resembling that of the beggar, taking on many
characteristics which the beggar exhibits.

This beggar is not a character in the traditional sense of the term. He
has no credible existence as a three-dimensional person apart from the protagonist. He is entirely what Flaubert's beggar is partially—an aspect of
the main character and an adumbration of his fate. He is the degradation
which the haughty protagonist dreads and the resignation which he has
not yet learned. He is the embodiment of the hero's repressed and unreal-
ized emotions and thoughts, and the personification of a possibility of
existence toward which the hero must move. He is the literal embodiment
of a leitmotiv, an aesthetic attribute in the disguise of a human shape, a
function of the dramatic idea.

A certain dehumanization is inevitable in this shift from sculpture to
music as the primary art. The human figure, chiseled or drawn with ana-
tomical accuracy, ceases to be the norm in the plastic arts. The human
character drawn with psychological accuracy ceases to be the norm for
literature. In the manner of the Cubist painting that distorts the human
figure beyond recognition, Kafka, who transforms a traveling salesman
into a cockroach, cries out: "Let us be done with psychology once and for
all!"; and the Expressionist Paul Kornfeld denounces psychological portrait art as a prime evil of literature. Modernist art and literature seek to
restore art to its pure essence. Art had always been and always had to be
a composition of formal relationships expressing an aesthetic idea. But its
pure nature, that which the Greeks called "poesy," the making of expressive shapes, had been confused with extraneous elements, such as morality,
religion, and, above all, mimesis, the imitation of nature. Modernism
seeks to abstract the essential nature of art by banishing all extraneous

considerations or, at any rate, making the artist conscious of the distinction between the essential and the nonessential in his practice.[5] In traditional literature a character may be conceived of as something else besides his aesthetic function; he may be a portrait of a living or historical person, a moral ideal, a psychological case history. In modernist literature his aesthetic function is simply much more consciously emphasized and even, in extreme cases, divorced from all other considerations. There are, of course, within modernism many degrees of abstraction.

The first Expressionist drama shows us not merely one character conceived entirely in terms of an aesthetic attribute, but—and this is of crucial importance—all the characters are so conceived. The drama is a composition of the hero's essential existence, and each character plays the role of a musical leitmotiv expressing an aspect or a possibility of the hero, who is called the Unknown Man. The Lady embodies the Unknown Man's link with life. She is nameless, like the hero himself, because she is not the portrait of a particular lady, but that amalgamation of the sexual and the sublime, the infernal and the celestial through which existence provokes, harasses, torments, and inspires the man. She possesses many concrete characteristics based on Strindberg's memories of his first and second wives. Her parents, for instance, live in the mountains even as the parents of Strindberg's second wife lived in the Austrian Alps. But these specific biographical features are used in a highly abstract way. They are not intended to illuminate the Lady's personality, but to define her function in the Unknown Man's existence. The Unknown Man once wronged her husband, the Doctor, who appears as the hated and dreaded leitmotiv of the hero's guilt and the barometer of his growing self-awareness and repentance. Caesar, a madman kept in the Doctor's household, functions as the leitmotiv of the hero's megalomania, which he caricatures, and he is indeed kept there for no other purpose than to anger and frighten the Unknown Man. For this madman is an adumbration of the danger which his own stubborn pride poses for himself. The Lady's parents function as mirrors of the hero's feelings. Their harshness toward him reflects his own hostility and guilt. The Mother's slowly awakening compassion mirrors his own slowly awakening humility and ability to love.

The characters in the Expressionist drama are often not lifeless abstractions. On the contrary, they often act in striking and unique ways. They exhibit strongly pronounced individual traits and bizarre idiosyncrasies. In the first German Expressionist drama, Reinhard Sorge's *The Beggar*

---

[5] This realization of the true nature of art Kandinsky calls "concrete art."

(1912), the Beggar's father, an insane retired engineer called the Father, races through the apartment beating on a castoff toy drum. He plans an enormous engineering project that would utilize the power of the Mars canals for the enrichment of the world and discusses these plans elaborately. He kills a bird on a Sunday morning because he has run out of red ink, the stores are closed, and he wants to use the blood of the bird for his drawings. But the very fact of its strikingly grotesque quality shows that this highly individual behavior is not intended as a description of character. The Father constitutes a musical variation of the Messiah theme in *The Beggar*. His megalomaniacal Messianic dream functions as a counterpoint to the Son's search for meaning and salvation. In contrast to the Son's idealism, the Father represents the materialistic counterpoint in the composition. He misinterprets the Messianic theme materialistically as technical progress and enrichment. His brutal killing of the bird is a chord that emphasizes this contrapuntal function of the Father theme.

The boundary line between these existential leitmotivs and dramatic characters in the traditional sense is not always easy to draw. Yet some strange detail, some distortion or implausible exaggeration, a grotesque twist, an intentional incongruity, appearances at empirically impossible times and places, again and again destroy our illusion that we might face three-dimensional persons of flesh and blood in these dramas. These characters resemble neither empirical personalities nor allegorical abstractions, but figures appearing in vivid dreams. Indeed, Strindberg called his first Expressionist dramas "dream plays."

Both Surrealism and Expressionism are deeply interested in the dream. Jacques Rivière's *Introduction to the Metaphysics of the Dream* in 1908 was the overture to Surrealism in France even as Strindberg's "dream plays" of 1898 and 1902 were the overture to Expressionism in Germany. Despite the strong similarity, there is a certain difference. French Surrealism was always more fascinated by actual dreams and hallucinations. Following Rimbaud's and even Gérard de Nerval's example, the French Surrealists sought to recapture actual dream images and hallucinatory scenes as the spirit dictated them. Nerval initiated this method in his novel *Aurélie*, assuming that the supernatural revealed itself in dreams. The aim of the poet, according to Rimbaud's "Lettre du Voyant," is to derange the habitual crust of the self and thus unleash the demonic powers of creation (as Schopenhauer and Nietzsche would say, "the Will"). Common sense with its ordered perceptions of a causally determined universe must be shaken up and displaced. The subconscious creativeness of the poet will then emerge in the form of visions and hallucinations, which will form a new universe created by the poet as the new God. Marcel Raymond has pointed out that these "illuminations" are not necessarily formless. Their form, like that of dreams, is given with the vision inherent in it. They possess a definite structure and the poet has only to be faithful to it and bar all the self-conscious reasoning and sentimentality of his empirical person. Nerval's and Rimbaud's method, based on the belief that poetry and the dream or hallucination reveal a divine, demonic reality, remained that of most Surrealists. André Breton systematized it in his Surrealist Manifesto of 1924 and equated the reality to be revealed with the subconscious of Freud and Jung.

Strindberg, more influential in German Expressionism on the whole than Rimbaud, had a somewhat different attitude to the dream than the Surrealists. In his preface to *The Dream Play* (1902) he writes:

> . . . *the author has tried to imitate the disconnected but seemingly logical form of the dream.* Anything may happen; everything is possible and probable. Time and space do not exist. On an insignificant background of reality, imagination designs and embroiders *novel patterns*: a medley of memories, experiences, free fancies, absurdities and improvisations. (Translated by Edwin Bjorkman. Italics mine.)

Strindberg informs us that he intends to copy the form and pattern of dreams, not their actual subject matter. He is less interested in revelation than in the free composition of a universe of pure expressiveness. He wishes to reproduce a universe in which the empirical laws of causality and relationship are suspended and only a single purpose rules: the will to express an invisible situation. The Expressionist dramatist, like the dreamer, concentrates entirely on the purpose of expressing an inner world and refuses to let conformity to external reality divert him from this purpose.

The physical stage, the protagonist's environment, ceases to be a fixed frame of a scene or act and becomes a projection of his inner self. For the idea of the set stage implies the concept of a fixed external nature in which the actions that art imitates take place. Strindberg and the Expressionists conceived of the world to be expressed in art not as a given space of nature but as a field of magnetic and gravitational forces radiating from the soul. The scenery of the Expressionist stage changes with the psychic forces whirling about in it, just as in the universe of relativity space is modified by the matter it contains; the Expressionist character is not a fixed individual personality, but the crystallization of psychic forces, modifying the scene surrounding him. Landscapes reflect the emotional situation of the characters. The mountains through which Strindberg's Unknown Man and his Lady in *To Damascus* travel on their way to her parents take on a savage and frightening look reflecting the hero's apprehensions of the impending visit. Scenes, therefore, change rapidly. What the characters remember is not merely talked about but is immediately presented as a scene flashing before our eyes. Expressionism, like the dream, replaces intellectual analysis by direct visual presentation. Consequently, it moves as far away from the three unities as drama can move. It is an extreme development of tendencies inherent in the Elizabethan and Baroque drama and especially of the Shakespearean form with its rapid changes of scene and narrative-historical rather than analytic structure. In some respects the "dream play" represents the culmination of the theatrical tradition descended from the miracle and Passion plays, Baroque drama and Baroque opera, *Faust*, *Peer Gynt*, Romanticism, and the Wagnerian *Gesamtkunstwerk*. Strindberg's conception of and preface to his *Dream Play*, in which he compares the whole world to a dream of the divine dreamer, suggest echoes of Calderón, the whole Spanish Baroque, Grillparzer, and, above all, the dramas of Shakespeare's late or "Baroque" period, *The Tempest* and *King Lear*. "We are such stuff as dreams are made of" is not very far from the assumptions of the dream play, and the heath scenes in the third act of *King Lear*, in which nature becomes a dynamic projection of a raving mind, are very close to Expressionism.

The Expressionist drama not only destroys the unity of place, time, action, and character; it changes time, like space, into a function of expression. It sometimes accelerates the flow of time fantastically or it reverses its direction. A young man, waiting for his girl with a bouquet of flowers in his hands, ages and turns decrepit before our eyes, still clutching at his bouquet; thereby he demonstrates the constancy of his love. An old man is rejuvenated on the stage expressing youthfulness in old age or longing to start life again free of the mistakes and ruins of the past.

The Expressionist translates the feelings of his characters immediately into actions. They do not merely blurt out their innermost thoughts, they act them out at once. In Paul Kornfeld's drama *The Seduction*, the hero meets a girl, very soon falls at her feet, declares his love to her, and tries to embrace her. A few moments later her fiancé enters the room. The hero immediately insults him in the most violent terms, pushes him out of the room, and strangles him in the hall. As in dreams, wish becomes act, emotion becomes event. The world is not the source of experience, but a structure designed for the purpose of expressing emotions.

To make expression more emphatic, the Expressionist, exactly like the dreaming mind, distorts features of reality by exaggeration. Walter Hasenclever's drama *The Son* (1914), the first stage success of German Expressionism, provides a good example for this technique. The drama expresses the bitter conflict between father and son endemic in German family life at that time, and already treated by the Naturalists of the previous generation. But Hasenclever drastically exaggerates, and thus abstracts the essence of the conflict from the incidental admixtures of empirical reality. The Father literally keeps the son a prisoner and appoints a governess as his jailer. The son is twenty years old, a fact which heightens the extreme grotesqueness of the situation since no real father, no matter how tyrannical, would think of employing a governess for a son aged twenty. The father forbids the son to leave the house at any time. A group of young men, however, helps him to escape through his window.

The Expressionist drama employs speech, too, functionally rather than descriptively. In the realistic drama each character has his more-or-less fixed idiom even as he possesses a more-or-less constant personality, molded by milieu, heredity, and sum total of experiences. Of course, his character may change in the course of the drama, but such changes are the effect of experiences shown by the plot of the drama. His idiom specifies the character's personality and milieu. As in real life, we can recognize and type a character by his speech. His speech distinguishes him from other characters; it marks the boundaries of his individuality, setting him off from other individualities. The realist aims at the variety of accents and idioms which the social and geographical diversity of actual life suggests. The Expressionist reverses this principle, since speech for him is not a means of characterization, but a function of expression. A character changes his speech as he changes his mood. While emotional nuances are mirrored in the speech of characters in the realistic drama, too, Expressionism exaggerates such changes enormously. In moments of despair, joy, illumination, or bliss, the Expressionist character takes on wings, as it were, both physically and linguistically. He rises from his seat, abandons his ordinary dry and bookish prose, and breaks out into hymnic, rhapsodic, or elegiac lyricisms. Most Expressionist plays exhibit such operatic arias, which Kornfeld expressly demands as an integral element of true drama. Horizontally, however, the Expressionist aims at a stylized uniformity of speech reminiscent of the classical drama. This sameness of idiom among all characters does not, as in the classical drama, reflect the cohesion of an idealized social-cultural elite, but underlines the fact that the characters appearing in it are fragments of a single mind.

Nothing is permitted to stay emotionally neutral in the Expressionist drama. Light, above all, becomes a vital actor in the play. In the chiaroscuro style of his old age, Rembrandt anticipates Expressionism by his functional use of light and darkness. Light serves to point out the essential in the picture. It puts a man, Peter, for example, "on the spot." The Expressionists carried Rembrandt's spotlight chiaroscuro into the theater. When a character issues forth into lyrical speech, the stage around him darkens and the beam of light singles him out. The first act of Sorge's *The Beggar* shows us the interior of a cafe. There are several groups in the cafe, literary people, prostitutes, pilots. In the center the hero sits at a table with the Elder Friend and the Patron. When the author wishes to illustrate a particular thought, which the discussion at the center table would either bring out or imply, he lets the various groups act it out. Then the rest of the stage darkens and the light is focused on one single group. By the functional use of lighting, the Expressionist reproduces the dream process. The sudden darkening or illumination of a particular corner of the stage indicates the leaps of the dreaming mind. The lighting apparatus behaves like the mind. It drowns in darkness what it wishes to forget and bathes in light what it wishes to recall. Thus the entire stage becomes a universe of mind, and the individual scenes are not replicas of three-dimensional physical reality, but visualized stages of thought.

The Expressionist dream play could be defined as a dramatization of the stream-of-consciousness or rather the stream of the subconscious. Expressionism is the dramatic alternative to the stream-of-consciousness technique, and both developed at the same time. Both seek to interiorize and vivify the traditional narrative method of presenting inner states in literature. The narrative method, as developed by the great nineteenth-century novelists, probes far beneath the surface behavior of characters and aims to comprehend their "soul." But it can do so only from outside, with the author in the role of psychologizing commentator and observer. It tends to intellectualize and may easily fail to convey the "inner feel" of the character's mind to the reader. To avoid its indirectness, Flaubert and the nineteenth-century Symbolists had introduced their functional symbolism from which, as we have seen, Expressionism developed.

The stream-of-consciousness technique was another way of meeting the same problem. Both stream-of-consciousness and Expressionism seek to get away from the analytical comments of the author to a greater forcefulness, directness, and immediacy. Both seek to present innermost thoughts and feelings from "inside out" instead of describing them from outside alone. The interior monologue seeks to attain this goal by exactly reproducing on paper the flow of associations and its immediate verbalizations in the character's head; Expressionism seeks to attain it by visualizing hidden emotions in symbolic scenes and embodiments. Whereas Expressionism descends from the "musical" or "leitmotiv" symbolism of Flaubert, Ibsen, Maeterlinck, and the Symbolist poets, the interior monologue was born in the consistent Naturalism of the brothers Goncourt and developed by Dujardin. It is Naturalism consistently applied to the inner life. The founders of German Naturalism, Arno Holz and Johannes Schlaf, introduced it into German literature, even as the brothers Goncourt and Dujardin had developed it in France. The clinical semi-Naturalist Arthur Schnitzler applied it consistently in his story *Leutnant Gustl* (*None but the Brave*) in 1900. Joyce, who perfected and transcended this method, was a fervent admirer of the Naturalist aspects of Ibsen.

Well adapted to narrative fiction, the stream-of-consciousness technique was less suited for the drama.[6] Expressionism, on the other hand, employing the visualization of the dream rather than the verbal patter of the waking mind, was eminently theatrical and suitable for dramatic experiment. The drama was to become its proper medium, where it found its strongest following and made its most lasting impact. It was no coincidence that the interior monologue celebrated its greatest triumph in a literature with a strong novelistic tradition, while Expressionism reached its greatest vogue in a culture notoriously weak in the novel but characterized by a strong flair for the theatrical.

For centuries the theater had played an enormous role in German civilization. In the Catholic South and West, the tradition of the miracle and Passion plays, the lavish Jesuit drama, and the Italian opera had created an ineradicable taste for the spectacular, while in the Protestant North the literary drama, fostered by Lutheranism as an instrument of education, became in the latter part of the eighteenth century the instrument for the recreation of a German national consciousness, and "stage German" became the official language and the unifying idiom of the German-speaking countries. Thus the theater achieved an eminence in German life unequaled in any other Western country. With their rediscovery of the artistic and literary traditions of the Catholic areas, the German Romantics discovered the taste for the popular spectacular theater as distinct from the literary drama of the Protestant classics Lessing, Goethe, and Schiller. The German-Catholic taste for the theatrical inspired the Romantics, and its influence can be detected in Goethe's *Faust II*. Wagner's idea of the *Gesamtkunstwerk,* the total work of art employing music, painting, scenic design, and literature, embodied a thoroughly Romantic ideal, foreshad-

---

[6] The Shakespearean monologue, especially in *Hamlet, Macbeth*, and *King Lear*, anticipates the stream-of-consciousness method to an amazing degree.

owed by Tieck and Brentano. Thus, German Expressionism drew on a rich heritage of the theater and two supreme showmen preceded and greatly stimulated its rise—Richard Wagner and Max Reinhardt. Expressionism also parallels Hugo von Hofmannsthal's attempt to revive the tradition of the *theatrum mundi*. Hofmannsthal, of course, sought to restore and revivify traditional forms whereas the Expressionists raced forward toward the new and unexplored. But the passion for the theater as a total work of art is common to both and would cause us to suspect further analogies. Hofmannsthal's late work *The Tower* (1926) indeed adopts many features of the Expressionist drama.

In choosing the nocturnal dream rather than the verbal flow of consciousness as their model structure, the Expressionists like the Surrealists opted for the dramatic against the narrative technique, for the visual against the verbal. Even when Expressionism becomes narrative art of the first rank, as in the tales of Franz Kafka, it draws its main strength from the vividness of individual scenes following one another in a dreamlike succession. Kafka's novels resemble sequences of stage settings or the reels of fantastic films. The effectiveness of a masterpiece like *Metamorphosis* resides to a great extent in its initial and key image—the mysterious transformation of a man into a giant bug. Some of the best lyric poetry of Expressionism is, like the poetry of Surrealism, imagist in character. The sharply outlined dreamlike image or image-scene forms its basis. It resembles in this respect the poetry of the Far East with its brief evocative scenes and largely visual appeal to the emotions. This similarity is not accidental. Rimbaud's *Illuminations,* which deeply influenced both Surrealism and Expressionism, were in turn influenced by Mlle Gautier's French translation of Oriental poetry, and strong interest in Chinese and Japanese poetry and art preceded the rise of Imagist poetry in English, Surrealist poetry in French, and Expressionist poetry in German. The Surrealist and Expressionist emphasis on the visual element of the imagination was also furthered by the rise of the cinema in the first two decades of our century. Franz Kafka was enthusiastic about the early pictures of Charlie Chaplin and the strong similarities between the world of Chaplin and the world of Kafka have often been noted. Surrealism and Expressionism lend themselves in turn extremely well to cinematographic treatment. Two of the most famous works of the two movements have been films, *The Cabinet of Dr. Caligari* and Jean Cocteau's *Blood of a Poet.* It is interesting to note that the Surrealist and Expressionist experiments in motion pictures largely ceased with the advent of the talkies, when the visual element became proportionately less important in films.

The strong emphasis on the visual in Surrealism and Expressionism is, of course, closely connected with the layers of mind with which, in contrast to the original stream-of-consciousness technique, they seek to deal. The stream-of-consciousness technique, in its original Naturalistic form, is, like the traditional dramatic method of narration, unable to show emotional tendencies and layers of mind of which the characters are not aware. Although it reveals thoughts carefully concealed from public view, it cannot reveal thoughts or emotions concealed even from a character's own consciousness. Since it is a stream of consciousness, it cannot show the subconscious, the seething volcano of things completely repressed and hidden. Because of its Naturalism and Naturalistic assumptions, interior monologue must ignore whatever is too shameful and horrible to be allowed across the threshold of consciousness. It digs beneath surface behavior but stops at a layer only once removed from it. Surrealism and Expressionism seek to push on to still deeper and more concealed recesses of the mind. They leave the area of consciousness and penetrate to the dream.

This difference in the depth of mental layers treated necessitates a profound difference of technique. Symbolic disguise takes the place of the direct verbalization of thoughts, which constitutes the stream-of-consciousness method. Pictorial language, the language of symbolic images, which characterizes dreams, takes the place of the flow of words and sentence fragments, which characterizes interior monologue. Instead of a narrative sequence of verbal thought fragments, we encounter a dramatic sequence of sharply visualized scenes. Thoughts become events. The most brutal desires are acted out in dreamlike scenes. The most monstrous fears become envisioned reality. Thoughts of parricide become parricide. Mothers are shown not merely daydreaming of their aged husbands dead and their strong young sons making love to them. In the Expressionist drama *Parricide* by Arnolt Bronnen, a mother seeks to seduce her son next to the corpse of her old husband, whom her fifteen-year-old son has slain. The *interior* monologue still seeks to preserve the distinction between external environment and inner self. Expressionism drops it. With the disappearance of this distinction the Naturalistic stream-of-consciousness becomes Expressionism.

We can observe this change in James Joyce's *Ulysses*. When James Joyce in the "Nighttown" part of his novel penetrates to the nocturnal side of his characters' minds, he abandons the verbalizing stream of consciousness for a symbolizing technique that is close to Expressionism. Joyce here gives body to Bloom's and Stephen's subconscious fears, desires, and repressed memories; he lets these appear as apparitions and shows deeply buried emotional complexes acted out in hallucinatory scenes. Here we can observe Expressionism arise from the author's desire to delve below the stream of consciousness to the subconscious. This immediately brings about the necessity to substitute dramatic visualization for the flow of verbalizing consciousness. In "Nighttown," the visual, imagist, and dramatic element assumes a far greater importance than in any other part of Joyce's ear- and sound-centered works. Exactly as the dream transforms the largely verbal stream-of-consciousness of our waking life into a theater of rapidly shifting scenes, Joyce's "Nighttown" comes close to being an Expressionist drama. Padraic Colum's dramatization of this part of Joyce's novel has made this kinship very apparent and Brooks Atkinson began his review of *Ulysses in Nighttown* by referring to the German Expressionist drama.

Yet there is still a very important difference between *Ulysses in Nighttown* and full Expressionism. The Naturalistic division between external environment and inner self is never dropped in *Ulysses*. In the "Nighttown" scenes, the reader knows exactly that certain associations caused by empirical objects gave rise to the visions. These fantastic symbolizations of emotional realities are contained in a framework of positivistic psychology. Joyce makes sure that we never forget that we are witnesses to the hallucinations of two Dubliners of 1904, whom we have come to know intimately as Naturalistic characters, and not to a magic transformation of empirical reality. We know exactly that the frightful apparition of Stephen's noseless mother represents a projection of Stephen's guilt feelings about his mother's death, with which the author has made us very familiar. We also know very well Mr. Bloom's yearning for his dead son before the boy's spectral appearance in the novel. Joyce's surrealist visions resemble Dante's in so far as both are rationally explained by their frame of reference. The positivistic psychology of Joyce corresponds to the Christian doctrine of Dante. Both provide publicly comprehensible and publicly accepted universes of discourse in which the fantastic events "make sense."

Surrealism and Expressionism drop the framework around the vision. The vision becomes an enigmatic magic universe, obeying the laws of the dream but not spelling them out. The distinction between outer and inner world, between universe and self, disappears as it disappears in the dream. The impossible happens as a matter of fact, and no explanatory frame of reference — theological, positivistic-psychological, allegoric-romantic — is supplied. There are, of course, varying degrees of transparency within the range of Surrealist and Expressionist imagery. Cocteau's famous image of the snowball that turns into a deadly projectile on its way to the heart of its victim can perhaps be understood more readily than Kafka's image of the wound in the patient's side in "A Country Doctor" or the famous transformation of a salesman into an insect. But all these images turn out to be extended metaphors, metaphoric visualizations of emotional situations, uprooted from any explanatory context. In the Surrealist-Expressionist universe no barriers exist between world and self. The snowball thrown with hate kills its victim as though it were a bullet.

Kafka's story of the mysterious metamorphosis of the traveling salesman Gregor Samsa into a giant bug belongs to the same order as Cocteau's example, though on a more complex scale. A brief discussion of this story will lead us to the heart of Expressionism not only because *The Metamorphosis* represents a peak of Expressionist artistic achievement but also because we possess an early pre-Expressionist version of its theme. By comparing the two versions we can study the genesis of the Expressionist form.

In Kafka's youthful semiautobiographical novel fragment *Wedding Preparations in the Country,* the hero, Raban, wishes he could split himself into two parts in order to escape the bothersome duty of visiting his fiancée in the country. His real self would be transformed into a bug, stay in bed, and wallow in irresponsibility. His pseudoself would drive out to the country and fulfill his obligations to the girl. Here the character's wish is described to us as a dream instead of being directly shown and acted out.

In the mature version of 1912, the story *The Metamorphosis,* Raban's infantile wish of turning into a bug becomes Gregor Samsa's mysterious fate. All references as to causes and meaning of this miraculous transformation are completely withheld. In a semi-Expressionist work, like, for instance, the "Nighttown" chapter of *Ulysses,* a character's wish of turning into a bug would also materialize; but we would know that we were witnessing a hallucination inspired by a wish for which the previous context of the work would have prepared us. Kafka, however, eliminates or, at any rate, veils all possible hints as to the causes of the metamorphosis and makes certain that we cannot mistake it for a hallucination, since Samsa's parents inspect his carcass after his death. He gives us absolutely no reason to doubt the physical, objective actuality of the inexplicable event. Thus, he creates a universe of his own which, exactly like the dream, exhibits similarities with our empirical world but is governed by at least one special law of its own.

If we compare the early with the mature version, we find that Kafka has abstracted his autobiographical hero's life from that in which he saw the essence of his hero's inner existence. Raban was many things besides his wish for irresponsibility and parasitic withdrawal from an active and mature way of life. Samsa, however, has become identical with his wish.

His empirical self has been abstracted to the point where it has become one with its essence. The diseased wish for parasitic irresponsibility has turned into an actual event. The character Gregor Samsa has been transformed into a metaphor that states his essential self, and this metaphor in turn is treated like an actual fact. Samsa does not call himself a cockroach; instead, he wakes up to find himself one.

Kafka presents us with a metaphoric visualization of a human existence. As Fritz Martini has pointed out, this is not a symbol in Goethe's sense of the term, for it is not a self-evident individual event (it begs for an explanation which is never supplied) nor does it represent a universal idea or type. Unlike Ovid's, this metamorphosis is not caused by the gods or fate; neither gods nor fate nor God is ever mentioned or implied. Unlike the fable, Kafka's tale does not teach or imply a lesson. In fact, Kafka never connects the miraculous event with anything whatever outside itself. The reader yearns for such a connection with a larger world, for an explanation, a ray of light from anywhere outside to break into the dim prison of Gregor Samsa's frightful existence. But nothing is allowed to pierce the boundaries of this enigmatic universe.

Since the metamorphosis does not symbolize a universal, it obviously cannot be allegory either. It is a symbol only in the sense in which events occurring in dreams are called symbols. Dream images are not symbols in Goethe's sense, since they do not represent general or public truths, but they are extended metaphors uprooted from their context. They are hieroglyphic signs, a pictorial script, which expresses, without revealing, the essence of a hidden situation. In fact, the dream image disguises as much as it expresses, and its expressive function is identical with its veiling function.

A careful reading of *The Metamorphosis* shows us that Kafka's symbolism precisely parallels that of the dream. Samsa's metamorphosis condenses his true existence into an image. The image expresses his existence but does not reveal anything about it, except in the veiled and indirect way of metaphoric disguise.

Gregor Samsa wished to abdicate his power in the family, together with the intolerable burden of hard work which his position entailed, and regain the love his parents once bestowed upon him before he had replaced his old father as the breadwinner and head of the household. At the same time he wishes to turn the tables on his family, who have parasitically exploited his drudgery, and to live himself like a parasite in simultaneous liberty and dependence. He never admits these wishes to himself. They flit through his mind to be quickly repressed and forgotten. But an all-pervasive feeling of guilt and self-reproach haunts him. We find then in Gregor's mind a number of repressed tendencies and attitudes to his family and his work which are mutually contradictory, and, in any case, are not allowed to come to the fore.

The metamorphosis accommodates all his repressed and conflicting tendencies and wishes and embodies, by the same token, his overwhelming feeling of guilt and self-contempt for nurturing his mutinous desires; and through his new shape of repulsive helplessness it provides an immediate punishment. As in Dante's *Inferno,* the punishment is the metaphoric visualization of the sin. Dante's thief becomes identical with the sneaky, thieving essence of his sin and turns into a snake. The sin, visualized and experienced in its naked essence as permanent existence, is the eternal punishment. The psychic or existential condition, which Kafka's *Metamorphosis* expresses in visual terms, however, is not, as in Dante, a specific sin categorized in a universe of sins and virtues, but an almost infinite ambivalence, an impossible emotional predicament. This and the lack of an explanatory framework are the two decisive differences between Dante's figurative and Kafka's Expressionist art.

The function of the metamorphosis is to express utter ambivalence, an empirically impossible task which only an empirically impossible event can perform. Satisfying each of mutually contradictory impulses, the metamorphosis accomplishes the literally impossible. It integrates disintegration, not by reversing or stopping, but by embodying it. Stream of consciousness can show ambivalence only as a sequence of impulses, not as an utter tangle. It has to separate conflicting emotions by time; but their destructive power lies in their interpenetration and complete simultaneity. But the metaphoric visualization, the "image essentielle" of existence, a parallel to Mallarmé's "parole essentielle," can accomplish such a task. By the judicious application and description of such a "strategic metaphor" or metaphoric event, the Expressionist is able to pack a very great emotional complexity and extensive meaning into a very small space with the resultant heightening of concentration and pungency. Kandinsky claims that this type of literature is "epochal," i.e., most appropriate for our time, an age of ambiguous and multifaceted personalities for whom the art principles of former times no longer suffice. The highly complicated modern sensibility wants to experience in art not the physical actualities of human life, but the mystery of the human soul. Kandinsky sees in Maeterlinck's abstract characters and dreamlike scenes the beginnings of an "epochal literature." Strindberg, Kafka, and Cocteau also would meet his demands.

Kafka's method of visionary abstraction, which we have analyzed in his masterpiece *Metamorphosis,* is typical for Expressionism. We find it in the lyric poetry of Heym and Trakl, in the *Ich-drama,* in Barlach's sculptures. Its fantastic use of metaphoric visualizations has its parallel in the Expressionist painter's use of color. Van Gogh formulated the basic principle of visionary Expressionism in the following way:

> For instead of trying to render exactly what I have before my eyes, I use color more arbitrarily in order to express myself powerfully. . . .[7]

Expressionist colors are plainly fantastic because they serve expressive rather than descriptive functions. They bear no relation to the empirical aspect of the original objects which served the painter as his point of departure. Flame-yellow or blood-red faces, orange hair, blue deer, and blue horses cause our attention to wander away from the object to the intense and unnatural color. Instead of the color describing the object, the object becomes a carrier of the color. Even as the metaphor describing Samsa's existence becomes his existence, the colors of Expressionist paintings absorb the bodies to which they are attached. The traditional relationship is reversed. Instead of a color attached to a body, quality attached to substance, we find body attached to color, substance a function of quality, or rather feeling. Finally, in Kandinsky's nonobjective painting, bodies have disappeared altogether and only their aesthetic attributes, colors, are left. The painting has ceased to be a representation of the world and become a pure composition of expressive values.

The Austrian poet Georg Trakl represents in Expressionist poetry an equivalent to Kandinsky's role in Expressionist painting. Just as Kandinsky creates pure compositions of colors and lines, so Trakl creates pure compositions of autonomous metaphors. Trakl's mature poetry consists almost exclusively of metaphoric disguises. Each metaphor has a more-or-less definite emotional tonality and combines with the other metaphors of which the poem consists not in a conceptually coherent sequence of thoughts, but in an incoherent stream of images. The syntactical subordination of sentences or phrases, which represents logical thought in language, is omitted. Trakl's poetry is not a system of communication of ideas, but a flight of images, or autonomous metaphors, resembling an incoherent dream.[8]

---

[7] Quoted by Myers, *The German Expressionists,* p. 25.

[8] The best works on Trakl and Expressionist poetry in general are: Lohner, "Die Lyrik des Expressionismus," in *Expressionismus,* ed. by Hermann Friedmann and Otto Mann, pp. 57–83; Schneider, *Der bildhafte Áusdruck in den Dichtungen Georg Heyms, Georg Trakls, und Ernst Stadlers;* Spoerri, *Georg Trakl;* Simon, *Traum und Orpheus.* The last two works deal with Trakl exclusively.

Yet each poem has an inner coherence, not the coherence of conceptual thought but of a musical composition. Each poem is a composition of aesthetic attributes which are almost entirely divorced from logical ideas. For example, in a number of Trakl poems, the metaphoric image "the petrified face" occurs. Upon careful reading of Trakl's opus, we find that this metaphor possesses a definite mood tonality. It usually expresses a transition from a major to a minor key, i.e., from a mood of joy, spontaneity, innocence, to inner deadness, guilt and hopelessness. The metaphoric image acts somewhat like a note in a musical score indicating that a certain tone or chord is to be played. Or it can be compared to a shade of color in an Expressionistic painting which does not describe the object to which it may be attached but designates a certain mood which the painter wishes to convey.

In revising his youthful poems, Trakl substitutes everywhere for the lyrical and personal "I" metaphoric disguises such as "the stranger," "a thing putrified," "a dead thing," "the murderer." He changes the sentence "I stepped out of the house" into "a dead thing left the decayed house." Trakl's metaphor "a dead thing" describes (or rather, *expresses*) an essential aspect of his existence: the poet has abstracted everything unessential, including the personal pronoun "I," from his existence and has packed the remaining essence into the metaphor, exactly in the way that Kafka in his *Trial* and *Castle* and the Expressionist dramatists omitted the personal name of their heroes as distracting from their essential situation, which alone is to be expressed. And as Kafka, by changing the metamorphosis from a reverie into a destiny, abstracts the incidental features of empirical reality from the truth of Gregor Samsa's existence, Trakl likewise abstracts his empirical personality, his "I," from his essential aspects or situations. Inwardly dead, the poet becomes "a dead thing." He rejects the word "I" because it contains aspects purely incidental and extraneous to the dead self. Similarly stressing the violent and cruel passion in himself, he calls himself not "I," but "the murderer." The metaphor abstracts the person from the feeling. It serves to objectify an intensely subjective content without losing its subjectivism, but, on the contrary, deepening and clarifying it.

Their intense subjectivism makes the great Expressionists Expressionists. Their ability to objectify through abstraction makes them modernists and distinguishes them from the naïve or rhetorical Expressionists who simply shriek out their feelings. Their tendency to abstract through dream-like visualization—through the "image essentielle" rather than through the "parole essentielle," the linguistic experiment—unites them with Rimbaud, di Chirico, and Surrealism, as contrasted to the word-centered modernism of Mallarmé, T. S. Eliot, Valéry, and Joyce, to which, however, other great Expressionists, like Gottfried Benn, conform.

The key concept of this main tendency within Expressionism, or Expressionism proper, is vision. Kasimir Edschmid, in his programmatic manifesto of Expressionism, defines the Expressionists in the following way:

They did not look.
They envisioned.
They did not photograph.
They had visions.
Instead of the rocket they created the perpetual state of excitement.

And further:

(For them) the sick man is not merely the cripple who suffers. He becomes sickness itself. . . .[9]

Edschmid's definition of Expressionism applies not only to Strindberg's dream play, Kafka's tales, Trakl's and Heym's poetry, but also to the sculptures of Ernst Barlach, which belong to the most remarkable and striking work produced by the Expressionist movement.

As Werner Haftmann has pointed out, Barlach's sculptures—mostly done in wood—are visions embodied in carved shapes. Unlike the works of the Greek sculptors, Michelangelo, Rodin, and Maillol, they do not impress us by the faithful recording of the splendor of human anatomy, but by the intensity of selected features or qualities—facial expressions, gestures, bodily tensions. In fact, Barlach's figures, like the characters of Expressionist dramas or Kafka stories, strike one as peculiarly bodiless. They are never shown in the nude, but form one single piece with the heavy, drooping garments which encase them. In his famous "The Avenger," for example, we do not see a body gripped by tension but rather a tension that has become body. The expressive gesture or movement possesses the figure to such a degree that the figure becomes the carrier of the expression, a means for making an emotional state visible. The expressive element swallows the representational; the aesthetic attribute becomes the aesthetic substance. In Expressionist poetry (and in the tales of Kafka), the aesthetic attribute metaphor absorbs the empirical self of the poet and the objective

---

[9] "Über den Expressionismus in der Literatur und die neue Dichtung," in *Tribüne der Kunst und Zeit*, I, 52, 55.

world of nature surrounding him. In Expressionist painting the aesthetic attribute color absorbs the represented objects. In Barlach's sculpture the aesthetic attribute — gesture, tension, facial expressiveness — usurps the human figure. In the Expressionist drama the character's existential situation absorbs the dramatic character in the traditional sense.

The characters of Expressionist dramas are embodied expressions of inner states as well as significant forms of human existence. The hero of the first German Expressionist drama, Reinhard Sorge's Beggar, has no name because he is identical with his "beggary," his spiritual search for the moorings of his existence; and the plot of the drama is the unrolling of all the spheres of existence in which his spiritual quest, his "beggary," takes place. It is an existential panorama, the totality of an existence displayed in encounters in which choices and decisions have to be made, and the hero changes his name—or rather his title—with the relationship in which he is involved. He is called the Son with his parents, the Poet in the company of the Patron of poetry, and the Youth when shown with the Girl. The plot could be summed up in the question: "What am I and how am I to find myself?"

"Is the death-wish stronger than the 'seduction' of life?" is the plot of Kornfeld's drama *The Seduction,* and the name of its protagonist, Bitterlich, is the label of an existence rather than a personal name. Even as Gregor Samsa, the bug, becomes identical with his wish for irresponsibility and self-punishment, in which his "essence" is contained, Bitterlich is identical with his bitterness, his disgust with life, his will to hate, and his will to die.

This abstract subjectivism of the Expressionists, which abstracts the empirical self from its basic problems of existence, anticipates the method of Existentialism as practised by Martin Heidegger in his *Being and Time* and by Sartre in his *Being and Nothingness.* In one of the most important programmatic essays of Expressionism, Paul Kornfeld sets up a dichotomy which seems like a nucleus of Heidegger's fundamental distinction between unauthentic and authentic existence. Kornfeld contrasts "psychological man" to "souled man." Psychological man is man *seen* from outside, as an object of portrayal and scientific analysis. "Souled man" is man *felt* from inside, in his ineffable uniqueness, or, to use Heidegger's term, man as *Existenz.* Martin Heidegger's *Being and Time* of 1927 is in many ways a tremendous elaboration of Kornfeld's Expressionist thesis. Applying the phenomenological method of his teacher Edmund Husserl, Heidegger seeks to define man "from inside," man as "soul." This parallelism derives from the contemporaneity of the genesis of the two movements of Expressionism and Existentialism: Heidegger developed the germs of his Existentialist philosophy as early as 1911, the year in which Expressionism got under way, and Jaspers published his first work in 1917, at the height of the Expressionist movement. Still more important are the identical intellectual influences affecting both movements: Schopenhauer and Nietzsche, Martin Buber's *Ecstatic Confessions* of 1911 and *Daniel* of 1913, the phenomenology of Edmund Husserl, Heidegger's teacher at the University of Freiburg, and, in the decade of the First World War, Kierkegaard's first impact upon Germany. Those who first appreciated him were the pioneers and founders of German Existentialism, Buber, Jaspers, and Heidegger, as well as the poet Rilke and the Expressionists Brod and Kafka.

For Heidegger the essence of man is his existence. Man exists in one irreversible direction. "Thrown" into time he travels toward an ultimate limit—death; and he is aware of this irreversible course of his existence. Thus defined from inside, man can never properly be understood by scientific research and analysis. If we treat man as an object we pass by that which distinguishes him from animals, machines, and gods—the awareness of his personal finiteness, his intimate, terrible knowledge that he will have to die some day, that every second of his life is irreplaceable, and that no one can help him to escape his death or take his place. Thus, human existence is the experience of an inexorable loneliness, a uniqueness for which the categories and methods of science, based as they are on the concepts of statistics, are completely irrelevant. But, and this is of crucial importance, though individual and unique, existence is by no means the same as individuality. Existence is not character. It is not at one with the quirks and idiosyncracies of personality; it is not originality; it is not that which sets a man off from other men. Rather it is that which he has in common with all men, but which each possesses as his own innermost truth. All men must die, yet each knows that he must die alone.

This view of existence shows an amazing parallelism to the method by which the Expressionist arrives at his vision. Both Existentialism and Expressionism are concerned with describing the ineffable. They seek to do justice to that which lies "beyond" or "beneath" conceptual understanding; both seek to define the "feel" of experience which is by definition incommunicable. The concept of existence, like the vision of the Expressionist, is the result of a peculiar process of abstraction; the incidental admixtures of external reality are abstracted from the essential self. This essential self, however, is neither a type (it is with some Expressionists, but by no means with the majority), nor an individual in his full empirical concreteness. It is an "inner feel," an awareness to which all categories and processes of logical thought are completely irrelevant.

The aim of Expressionism is to give voice to this indefinable "inner feel," this translogical essential situation, either by the dreamlike metaphoric visualization or—in a more old-fashioned way—by the parabolic demonstration, or by direct shriek, or by still other forms which we shall encounter. But what is this "inner feel"? What are the essential situations which we encounter in the works of the Expressionists? And how do they account for the various forms of distortion and abstraction in this rich and multifaceted movement?

CHAPTER THREE

Poeta Dolorosus

IN 1917, WHEN THE EXPRESSIONIST MOVEMENT WAS AT ITS HEIGHT, THERE appeared a drama by Hanns Johst with the significant title *Der Einsame: Ein Menschenuntergang* (*The Lonely One: Decline and Fall of a Human Being*). In a very free manner it dealt with the wretched life of Christian Dietrich Grabbe, a nineteenth-century poet and misunderstood genius in whom the Expressionists saw a kindred spirit who had experienced before them their own plight, their insights, and their ecstasy.[1]

At first sight, *The Lonely One* does not seem to be a typically Expressionist play,[2] dealing as it does with a definite historical character whose tragedy, moreover, is caused by a particular event (the death of a beloved wife), instead of being rooted in the hero's very nature. However, if we look more closely at this hero's dismal career, we find that we are dealing here not with an historical character at all, but with *"the poet . . . whose tragic fate it is to perish on the shoals of rigid bourgeois society."*[3] We recognize in him a type of writer, artist, or intellectual who, in many variations, appears throughout Expressionist literature. Hermann Hesse in his semi-Expressionist novel has called his embodiment of this type *Steppenwolf,* the wolf of the steppes, an outcast from the sheltering warmth of society, roaming the barren wastes of his loneliness. Sensitive, gifted, creative, the Expressionist hero is superior to the self-satisfied majority. But his superiority is the bane of his life, the stigma which singles him out from among men; his superiority casts him into outer darkness. His nature is unique; his words find no echo. The few who do befriend him are outcasts like himself, down-and-out tramps like Waldmüller in *The Lonely One;* prostitutes like Hermine in *The Steppenwolf;* Jews, themselves victims of ostracism, like Dr. Benda in Wassermann's *Gänsemännchen* (*The Goose*

---

[1] Kasimir Edschmid cites Hölderlin, Grabbe, Lenz, Kleist, Büchner, and Nietzsche as "unsere Dichter . . . die nichts hielt, nichts begriff und niemand liebte." "Über den Expressionismus in der Literatur und die neue Dichtung," *Tribüne der Kunst und Zeit,* I, 19.

[2] Mathilda Hain calls it "still strongly rooted in the life-feeling of Neo-Romanticism. . . ." Hain, *Studien über das Wesen des frühexpressionistischen Dramas,* p. 44.

[3] *Ibid.*

Man).[4] The poet himself often lives as a vagabond, like Werfel's Laurentin in *Die Mittagsgöttin* (*The Goddess of Noon*), forever suspect to established society and the police. His lot is compared to that of the Jew.

The poet is one who is scattered among the nations . . . an exile. He is, in our time especially, a stranger dwelling in insecure domiciles. . . .[5]

His own family berates and disowns the Expressionist poet. The artist's relationship to his family is highly important for an understanding of that intense sense of isolation which is such an extremely characteristic element in the life and works of Expressionist writers though, as we have seen, not limited to Expressionism or unique in modern times. Many aspects of that movement can be traced to it. It is in his family that the poet meets for the first time and most starkly those forces of bourgeois society which will hound him all his life and finally crucify him. The violent conflict between the generations has generally been conceded as a dominant theme in Expressionism. This conflict has two distinct facets, which of course cannot be completely divorced from each other, being interlocked in a vicious cycle: rejection by the old of the young who are unable to conform, on the one hand, and, on the other, the rebellion of the young who are unwilling to conform. The first aspect of the conflict is intimately connected with the opprobrium attached to a nonlucrative vocation such as poetry or art: Grabbe's mother in Johst's play cannot understand why her son has chosen the shameful vocation of poet. In her world, art can be tolerated only as a spare-time activity; man should fulfill his "real" role in life in a useful job, as, for example, the privy councilor von Goethe had done. Yes, she has heard of Goethe and she respects him, even though he is a poet, for his poetic aberrations had been offset by his great accomplishments as a civil servant. But, alas, in her son she can see nothing but a misfit unable and unwilling to work in a normal, accepted profession. "Where is the house you promised to build for my old age?" she reproaches him. "Where is the money you promised me, so that my gnarled and shaking old hands might find rest at last . . . . Lies. Nothing but lies."[6] She would rather see him buried than jobless and despised, nursing his megalomaniacal dreams of immortality.

Grabbe's degradation is so deep that he does not shrink from taking her hard-earned pennies from her to buy the liquor he depends on for a source

---

[4] Wassermann's novel, which appeared in 1915, has a demonic atmosphere despite stylistic realism and is by theme and message closely linked to the Expressionist outlook.

[5] Wolfenstein, "Jüdisches Wesen und neue Dichtung," in *Tribüne der Kunst und Zeit*, XXIX, 10.

[6] Johst, *Der Einsame: Ein Menschenuntergang*, p. 50.

of inspiration. "To work!!! That I might forget reality and partake once more of my truth—and live! Brandy! Brandy! Brandy! Oh, thrice-holy daemonium!" He sinks to the level of a boozing tramp. A beggar musician, Waldmüller, his only companion, addresses him with a deep ironic bow: "Ecce poeta dolorosus!"—an epithet that could be applied to all the artist-outcasts, living and fictional, whose complex relationship to society is the subject of our present investigation. Various stylistic characteristics of Expressionism can be traced partially to this tense relationship between the poet and his environment.

The precarious social situation of the artist is forcefully dealt with in Frank Wedekind's one-act play *Der Kammersänger* (*The Tenor*). Two types of artist confront each other: the successful tenor Gerardo, darling of society and idol of the ladies, and the aged composer Dühring, who has been writing music all his life without having seen any of his works performed or published. While Gerardo is the object of nightly applause, Dühring languishes in lonely gloom. Now, at seventy, he begs the famous singer to help him arrange a performance of one of his operas. But Gerardo despises the old composer. It was stupid of Dühring to continue to compose after his initial rejection, explains Gerardo. To Gerardo, only success is real. "A healthy man does what he is *lucky* in. If he's unlucky he switches to something else."[7] To Dühring's plea that Art is the supreme value to which he has sacrificed his life, Gerardo answers shrewdly: "We artists are a *luxury article* of the *bourgeoisie.*" For the bourgeois the archsin is waste. The artist who values his creations as something apart from and even superior to the cash they may bring commits that archsin: he sacrifices reality to a conceit. In return, bourgeois society condemns him to a shadow-life. Therefore, with great moral self-righteousness, Gerardo refuses to lift a finger for Dühring.

In the money-determined society of today, the artist can maintain himself only as entertainer. The performing artist is esteemed more highly than the creative artist; if it were not for the singer's voice and talent, Gerardo remarks, Wagner's operas would already be forgotten. Even the creative artist is forced to vie with the tricks of the performer. He must compete with the boxing ring and the dance floor, with the acrobat and the clown.[8] As a retailer of amusement he has a modest place in the bourgeois scheme. He has been pushed to the periphery, to the margin of life.

---

[7] Wedekind, *Gesammelte Werke*, III, 216 ff.

[8] For the great importance clown and circus have in modern art, compare Leoncavallo's opera, the paintings of such modernists as Toulouse-Lautrec, Picasso, Rouault, and Beckmann, the Elegies of Rilke, the drama of Wedekind and Andreyev, the poetry of Lasker-Schüler, the prose of Kafka.

But while the public expects entertainment for its weary hours, the modern artist, bereft of a spiritual center and of a meeting ground with his fellow-men, has nothing to give but his own private soul. The gap ever widens between the public which desires from art nothing more than buffoonery or the tickle of the obscene[9] and the artist who moves ever further toward the purely private and unintelligible. Wassermann formulated the situation in 1910:

The writers . . . sensing their isolation, their alienation, the absence of social coherence and an inner legitimacy based on myth, withdraw into their inner life as into a cave, or proclaim a tyrannical self-sufficiency without finding a bridge to their society and to mankind. On one side a people in feverish activity, all action, all drive, but also wholly without God; on the other side the poet in feverish torment, activated by his dreams, lonely, and deifying himself.[10]

This complete lack of contact between artist and audience, so keenly felt by the writers with whom Expressionist tendencies begin, is presented with poignant irony in Wedekind's tragicomedy *König Nicolo oder so ist das Leben* (*King Nicolo or Such Is Life*). The former king, dethroned and exiled by a revolution of shopkeepers, wanders anonymously through the land, gets a job with a tailor but cannot adapt himself to the bourgeois scale of values and loses his job. Reduced to misery, the onetime king, now in rags, appeals his case to the people.

The effect his solemn poetry has on the audience is the opposite of the expected. His eloquence moves them not to tears but to laughter. His tragic story turns into a comedy hit. In vain does the king assure his listeners that he has revealed to them his "most precious secret which I have kept locked in the depths of my heart." His pleading only heightens their merriment. They no longer are able to accept the tragic except as parody. The king resigns himself to his unwanted success as a clown and permits himself to be hired by a producer. He reaps great applause and ends his days as court jester to a wealthy butcher who has become the new king. In the bourgeois world the natural hierarchy of values is reversed, for "when the butcher is king . . . then the only role left for the king is that of a fool." The vulgar wear the crown; the noble wears the jester's cap. The tragic muse can survive only in the guise of the comic.

---

[9] See the tavern scene in Johst's *Der Einsame,* pp. 55 ff.

[10] Wassermann, "Offener Brief," *Die neue Rundschau,* XXI/3 (1910), 999. See also Rehm's excellent article "Der Dichter und die neue Einsamkeit," *Zeitschrift für Deutschkunde,* XLV (1931), 545 ff.; Rosenhaupt's painstaking elaboration of Rehm's theme *Der deutsche Dichter um die Jahrhundertwende und seine Abgelöstheit von der Gesellschaft;* and the same author's essay on Heinrich Mann in *Germanic Review,* XII (1937), 267 ff.

While *King Nicolo* ends on a note of reconciliation, Wedekind's next play, *Karl Hetmann, der Zwergriese* (*Karl Hetmann, the Dwarf-Giant*), treats the same theme with savage bitterness. Hetmann, a crippled writer with a social mission, in turn cajoles and insults the hostile public until he suffers a nervous breakdown and is committed to a sanitarium. After his release, already skeptical and weary of his mission, he is approached by the manager of a big circus, who offers to employ him as a clown. Hetmann, in utter disgust, hangs himself.

King Nicolo, Hetmann, the writer Buridan in *Die Zensur* (*Censorship*), the composer Dühring in *The Tenor,* are disguises of Wedekind. The theme of the great artist ignored by his public or at best taken for a clown haunts Wedekind in the middle years of his life because it represents his own fate. The author of some of the most interesting plays of modern German literature lived for many years in extreme poverty made all the harsher by obscurity. The public knew him as performer in the Munich night club The Eleven Executioners. His comic talent, his jokes and songs were greatly appreciated, and he was for a time a star of Munich night life. Gradually, his constant troubles with the censor became known and earned him a reputation for obscenity. He was also known as a contributor to the liberal-satirical magazine *Simplizissimus* and spent a term in jail for a liberal cause in which he did not wholly believe. The one thing he believed in, the one thing he wanted to be known for, his drama and its message, remained unknown, unperformed, a vague rumor of scandal and pornography. "Imagine my situation," he writes, "having to introduce myself to the Berlin audiences as clown and jester while my lips may not utter the best I have to say as a serious man."[11]

This continued obscurity and misunderstanding of his art made him so desperate at times that he wanted to stop writing altogether. Neglect poisoned his mind, shut it to larger issues, beclouded his sense of proportion, soured his humor, and thus contributed to the deterioration of the quality of his work.

It has been argued by Julius Bab that Wedekind's creative endowment was so small as to be exhausted after his two or three great plays, *Frühlingserwachen* (*Spring's Awakening*), *Erdgeist* (*Earth Spirit*), and, possibly, *Der Marquis von Keith;* the rest was repetition of former themes or angry complaint at the public's neglect. But the astute and rather "Expressionistic" drama critic Franz Blei delves deeper by linking Wedekind's crisis to the general situation of the artist in our day.

---

[11] Quoted by Kutscher, *Frank Wedekind*, II, 91.

Such crises [of the creative personality] can often be found at the turning point of a modern artist's life; they have their basis in the rootlessness of modern art which does not belong to a definite culture-pattern but leans at best upon the prop of the so-called educated class, a very shaky and insecure support indeed.[12]

Modern art, Blei wrote in 1915, has long ceased to be "the expression of a community." "The people have no literature today and what we call literature does not have the people." Today, the writer cannot take for granted any community of interest with an audience which, instead of passionately participating, leans back in the dark orchestra and waits to be entertained. Modern man holds the conviction that "art is not life but merely appearance; that art exists for art's sake; and that the thing does not have the same degree of reality as a corner at the New York stock exchange."[13] The author unable to cope with the business-centered "grownup" world raves at its banality and indifference; hatred often becomes the inspiration of his work. But the casual public merely smiles condescendingly at his wrath, and the author's malaise rises to a crisis. However, Blei continues, "the resolution of these crises depends on fair entries of credit and debit. Wedekind grimly entered the debit in the column of the others. His own column he left blank and pure like the garment of the prophet, of the true hero."

Here Blei hints at an element that is vital to an understanding not only of Wedekind but of Expressionism as a whole. It could be called the "martyr complex." The feeling of martyrdom cannot, in Wedekind's case, be attributed exclusively to public indifference or hostility to his work. It was with him from the very beginning,[14] and the reading of Wedekind's biography gives the impression that, deplorable as censorship was and backward as the attitude of the public appeared, he himself went out of his way to provoke them. Even his best friend, the composer Weinhöppel, advised him to "step down a little and aim for a more popular style. . . . In general I would, for the time being, try to make the citizens believe I intended to adjust myself to their institutions."[15] Wedekind, of course, abhorred such advice. To the critic Kurt Martens, who had tried to prove to him that a

---

[12] Blei, *Über Wedekind, Sternheim und das Theater*, pp. 43–44.

[13] *Ibid.*, p. 13. Cf. Blei's analysis of the German situation of more than a generation ago with the strikingly similar analysis of the contemporary American situation in Lionel Trilling's essay on Dreiser in *The Liberal Imagination*.

[14] See Wedekind's high-school essay (Kutscher, *Wedekind*, I, 57 ff.) in which the youthful student shows a Philistine objecting to the teaching of classical languages and complaining about the insufficient time devoted to chemistry and other "useful" subjects. The Philistine wants Heine's bust replaced by that of Edison, "mankind's benefactor." The things of the spirit are, so it appears to Wedekind even in his earliest youth, under constant attack from the archenemy, the bourgeois.

[15] Kutscher, *Wedekind*, II, 15.

sense for the tragic was out of place in modern life, since any cause of personal tragedy could be circumvented by energy, "smartness," and circumspection "unless, of course, one takes himself too seriously," Wedekind replied furiously that he would remain a beast with strong instincts and proudly accept his fate as a beast. He courted the disfavor of the *bourgeoisie* on whom he had to depend for his audience by ridiculing their sexual taboos and trampling underfoot their whole moral system. He perplexed their sensibilities, barely accustomed to the Naturalist fare, by fantastic scenes, psychological incongruities, grotesque irony, and above all a ferociously cynical dialogue. Wedekind's style of dialogue is of enormous importance for the development of the Expressionist dramatic style of Sternheim, Kaiser, and Toller. It is based, as we shall see, upon two main factors: aggressiveness against the *bourgeoisie* and rootlessness.

Wedekind wrote his first and most important dramas in the eighteen-nineties, a period when Ibsen's and Hauptmann's Naturalism had barely been accepted on the German stage. What distinguished Wedekind's plays from Naturalism, despite their highly modern, semi-Naturalistic subject matter, was the grotesqueness of situations depicted in them and the quality of the dialogue. Wedekind applied the identical idiom of stilted phrases and caustic epigrams to all his characters from newspaper publisher to rag-picker. From the point of view of Naturalism, this was outrageous ineptitude. But Wedekind's purpose was not to present actual society on the stage. By his peculiar idiom he created a closed world similar to the autonomous space of the Cubist or the closed universe of Kafka and Trakl. In contrast to Kafka, Trakl, and the Strindbergian drama, however, Wedekind built his closed world not for the purpose of visualizing existential situations, but for the purpose of exaggerating and distorting social reality. Like the figures of the Cubist, Wedekind's characters correspond to objectively existing reality, but they are seen and presented in their essential structure rather than in their empirical surface appearance. Wedekind sees sex and drive for power and prestige as the basic conflicting forces dominating life. He distills these forces from actual society in which they are hidden in layers of hypocritical convention and, with provocative glee, exhibits their "pure essence" embodied in empirically impossible specimens. Lulu, his "earth spirit," is nothing but the tyranny of sex become flesh and blood, and his incredibly domineering and successful newspaper publisher Schön is the embodiment of the relentless drive for power that rules modern society. Wedekind demonstrates the basic conflict between the two in the "test tube" of his drama which his artificial but ruthlessly expressive dialogue creates. In the prologue to his drama *Earth Spirit,* he compares himself to an animal tamer in a circus. Here, as in all other Expressionist works, distortion reveals essence. But in the drama of Wedekind, and that of his successors Sternheim and Kaiser, essence lies less in visionary fantasy than in the uniformly exaggerated, epigrammatically concentrated quality of speech.

The ferocity and provocative cynicism of Carl Sternheim's idiom far surpassed Wedekind's. Exaggerating the clipped, dry, and arrogant speech with which the Berlin *bourgeoisie* aped the Prussian ruling caste, Sternheim forged a linguistic weapon with which to flail the hated *bourgeoisie*. He created a new language, a telegram language of utmost concentration, which sharply deviated from customary syntax and word order. Yet the commando tone of the monocled Prussian officer and the Berlin business man can still be heard in the harsh, heartless, and aggressive economy of Sternheim's dialogue, which, through the drama of Wedekind's and Sternheim's disciple Georg Kaiser, was to become one of the most important styles prevailing in Expressionism. Sternheim's dialogues are the literary equivalent of George Grosz's paintings. Both Sternheim and Grosz observe real objects with a caustic, bitter temperament and by exaggerating certain features produce parody and highly stylized social criticism. Bert Brecht is the direct descendant of this parodistic trend within Expressionism, which Wedekind originated and Sternheim developed.

Wedekind was deeply influenced by Büchner's and Nietzsche's aphoristic, ironical style; and Nietzsche's style in turn continues an often-ignored tradition in German literature, the aggressively epigrammatic tradition which includes Büchner, Heine, Schiller, and ultimately descends from Lessing and Lichtenberg. But Kadidja Wedekind, the author's daughter, traces Wedekind's amazing idiom to the complete rootlessness of his background. Born of an eccentric political *émigré* and a cold, tyrannical, San Francisco German opera singer, Frank (abbreviated for Benjamin Franklin) Wedekind was brought up in a lonely castle in Switzerland, which his eccentric parents had bought upon their return to Europe. Cut off from any natural contacts with the speech of the Swiss people surrounding them, the Wedekind family, twice exiled, continued to speak their own caustic and bookish idiom which, with its stilted syntax and paucity of concrete vocabulary, resembled the German idiom spoken by Jews one generation removed from the ghetto. This idiom was to become the linguistic medium of Wedekind's startling dramas. Wedekind's idiom, seen in this light, is distilled homelessness and isolation. It expresses the utter lack of community which gave it birth, not only by its artificiality, but also by the fact that Wedekind's characters do not talk "to" one another but "past" one another and never really communicate. A Berlin Jew, Carl Sternheim, and an invalid languishing in a sick room for years, Georg Kaiser, adopted

Wedekind's type of dialogue and developed it into a prominent feature of Expressionism. In their dramas, each character, isolated in his own current of thoughts, bombards others who never truly answer him. All are united, however, by a language never heard in actual life and yet remarkably expressive of the alienation, confusion, and hysteria characteristic of modern life.

Wedekind expected the very people whom his style and views outraged to applaud him. In this context we also should note that he rebelled against his father, who was himself an eccentric, and preferred being cut off from all parental support to a possible compromise. In view of all this, the thought suggests itself that Wedekind's talent was associated with and partly nurtured by a rebellious wish for martyrdom. Wedekind was uncomfortably aware of the provocative exhibitionism of his work. In the dialogue between the writer Buridan and the Reverend Dr. Prantl in Wedekind's play *Censorship,* Buridan, perhaps the author's most obvious self-portrait, complains of the "ineradicable curse" he must drag with him through life. It is the typical Wedekind tragedy, the author misunderstood by his audience. But the priest answers: "Who can trust a man who for a fee exhibits to the whole world what he should solve for himself in the privacy of his home?"

Disaffection with the bourgeois environment, accompanied by the wish to attract attention, to provoke the enemy, and to be crucified by him, fits in well with the analogies in Expressionist literature between misunderstood artists and Christ. Johst's Grabbe horrifies his mother by comparing his life to Christ's martyrdom. In Leonhard Frank's first novel, *Die Räuberbande* (1914), the Stranger, a projection of the struggling artist's ego-ideal, compares the young artist to Christ.

. . . as long as a man treads the lonely road of self-realization, people stand on the roadside and jeer at him. And his father is ashamed of him. But after he has struggled all the way to the end of the road and attained self-fulfillment . . . men hail him with their hypocrites' shout and tell each other that they never despised him. And his father acclaims him as his son. Scorned and mocked, Jesus Christ bore his cross of loneliness up to the high summit. Today the hypocrites cry hosanna for him and shout their contempt for you because you have not yet carried your cross of loneliness to the end.[16]

The crucified is also the savior. Persecuted at present, he will inherit the kingdom of the elect. Those who scorn him now will one day throng to the theaters and museums to worship him.

---

[16] Frank, *Die Räuberbande,* p. 291.

If the artist is compared to Christ it is, to be sure, a Christ seen through the lenses of the Storm and Stress and its worship of genius; Faust, in the first scene with Wagner, speaks in terms almost identical to the Expressionist author Frank's of the martyrdom of genius, and in his speech the image of Christ merges with that of Socrates, likewise sacrificed by the mob. It is a Christ seen also through the lenses of Young Hegelianism and Historism which negated the absolute validity of any particular artistic style and taste and affirmed the rightness of the future and its pioneers against the traditions of the past and the limited vision of the present. Finally, it is a Christ seen through the lens of Nietzsche and become identical with Zarathustra. All three traditions blend in the proud self-vindication of misunderstood and ostracized genius. Historism especially is a basic assumption of Kandinsky's theory of modernism. Kandinsky sees history as an ever-progressing movement. At any given time of history the spiritual awareness of mankind presents itself in the form of a triangle. The basis of the triangle represents the spiritual level of the mass of contemporaries. The apex of the triangle represents the most advanced insights of the period, limited to a minute creative minority of genius. The triangle moves upward. The basis of today will rise to the level of the apex of today and that level will be the base line of tomorrow. Meanwhile the creative minority will have moved upward far beyond the apex of today, and a new discrepancy between the apex of today, which will have become the base line of tomorrow, and the apex of tomorrow will exist. At no time in history can the majority understand and appreciate the level of the pioneering minority of its day. The lawgiver of tomorrow must by necessity be the martyr of today.

This Left-Hegelian version of an ancient Judeo-Christian belief in the persecuted prophet-savior and the progressive movement of God through history is of tremendous importance for the psychology of the modernist artist and those who sympathize with him. It encourages him to withstand the ignominy and indifference which greet his unconventional work, and, indeed, it compels him toward originality and experiment since his view of history and the human spirit almost precludes the possibility that greatness and immediate recognition can be compatible. Such a view gives historical perspective and social significance to the romantic deification of genius. It runs, of course, completely counter to the theory of mimesis, which presupposes a symbiosis between the artist and the surrounding world, while the historical justification of genius assumes an inevitable discrepancy between the artist and his environment at any given moment of history.

The Hegelian view merges in early Expressionism with the Nietzschean-Zarathustrian myth of the isolated superman, who on his icy summit knows a glory of which only feeble rays penetrate to the common-place world below. Whatever he may suffer is more than outweighed by the sublime joy of the creator eulogized so eloquently by Nietzsche. In the same speech in which Frank's Stranger compares the outcast-artist's martyrdom to Christ's, he also speaks of the heights upon which he stands, looking down at the malodorous pall of the city far below him. "And I am alone," he adds proudly. Setting and outlook are strikingly Zara-thustrian. The same reaction to the bourgeois world which is character-istic of Nietzsche also characterizes Frank (and other Expressionists) and establishes an almost identical metaphorical landscape. The varied and complex reaction of Expressionism to Nietzsche will never be far from the center of our analysis. Here we are concerned with Expressionism's direct succession to Nietzsche as the herald of the amoral creator who is law unto himself.

In February 1921, a sensational trial took place in a German courtroom. The defendant was Georg Kaiser, leading dramatist of Expressionism, whose plays were not only among the most frequently performed in Ger-many itself but also among the vanquished country's first exports to Green-wich Village and Broadway. In feverish haste, Kaiser penned play after play whose novelty hit the public with a terrific impact. A time out of joint seemed to be mirrored in these terse dialogues in which the characters spoke without paying attention to one another, thus giving expression to the tragic suspension of genuine communication between man and man in modern life. An air of breathless modernity emanated from these scenes, some of the world-shaking discoveries and upheavals of the age seemed to be projected onto the stage. And the plays were poured out in rapid succession, sometimes several a year, as though a playwriting machine, which could have been one of Kaiser's Cubist stage inventions, were sput-tering them forth. He was called "the exponent of our technical age,"[17] "the writer of the abstract drama (*Denkspieler*) who applied the technique of the cinema to the play of ideas," "the engineer of the machine-drama . . . the most timely artist-type and the most untrammeled by any tradi-tion."[18] But all this time, while his fame blazed across Germany and beyond, Georg Kaiser sat "at his lonely desk in a luxurious villa . . . and starved."[19]

[17] Lewin, *Die Jagd nach dem Erlebnis: Ein Buch über Georg Kaiser*, p. 183.

[18] Diebold, *Der Denkspieler Georg Kaiser*, pp. 19, 21.

[19] *Ibid.*, p. 29. For the subsequent report on Kaiser's life and trial the following sources have been used: Diebold, *ibid.*, pp. 29–31; Lewin, *Jagd nach dem Erlebnis*, pp. 178–79;

Kaiser was nearly forty when success finally came. For fifteen years he had been writing in obscurity, living on borrowed money and the financial sacrifices of his wife. For his work he needed "a negation of reality," as he called it, a certain luxury which was to serve him as an indispensable screen between himself and the vulgar world. Without it, he could not be certain of his inspiration. But debts had to be paid, wife and children had to be fed. Threatened by the interruption of his work because of financial difficulties, Kaiser sold the rugs in the villa he had rented: now he could once more create in peace.

He was sued and brought to trial. Kaiser turned the tables on society. He, the thief, became the accuser; the law stood accused. The law had no sense of the essential, was blind and crude, he claimed. He, Georg Kaiser, was "not just anybody." "The assumption: 'All are equal before the law' is nonsense," he proclaimed.[20] He was a creative genius whose sacred mission it was to produce. He was a national asset; a verdict of guilty against him would be "a national calamity. . . ." "We have so few original and productive minds that none of us should be allowed to be thwarted in his creative effort. The creative man has the duty to produce even if his wife and children should perish because of it."[21] His life was martyrdom on the altar of his work. The force that whipped him on, the pangs of productive labor, were an ever-present chastisement, a sacrifice for the exaltation of mankind. The lachrymose note of the martyr complex was an insistent leitmotiv in his arrogant plea. "Do not hurt the intellect," he cried pathetically to his judges, "because intellect itself is an incurable wound!"[22]

Kaiser's defense at his trial amounted to a question. What was more important: that some bourgeois keep his rugs or that a great writer be enabled to shed light on the dark chaos of life? Several years later he elaborated his ideas about the creative genius in an article called "Historientreue" ("Faithfulness to Historical Fact"), in which he claimed that the poet "corrects the confusion [of raw life]."[23] The poet distills meaning out of the jumble of accident and brute fact. Therefore, he cannot be judged as other mortals are judged. He stands beyond good and evil.

Bitterlich, a superior-outcast type in Paul Kornfeld's *Die Verführung* (*The Seduction*) (1913), carries the "logic" of this argument far beyond

---

Fivian, *Georg Kaiser und seine Stellung im Expressionismus*, pp. 255–62; Soergel, *Dichtung und Dichter der Zeit; Eine Schilderung der deutschen Literatur der letzten Jahrzehnte. Neue Folge. Im Banne des Expressionismus*, p. 663.

[20] Fivian, *Georg Kaiser*, p. 261.
[21] Lewin, *Jagd nach dem Erlebnis*, pp. 178–79.
[22] Diebold, *Georg Kaiser*, p. 31. Kaiser was sentenced to several months in jail.
[23] *Berliner Tageblatt*, September 4, 1923.

Kaiser's position. He arrogates to himself the right to kill a bourgeois simply because the latter disgusts him. Another example of the outcast-superman who puts himself beyond good and evil is the hero of Gustav Sack's drama *Der Refraktär* (*The Objector*) (1914). Since Sack's works represent various stages of his autobiography,[24] it is Sack's own antisocial attitude which comes to the fore in each of them. He says in a novel fragment:

It must be pure and free around me, and ever cool. Life, however, is a tepid broth, it's one of the most grotesque aberrations of the world. . . . Life is the plebeian side of the world.[25]

In the play *The Objector,* Sack works out neatly the problem of the isolated artist and his civic obligations. Egon, a penniless writer who lives on his businessman father-in-law's money, refuses to leave Switzerland to join the German army when war is declared. His father-in-law threatens to withdraw his financial support and Egon's wife presents her husband with an ultimatum: either he gives up his claim to special status or she will leave him. He does not surrender. She leaves; he stays behind, penniless, ostracized, adamant in his splendid isolation. Egon's objection to military service is entirely selfish, i.e., centered around his artist's self; it not only has no social significance whatsoever, but it also stands in direct opposition to humanitarian pacifism. His objection is Nietzschean, not Tolstoyan, Quaker, or Socialist. The dual standard invoked by Kaiser to justify his theft is invoked by Egon to justify his refusal to serve his country. He has no truck with the others; he has never thought like them, never felt like them. Why should he now? The fate of the masses does not matter to him; he has only contempt for them. They deserve this war; its outbreak merely proved their incorrigible stupidity. They have been shown to have the souls of slaves, and any effort to raise them is wasted. Their rulers are the kind they deserve. These modern rulers, businessmen and politicians, have the same mentality as the masses. In the Nietzschean vein he asks:

Are those oligarchs, craving for customers and not for subjects, worthy of leading the peoples in this war? . . . Are they such radiant stars of the species Man? . . . Just look at their books, their houses, their clothes! Their amusements, their plays, their music! Just look at their mistresses—But most of them anyway are only under-sexed family men![26]

---

[24] Sack, *Gesammelte Werke*, ed. by Hans W. Fischer, I, 43.
[25] Quoted by Fischer, *ibid.*, p. 47.
[26] *Ibid.*, p. 95.

They are greedy, stupid, vulgar. They wage war for purely commercial purposes. They do not desire new souls to rule, but new customers to whom to sell.

Sack, like Nietzsche, is not opposed to war as such. He would welcome an apocalyptic war arising out of universal despair and nihilistic disgust, a war that would be the suicide of the bourgeois world, on whose ruins a nobler world might arise. The hero of his first novel, *Ein verbummelter Student*[27] (1910), thinks:

Let war come! It's lurking all about in glittering spires of clouds—: let a star awaken and arouse it from its lurking slumber . . . ! Nation against nation, country against country—one star, nothing but one raging storm, a twilight of mankind, a rejoicing destruction—! oh, perhaps then something higher [will be born].[28]

But the First World War was, according to Sack, no such war. It was a picayune wrangle for markets and profits. Nihilism had not gone nearly far enough. (It would be interesting to speculate whether the Second World War would have met Sack's requirements.)

Before Egon's final decision, his brother Albert, scientific, liberal, intelligent, and well adjusted, reasons with him. Why, asks Albert, does a writer create? Obviously because he wants to be read. Therefore, he cannot really wish to cut himself off from society. He must stay close enough to his fellow men to be understood. He can be understood only if he shares at least some of their great experiences. For the sake of his work Egon ought to enlist and participate in his nation's collective experience. But Egon replies, "What I write, I write for myself; indeed, only for myself and in order to find myself."

We are here at the crux of the problem of obscurity in Expressionist and, in general, much of modern writing. Art is no longer communication. The chasm between the artist and society has been widened to the point where even the desire to bridge it is lost. Egon, the Objector, for whom writing is a means of "getting to the bottom of things" or "curing his sick heart," a device for self-analysis and self-exploration, represents, like Rimbaud in his "Lettre du Voyant," a stage on the modern writer's road toward the purely private and obscure.

---

[27] There is no English equivalent for the word "verbummelt" because Anglo-Saxon university life differs from the German system. "Verbummelt" is a term used for the perennial student who drifts about aimlessly from one university and course to another, haunts the beer cellars, gathers dueling scars on his face and years in his life without hope or purpose.

[28] *Werke,* I, 291.

Egon, this unusual pacifist, continues the Faustian-Byronic attitude, which had been sharpened by Nietzsche, the attitude of the godlike pariah who stands up, alone and immensely self-confident, against the whole world. At the beginning of the play Egon calls himself a "Faustus redivivus" and someone compares him to the Byronic Manfred. But Sack no longer accepts the Romantic attitude without irony. He peers beneath it and finds it to be a gesture of desperate and ineffectual self-defense. Egon's work, for the sake of which he has accepted absolute loneliness, appears to him, in the end, as nothing more noble than the sublimation of his needs. On the Alpine summit to which he has fled, Egon is confronted by the shades of the characters he has created. They sneer at his illusions about them and himself. Why had he created? "To get to the bottom of things," as he assumed? Not at all. He created because he longed for fame and love. Writing was a roundabout way of attaining what he lacked in real life. "You happened to have no living woman around—so you fornicated with me," says a woman character to him. The proud claim he made in the valley below does not hold true in the icy air of the heights. His "complete emancipation" from his species was rooted not in strength but in weakness.

The Expressionists lived after Nietzsche's and Freud's unmasking of artistic genius. Nietzsche and Freud saw in the artist a congenitally inferior type whose greatness lies in his ability to avenge himself for his shortcomings or to sublimate his unfulfilled needs. Schopenhauer's philosophy implies this denigration of genius. For if the truth of the world is horror and meaninglessness, then the musician as well as the philosopher, both of whom reveal the blind futility of all existence, perform a very dubious service to mankind. If the truth is horror, would not illusion and ignorance make man happier? Thus, not only the artist's motives, but also intelligence itself, become suspect.

The Expressionists have lost the superman's "good conscience," which earlier Romantic generations still possessed. Their pride is insecure, and their arrogance appears to them as disguised self-contempt. They suspect that the boundless self-esteem of the superman may be the compensation of the subman. Immediately upon completing *The Objector*, Sack planned a satirical novel in which a writer-intellectual would consider himself "lord of the world," entertain wild dreams, rave on mountain tops about Nietzschean concepts, and prove actually to be a victim of dementia praecox. The grandeur of his hallucinations would result from the deterioration of his mind.

The precarious nature of the Expressionist poet's dream of grandeur is a prominent aspect of the work of one of the movement's most delicate lyric talents, that of Else Lasker-Schüler. It has been said of her:

Her fancy ambulates within the walls of Thebes of the one-hundred gates; in the shades of Pharaonic groves . . . she is thrown into a reality alien and incomprehensible to her and her heart is filled with unquenchable homesickness.[29]

In this discrepancy between dream world and reality, F. J. Schneider sees the peculiarly Expressionist quality of her work.

Else Lasker-Schüler created a make-believe world for herself and tried desperately to integrate it into her life. She was alternately Tino, poetess-princess of fabulous Baghdad, and Jussuf, Prince of Thebes. She addressed her fellow Bohemians as kings and princes and was happy when she was hailed in return as a fantastic and exalted personage. "The King of Bohemia Paul Leppin," she writes about one of her friends, "gave me his poem 'Daniel Jesus.' I opened it and read: To the dear, dear, dear princess. I wrote him upon a cerulean sheet: Oh, sweet Daniel Jesus Paul."[30] After a performance at the Berliner Theater, she sends a poem to one of the actors: ". . . Only poets and poetesses may think of you, / Only kings and queens may mourn with you."[31] About her origin she says: "I think, in the beginning, I fell from a golden star, a sparkling giants' palace, upon this shabby earth."[32]

The world of the circus fascinated her as it enthralled Wedekind. It threw a ray of magic into the grayness of modern life. "It's like a flowering adventure," she writes to the painter Franz Marc. "I feel as though I were drinking foaming dark wine, and forget all that's gray and hobbling in the world."[33] She clung to the cabarets and circuses and the playful pretenses of the Bohemian cliques, but the "gray hobbling" world ever lay in wait with money worries, humiliations, vulgarity, and lovelessness. If only the world could be shut off, the vulgar, nagging, menacing world of the real. Deliberately she looked away and buried herself in fantasies of childhood. These lines in her poem "To the Prince of the Grail"

> We are framed by stars
> And flee away from earth[34]

could be the motto for her entire work.

---

[29] Schneider, *Der expressive Mensch und die deutsche Lyrik der Gegenwart*, p. 27.
[30] *Die gesammelten Gedichte*, p. 114.
[31] *Ibid.*, p. 155.
[32] *Gesichte*, p. 35.
[33] *Ibid.*, p. 90.
[34] *Gedichte*, p. 161. "Wir sind von Sternen eingerahmt/Und flüchten aus der Welt."

Like the Neo-Romantics and *fin de siècle* artists, she hated the vulgar masses. "We artists are aristocrats to the bone . . . God's favorites, the children of the Maries of all lands."[35] "A potato would understand me sooner than such a primitive person," she said about her maid.[36] The thought that common people like maids, janitors, shopkeepers dared to call their sexual affairs love seemed to violate the very idea of love in her mind. Love was reserved for the few, the isolated and sensitive, who were able to taste to the fullest its sweetness and tragedy. It was a luxury, a refined poetic system of sensations which could never be grasped by the *vulgus profanum*.

I hate love among the common plebs. . . . Love is for Tristan and Isolde . . . Romeo and Juliet, Faust and Margarete, Mephisto and the Venus of Siam.[37]

She poked fun at the Germans' preference for the folkish and untutored. Coarseness was for her the sin that drives man out of paradise. Berlin's big-city vulgarity constantly jarred on her nerves and made her want to escape to her imaginary cities where "dark-skinned slave girls stood around me like black marble columns."[38]

But only a thin line divided the isolated outcast's proud daydream from the nightmare. The tension between dream and reality gave rise to the grotesque self-irony which distinguishes her work from Neo-Romanticism. Her friends have deserted her and she contemplates suicide. She would turn on the gas, but the gas bill has not been paid and the gas is shut off. She wants to drown herself in milk, but the unpaid milkman has stopped making his deliveries. Her poverty makes suicide impossible. Or: "It was night when your letter came. I had just hanged myself. Next morning I couldn't find the tree."[39] Or: "Today I asked the psychiatrist to take me out in his baby-carriage. . . . Sometimes I have such a longing; to sit in the afternoon at a great round table next to Mama and close between my brothers and sisters, and Papa sits at the head . . . and we are sitting so close, like an island, all out of one piece. Nothing alien any more, we are flowing into one another . . . and are not afraid of death."[40] And: "I've stopped speaking without a fee except in conjunctions. If I could only find one that would conjoin me."[41]

Some of her most tragic self-revelations are clothed in that witty gro-

[35] *Gesichte*, p. 23.
[36] *Mein Herz*, p. 79.
[37] *Ibid.*
[38] *Die Nächte der Tino von Bagdad*, p. 9.
[39] *Mein Herz*, p. 106.
[40] *Gesichte*, p. 59.
[41] *Mein Herz*, p. 107.

tesque idiom which, while begging for human sympathy, cannot take itself seriously. There is flirtation in her melancholy and sadness in her exuberance. Her romantic aloofness, like Sack's, lacked the robustness that comes from belief in one's own exceptional status. She stayed in an obvious make-believe world, indulging in a childlike and melancholy masquerade. Reality intruded, tore the crowns off the self-styled princes and princesses, and bared, under Oriental splendor, the struggling habituée of the cafés, starved for love, sometimes for food. She fled from the cruel glare of day to Thebes and Baghdad, palaces and caravans, black slave girls and knights eager to serve her. And again and again, her Tristan, her Prince of the Grail, and all her kings and knights and bishops changed into indelicate fellows who forgot that she was not only a Pharaonic princess but also a woman craving affection. Then the curtain painted with her royal dreams was suddenly rent to reveal an almost Biblical despair.

Soon I will be quite empty, quite white, snow fallen in Asia. . . . I am blown away and past, they can't build another temple with my bones. . . . O world, thou garden of illusions, I no longer want thy fragrance, it feeds false dreams.[42]

The romantically conventional, stylized disguises of Else Lasker-Schüler give way to the metaphoric disguise in Trakl as well as in Heym and the prose poet Kafka. The metaphoric disguises of these full-fledged and greatest Expressionists are to Else Lasker-Schüler's Neo-Romantic disguises what the night dream is to the daydream. The night dream expresses the deepest concerns of the self while shielding it in the unrecognizable costume of the uprooted and extended metaphor, which assumes the role of a hieroglyphic secret script and corresponds exactly to the metaphoric method of Trakl and Kafka, already discussed in the previous chapter. Like the dialogue of Wedekind, Sternheim, and Kaiser, the metaphoric Expressionism of Trakl and Kafka shows a significant relationship to the essential patterns of their existence.

When Georg Trakl's bourgeois family learned that he wrote verses, they heaped ridicule upon him.[43] As a consequence, the already introverted youth withdrew even farther into his shell. His shyness became so great that he was terrified in the presence of strangers. The isolation which may have been in part responsible for his looking to poetry as a means of communication and self-expression became still more profound as a result of this very withdrawal into poetry. The neighbors shook their heads and

    [42] Ibid., pp. 113–14.
    [43] Trakl, Gesammelte Werke, ed. by Wolfgang Schneditz, III: Nachlass und Biographie, 69.

thought him "crazy."[44] This further confirmed him in his aloofness. The vicious cycle begun within his family circle was never to disappear throughout his life. Failure, which had already marked him as a boy, clung to his heels. Johst's Grabbe had been driven to alcohol to forget reality; Trakl took refuge in drugs. He never came to terms with his environment.

The bitter conflict between the necessity of earning a living and the inner duty to his creative urge played havoc with the life of Franz Kafka, as it did with that of Trakl. Kafka went under the yoke and, at disastrous cost to his inner life, tried to keep up the appearance of the respectable existence which his parents expected of him until tuberculosis, like the metamorphosis of his hero Samsa, released him from his prison at the cost of his life. Trakl fled the prison of his home and of bourgeois society to live an entirely erratic existence which, when he was twenty-seven, he ended by suicide. Trakl's and Kafka's isolation from their environment, the inability of their families to accept and understand them, contributed to their anguish of spirit, which expressed itself in the shielding and protecting metaphor. The work of Trakl and Kafka successfully veils the wound of existence in the process of defining it.

Withdrawal and disguise, the keynotes of Trakl's existence, determine the formal principle of his poetry. His visions tantalize the understanding as dreams do, with undecipherable messages. The gate to Trakl's garden is locked, but through its trellis of imagery and metaphoric music we catch glimpses and outlines of a strange, perturbing world. The garden or garden-like park with crumbling statues, symbol of the ancient and secluded, often occurs in Trakl's poetry. The nocturnal garden, the candle-lit room in the patrician house, the empty moon-lit street of a Baroque city, the lonely forest—these are the favorite settings for the poet's private myth. This myth is centered around the self and its intense emotional and spiritual experience. It is anchored in childhood and certain dreams and visions that must have originated there. Phantoms, not humans, people the myth. Upon the visionary screen a carefully masked biography of the poet's essential existence is projected in fragments.

This is how Trakl describes his childhood in "Traum und Umnachtung,"[45] one of the few relatively obvious autobiographical documents in his poetry, even though he talks of himself in the third person: "Filled with disease, terror and darkness, playing secret games in the star-lit garden." He speaks of the "hard hand" of the aged father and the "stony face" of the mother, from whom he stole away to feed the rats in the yard.

---

[44] *Ibid.*, p. 69. ". . . er spinne."
[45] Trakl, *Die Dichtungen. Gesamtausgabe*, ed. by Kurt Horwitz, pp. 151 ff.

He liked to walk around the "crumbling (*verfallenen*) graveyard" in the evening, or look at the corpses in the dusky morgue. In his "chilly bed" at night, ineffable sadness welled up in him and poured out in tears. But there was no one to put a hand on the boy's brow. He loved autumn, when he would walk under the brown foliage by the water. "Oh, these ecstatic hours, these evenings by the green river. . . . The music of his footsteps filled him with pride and contempt for mankind. On the way home he came upon an uninhabited castle. Crumbling statues of gods in the garden, mourning in the twilight." There, he thought, he must have lived in forgotten years.

The poet who so describes his youth remained lonely all his life. "As long as he lived [he was] despised by most, misunderstood by many, genuinely esteemed only by a few," writes one biographer.[46] Even among his friends he seemed alone. His conversation was like a monologue.

This alien in any society, and particularly in bourgeois society, whose favorite metaphoric disguise of himself was "the stranger," reacted to the indifference of his environment by withdrawing into his personal kingdom of dreams and visions until his alienation from life was climaxed in the alienation of his mind. "The music of his footsteps filled him with pride and contempt for mankind." But his self was no less an agony to him than the world. In his early work the idyllic prevailed; the later work is full of terror and regret. As we have already pointed out, the proud Nietzschean faith in the exceptional self, which had sustained Trakl for a while, does not rest on firm foundations with the Expressionists. It is as peripheral to the mature Trakl as is his Christian faith in love. He calls his character "incessantly vacillating and despairing of everything."[47] Periods of feverish intoxication helped on by drugs when "a chaos of rhythms and images" assails him, leaving him no time to live, alternate with others of "ineffable desolation." "What a senseless, torn life . . . !" he exclaims.[48] His despair is so great that he thinks of cutting all ties to Europe, abandoning his poetry, and emigrating to Borneo as a pharmacist, in emulation of Rimbaud, who had abandoned art when he was nineteen and had gone to Africa as a trader. Friends of his art dissuaded Trakl from carrying out his plan.

We meet in Trakl the symptoms of what the devil in Mann's *Doctor Faustus* calls "the extravagant life." His martyrdom comes not only from outside. It is also imposed on him by his very nature, by the way his genius

---

[46] Mahrholdt, "Aus einer Studie über Georg Trakl," in Trakl, *Dichtungen*, ed. by Horwitz, p. 203. An excellent study of Trakl's personality in relationship to his work is Theodor Spoerri, *Georg Trakl*.

[47] Trakl, *Briefe*, ed. by Schneditz, in *Gesammelte Werke*, III, 20.

[48] *Ibid.*, p. 23.

manifests itself. There is in it that high-pressure fury that drives him back and forth between the gasping euphoria of his visionary states and the utter anguish of complete sterility. The poet is under a terrific pressure and the tension that whips him on makes life impossible, for when it relents, there is not the comfort and peace of relaxation, but a complete emptiness, a vacuum whose walls are self-rejection and despair. The Nietzschean jubilation and self-deification on icy peaks is only one, and usually the more ephemeral, part of the life of this *poète maudit*. The other part is spent in an abyss into which neither Zarathustra nor Christ sends a ray of light. Plunged to that awful depth, the poet feels condemned, utterly hopeless, and beyond help.

Gloomy self-doubt and an all-pervading sense of guilt grew more oppressive in Trakl's life as the years carried him away from the state of godlike bliss that was his in childhood and early youth; the purity and splendor of visionary power which he then possessed are symbolized by the mythical figure of Elis. To a poet like Trakl, maturity with its waning capacity to impose vision upon reality comes like a cloud of gloom that settles in the mind and brings about what the Germans call "Umnachtung,"[49] the twilight of reason, the mental night. The theme of madness is already sounded in Trakl's early poem "In ein altes Stammbuch," in which the similarity to Hölderlin is striking:

> Again and again you return, O Melancholy,
> O gentle mood of the lonely soul.
> A golden day glows to its dying.
>
> Humbly the patient one bows to his grief,
> Sounding of euphony and gentle madness.
> See! Twilight already has come.
>
> Again night returns and a mortal thing wails
> And with it another one suffers.
> Shuddering under autumnal stars
> The head bows deeper every year.[50]

---

[49] See the above-mentioned prose poem "Traum und Umnachtung" with its significant title.

[50] *Dichtungen*, ed. by Horwitz, p. 51.

> Immer wieder kehrst du Melancholie,
> O Sanftmut der einsamen Seele.
> Zu Ende glüht ein goldner Tag.
>
> Demutsvoll beugt sich dem Schmerz der Geduldige
> Tönend von Wohllaut und weichem Wahnsinn.
> Siehe! Es dämmert schon.
>
> Wieder kehrt die Nacht und klagt ein Sterbliches
> Und es leidet ein anderes mit.
> Schaudernd unter herbstlichen Sternen
> Neigt sich jährlich tiefer das Haupt.

Even in this early poem we see the circumlocutions for the self so typical of Trakl's style, "the patient one" and "a mortal thing." "Another one suffering with" the self, mentioned in the third stanza, is probably a disguise of the poet's sister. "Shuddering under autumnal stars / The head bows deeper every year" strikes the sad note of resignation and despair which is to sound ever more insistently in Trakl's work until it merges with the note of "gentle madness." Not long before the end of his life, Trakl cried out like one completely humbled and broken:

It is such an unspeakable misfortune when the world falls apart in our hands. O my God, what judgment has been visited upon me! Tell me that I must have the strength to live on and do what is right. Tell me that I am not mad. Stony darkness has come over me. O my friend, how small and wretched I have become.[51]

Despair like this, coupled with the fear of madness, is felt as a punishment for the proud isolation, the joyous self-sufficiency he experienced in his creative periods. For the more-than-human status he rose to in his inspired moments, the less-than-human, the degrading fate of insanity, is retribution. Spirits like Trakl's, exiles from heaven, bypass earth in their fall and end in the night of hell.

The fear of insanity hung like a black cloud over Trakl's life. In the end it overtook him. Deeply shaken by the sights of war, he broke down in a fit of hysteria and threatened to kill himself. Committed to the psychiatric division of a military hospital, obsessed by the irrational fear that he would be court-martialed and shot, he finally succeeded in putting an end to his life.

Symptoms of this persecution complex can be spotted throughout his life and work. His obsession and identification with Kaspar Hauser can be viewed as such a symptom.[52] When Trakl refers to himself, in a letter, as "a poor Kaspar Hauser," he has in mind the same helpless alienation that characterized that mysterious youth. The poem "Kaspar Hauser Lied," in which, as in Wassermann's almost contemporary novel, the watchword of Expressionism, "O Mensch," occurs, contrasts the innocence of Kaspar Hauser, i.e., of Man, to whose heart God spoke as "a gentle flame," with

---

[51] *Briefe*, p. 50.

[52] Trakl, *Briefe*, p. 27. See also Trakl's poem "Kaspar Hauser Lied," *Dichtungen*, p. 109. Kaspar Hauser was the tragic and mysterious youth of early nineteenth-century Germany who claimed to have spent the first eighteen years of his life in a dark hole; who when discovered was at the mental level of an animal; who grew within a short time into a handsome and poetic youth; and who was probably murdered soon afterward. The mystery which shrouded his origins, as well as his tragic end, fascinated not only Trakl's but also Wassermann's imagination.

the guilt of the murderer who stalks him and lies in wait "in the shadows of the dusky hall."[53] Quite in keeping with the schizophrenic personality type to which Theodor Spoerri relates so many characteristic features of Trakl's work, the poet expresses himself by a twofold metaphoric disguise: both Kaspar Hauser, the victim, and the murderer who stalks him are symbols of the poet's self.

The metaphor of the murderer and the atmosphere of mortal terror connected with it occur in other Trakl poems, as in the early "Romanze zur Nacht":

> The murderer palely smiles in the wine,
> The sick one is gripped by horror of death.[54]

The theme of an "unspeakable guilt" seems to wind like a bloody thread through Trakl's poetic work, closely connected with the murderous fear. This guilt (expressed in "Das [or der] Böse") is connected with incestuous dream experiences with the poet's mother and especially his sister.

. . . the blue rustle of a woman's garment petrified him. The nocturnal shape of his mother stood on the threshold. Above him rose the shadow of Evil. . . .[55]

The prose poem goes on, lamenting the guilt revealed by that scene, and then continues:

. . . as he, meditating passionate ("glühende") things, walked down along the autumnal river . . . *his sister*, a flaming demon, appeared to him in a hairy cloak. The stars faded over their heads as they awoke. . . . Woe to the accursed family. When in the *polluted rooms* every destiny has run its course, death enters the house.[56]

There are other apparitions of "the sister" in Trakl's poems and often they are associated with a mood of regret, fear, guilt, or a melancholy joy.[57] On the other hand, there are no love poems, in the usual sense, in Trakl's work. Where love is mentioned or where a poem is charged with emotions of love and tenderness, it is connected with a "rosy angel" or with "the boy Elis," not human beings of flesh and blood. The furtive sister fixation, involved

---

[53] *Dichtungen*, p. 109.

[54] *Ibid.*, p. 27.

> Der Mörder lächelt bleich im Wein
> Den Kranken Todesgrausen packt.

[55] *Ibid.*, pp. 156–57.

[56] *Ibid.* (Italics mine).

[57] The poem entitled "Traum des Bösen" concludes with the line: "Im Park erblicken zitternd sich Geschwister." *Ibid.*, p. 48. See also the poems "Psalm," pp. 58 ff., and "Unterwegs," pp. 96 ff.

in ambiguity, guilt, and terror though it is, is the closest approximation to love for another human being. It is not certain whether actual incestuous relations existed between Trakl and his younger sister Margarete. At any rate, she was the only woman who played an important part in his life. She was his only confidante, sole sharer with him of the pains and voluptuousness of his creation. Margarete, who had once suggested that they die together, committed suicide after showing signs of insanity. Some years later the poet, too, died by his own hand.

The incest motif in Trakl is symptomatic of the erotic dilemma which was an important aspect and motive power of Expressionism. One's sister is perhaps even more than one's mother (because of the greater closeness in age) the woman closest to oneself. If she resembles one physically and mentally as closely as Trakl's sister resembled the poet, one can see and love in her his own self disguised in the opposite sex. Moreover, in Trakl's visions his sister sometimes turns into a youth, i.e., into her brother, into himself. On one such occasion, the sister appears, a dying youth in a broken mirror, and night devours "the accursed family." Could it be that Trakl shuddered at the realization that it was only himself he loved, and no one else in the wide, empty world? At any rate, the exclusion from normal life, the Expressionist's fate in the modern bourgeois world, finds in Trakl its aesthetic and psychological correlative. To the obscure private symbolism of the Expressionist's work corresponds the narcissism of his life, the withdrawal of love from the world to the self. In this withdrawal we shall find the root of the Expressionist's feeling of guilt. Thomas Mann possessed a profound knowledge of this type of artist and his work; and three decades after the Expressionist period he created in his Adrian Leverkühn one of the purest and finest examples of the Expressionist, experimental type of artist to be found in German literature.

In his discussion of *Doctor Faustus*, André von Gronicka has convincingly shown why Adrian Leverkühn must be considered Mann's portraiture of an Expressionist artist.[58] In the section of the novel dealing with Leverkühn's great oratorio, *The Lamentation of Dr. Faustus*, his kinship with Expressionism is made especially explicit. Describing the structure of that work, the narrator uses the terms "Ausdruck" and "expressiv" and "Durchbruch," the last reminiscent of the Expressionist "Aufbruch" and used in the same sense. Leverkühn, like the Expressionists, was accused of "nihilism," "criminality," "cultural bolshevism." Like them, he was misunderstood, ignored, derided by critics and public; and although he pined

---

[58] "Thomas Mann's Doktor Faustus," *Germanic Review*, XXIII/3 (October 1948), 206 ff.

for a new kind of art based on the artist's integration in the community—a fundamental longing of the Expressionists as we shall see—he stayed as esoteric as they did. Connoisseurs and intellectuals remained his public as well as theirs.[59]

Here we come to the link between Leverkühn and artist types like Trakl or Sack's Objector. They do not write for a public. They create for themselves, in a vacuum. Leverkühn accepts this as a natural condition of art in our time. He even goes further and erects obstacles between his art and any possible popular appeal, because "he altogether declined to imagine a contemporary public for his exclusive, eccentric, fantastic dreams."[60] He attaches unacceptable stipulations to public performances of his works, declines the offer of a concert tour, and makes enormous demands on the virtuosity of his performers. His late trio for violin, viola, and violoncello is called "scarcely playable, in fact to be mastered technically only by three virtuosos." "Impossible, but refreshing," he characterizes it himself. Thus he takes a devilish delight in making the barriers between himself and the people well-nigh insurmountable. His music is of the same esoteric type as the poetry of Trakl.

The isolation of the artist is then no longer imposed by society but by the artist himself. An "advanced" artist like Leverkühn has an inborn contempt for humanity. "All about him was coldness," says his biographer at the beginning of his story. Leverkühn is rarely aware of what goes on about him or what company he is in. "I might compare his absentness to an abyss, into which one's feeling towards him dropped soundless and without a trace." (p. 6) Unlike Wedekind, who persistently wooed the world which scorned him, Leverkühn himself is wooed by the world and rejects its embrace.

Adrian Leverkühn knows that his lack of feeling is a forbidding barrier to creation, and he hesitates a long time before he embarks on a composer's career. "I fear to make promises to art because . . . I must disclaim the robust naïveté which, so far as I can see . . . pertaineth to the nature of the artist." (p. 132) Moreover, he despises those elements in art which are based on tradition and the conventions, which appear insipid to him even in the work of genius. The ordinary, the easy, the nothing-but-human in art, bore him and bring on his headache. His interest in mankind is not sufficient to kindle even the elementary artist's emotion: exhibitionism, the longing for renown.

---

[59] There are, of course, exceptions like Werfel who captured a comparatively great number of readers from the start.

[60] Thomas Mann, *Doctor Faustus*, tr. by H. T. Lowe-Porter, p. 165.

Why then does he, conscious of his want of the outgoing emotions, choose art, and above all music, the most emotional of arts, as his career? All other professions deal with life, in one way or another, and life is too explicable, too transparent; it brings on "satiety" and "cold boredom." But musical notation, like theology and mathematics, abides in its own abstract realm, intangible, bewildering, and remote. What draws him to music above theology and mathematics, however, is the special paradox in its nature as both the most abstract and the most tonic of all the arts. It is his longing for the demonic, "the magic square," that which cannot possibly cause boredom.

The ambivalent attitude of Expressionism, and all modernism, toward form, its desire to embrace the most abstract and rigid, the functionalist and Cubist, along with the most primitive and licentious, is epitomized by Leverkühn's relation to music. Leverkühn lacks, as we have seen, "the soul" for artistic creation. "I am a lost soul, a black sheep; I have no warmth," the youthful Adrian writes to his teacher. "Natures like Adrian's have not much 'soul,'" says Zeitblom. He lacks the passionate, the elemental, the "robust naïveté." But he yearns for it as Tonio Kröger yearned for the "normal" bourgeois life. He yearns for the "breakthrough," the liberation from his icy skepticism, which he shares with his age. For in this he is one with his age. The scientific century, the ever-increasing rationalization of culture (culture in Leverkühn's sense is defection from the cultic), make the task of the artist ever more difficult. For if his intellect is on a level with the most advanced of his age, the progressive hygienization of the subconscious life, the taming and "civilizing" of the tumultuous jungle of instincts and emotions from which inspiration derives, are bound to dry up the mainsprings of his own creativeness. With the triumph of rational control over man's nature, the symbolic and intuitive thinking of the poetic, i.e., the prescientific "magic" mind, becomes an anachronism, an absurdity.[61]

The question is whether at the present stage of our consciousness, our knowledge, our sense of truth, this little game [of art] is still permissible, still intellectually possible, still to be taken seriously. . . . (p. 180)

Thus Leverkühn defines the crisis which the modern artist has to face. And with his radical skepticism, he goes further and asserts that the work

---

[61] This does not mean the disappearance of all art, but only of that type of art fed from subconscious longings and dreams, the so-called Dionysiac or romantic art, which the Germans call *das Musische*. The technical, constructivist type of art born from a desire to exercise muscular and intellectual faculties and to beautify life by functional, rational means and techniques has nothing to do with this.

of art has become a fraud, a pretty lie that lacks any legitimate relation to social reality, i.e., to life. For a while the parodistic and ironical art forms will be left, and then—the void.

One of the solutions for the artist's dilemma was devised by Rimbaud as early as 1871. In his so-called "Lettre du Voyant" of May 1871, the young poet develops a theory of becoming a *voyant*, a visionary, which consists in making one's soul something monstrous.[62] It is a "reasoned derangement of the senses." Love, suffering, madness have to be explored with one's whole being, the poisons of life have to be known and exhausted. Rimbaud buttresses this doctrine of "passing through malady, crime, and blasphemy"[63] in order to reach contact with inspiration with a supplementary linguistic theory. According to Rimbaud, language is "a means of forgetting ordinary knowledge, a means of losing oneself and discovering one's monstrous nature." It is "fairly comparable to the method of incantation in religious practice by means of which one arrives at the inexpressible."[64]

Leverkühn, too, in order to overcome his sterility and retrieve the "magic" and "incantatory" essence of music, "passes through malady, crime, and blasphemy." He injects into his blood the poison which will heat it to the boiling point of inspiration, before his mind is burned out. The devil (or his disease) allows him the exaltation that will carry him to heaven before it takes him to hell. Cerebral syphilis, that latter-day equivalent to Dr. Faust's blood-letting, is to stimulate powers too sluggish, too hemmed in by self-critical intellect to burgeon into greatness. Syphilis can still inspire the late-born artist to "towering flights and illuminations . . . upliftings and unfetterings . . . freedom, certainty, facility, feelings of power and triumph." (p. 230) He can still reach a state of euphoria, in which he feels like God. In such moments of ecstasy, which Nietzsche experienced on his Alpine wanderings, Leverkühn is carried like Faust of the chapbook on the devil's carpet high above the world of man. Ideas foam and bubble in his brain and instantaneously become music; and in the transport of creation he is swept toward union with eternity.

But as we have observed in Trakl's case, this euphoria is bound to alternate with periods of bleak depression, sterility, despair; Leverkühn lives through weeks and months during which he thinks he will never again be able to invent a single chord. Far from invalidating his moments of godlike power and grandeur, these states of depression are their *conditio*

---

[62] Fowlie, *The Age of Surrealism*, pp. 54 ff.

[63] This doctrine has a Christian parallel subscribed to, for example, by Dostoevski.

[64] Fowlie, *Age of Surrealism*, p. 55.

sine qua non. One flying so high cannot possibly fall back to moderate bourgeois comfort and low-pressure living; he has to drop infinitely below into a pit of nausea and hopelessness which is "hell in advance . . . already offered on earth." Says the devil: "It is that extravagant living, the only one that suffices a proud soul."

But in the end only desolation remains. Rimbaud, after spending his season in hell, gave up art and left Europe. Leverkühn, at the end of his colossal tour de force, collapses. The aphrodisiac for art has proved too costly; the crisis has not been overcome. Leverkühn's cosmic despair is only a variation, on a grandiose and monumental scale, of that portrayed in Wedekind's Hetmann and Buridan, Sack's Objector, and exemplified in Trakl's paranoia and suicide. In all of them the lordly effort of genius ends in a breakdown. The work which was to fill the vacuum of life proves mere nothingness: "a false dream," as Else Lasker-Schüler once exclaimed; "devil's work, infused by the angel of death," as Leverkühn calls it in his heartrending confession. (p. 497) The lonely "superman" has lost the power to believe in his own myth; and with this loss he has fallen infinitely below his ordinary, unilluminated brother, the scorned bourgeois. The tables are turned. He who has risen higher than other men is now abandoned by them, rejected by himself, and condemned by God.

But only mark . . . heartily respected loving friends, that you have to do with a god-forsaken and despairing man, whose carcass belongeth not in consecrated earth . . . but on the dung-heap with the cadavers of dead animals.[65]

Long before his end, Leverkühn knew that it was weakness, not strength, that distinguished him from others. "You will not believe that I hold myself too good for any profession. On the contrary, I pity that which I make mine own."[66] Artistic genius, traditionally conceived of as reveling in excessive vitality, has become exactly the opposite. The Expressionist artist not only feels superior to the average man, but he also feels inferior to him. Does he even have a right to exist? He doubts it.

---

[65] *Doctor Faustus*, p. 499. Lowe-Porter has "horse-dung" in her translation. I changed this to "dung-heap."

[66] *Ibid.*, p. 130. Lowe-Porter has ". . . I am pitiful of that I make mine own." I changed this to ". . . I pity that which I make mine own." This change has been made in the belief that it will help to clarify the meaning of the phrase for the reader.

CHAPTER FOUR

The Thorn of Socrates

W. H. AUDEN ONCE REMARKED THAT THE ESSENTIAL DIFFERENCE BETWEEN THE nineteenth-century and the twentieth-century hero of autobiographical poetry was that the former regarded self-awareness as a boon, while the latter regarded it as a burden; and that, conversely, the vitality which had once belonged to the poet and been lacking in the Philistine now belonged to the Philistine and was lacking in the poet.

Auden's concept of the twentieth-century poet has special relevance to the concept of the artist in Expressionist literature in Germany. A deep conviction of unworthiness runs as a constant theme through the works of the Expressionists. In fact, Expressionism can be viewed as the attempt of a generation to come to grips with and somehow transcend the calamitous self-contempt that has overtaken the modern poet. Contempt of the bourgeois gives way to envy and even admiration of him. The poet stands on the margin of life, longing to be in the center. But something in himself bars him from ever reaching it, from ever partaking of the world's warmth and love.

His relation to the opposite sex reflects his general feeling of inferiority. If he is not altogether unable to gain a woman's love, he is incapable of holding her affection for any length of time. Convinced of his ugliness (for would he have to write poetry if he were handsome and lovable?), he gazes wistfully at a simple girl and thinks that if she only condescended to love him she could redeem him from the artist's congenital ugliness.[1]

The poet's chronic inability to win a woman's love constitutes the almost exclusive theme of the Viennese Expressionist Albert Ehrenstein's poems and prose sketches. In one of these sketches the poet admires a lovely girl from afar. It is a great feat of courage for him to say "How do you do?" as she passes him in the street. He has clothed her in the splendid garments of his dreams. But an uncouth manufacturer of leather goods marries her and takes her away. "And I was among the congratulating guests," the poet

---

[1] See Franz Werfel's untitled poem in *Die Aktion*, IV (1914), 40.

concludes with Heine-esque self-mockery.[2] For Ehrenstein, woman is the incarnation of the sweetness and loveliness of life; she is life itself, "laughing, swaying, dancing and blooming in all its glory."[3] But the cruel divinity, conspiring with a merciless God, has decreed a celibate's horrible fate for him. Bedbugs visit him, taking pity on his loneliness, but women have no compassion. They do not love the poet; they admire the vulgar, robust extrovert. Women do not care for the things of the mind, and they deny their tantalizing bodies to those who are not strong and simpleminded. Literature and life are divided by an unbridgeable gulf for the Expressionist poet; in his despair he curses literature and praises life: "Ink is bitter / Life is sweet."[4]

He turns in hate against the world, and especially against the women who torment him. He gnashes his teeth at them and maligns them with savage fury resembling the wrath his faithless girl inspired in François Villon. He calls Woman the evil of the earth, wishes he could trample on her face, thrust a dagger into her throat. And he curses himself.

> Rats! Eat up my bowels!
> Break me, rock, and river drown me!
> Why did I not die before my birth?
> Never for me will shine the land of joy.[5]

Franz Kafka, too, was never allowed to enter "the land of joy," and, as with the other Expressionists, the conviction of his unworthiness was intimately linked with erotic failure. Max Brod's biography and Kafka's diaries, as well as his letters to Milena, tell of his unhappy relations with the other sex; and the disastrous story of his engagements has become common knowledge. In contrast to Ehrenstein, however, who pities himself and curses the world and his fate, Kafka looks for the causes of his unhappiness in himself. What are these causes? What is the basis of the deep-seated conviction of inferiority and guilt which receives its most potent expression in such works as *The Metamorphosis* and *The Trial?* What is it that seems to bar the Expressionist from receiving his share of the world's warmth and love?

---

[2] Ehrenstein, "Passion" in *Der Selbstmord eines Katers*, p. 80.
[3] Ehrenstein, *Tubutsch*, tr. by Eric Bosselt and Era Zistel, p. 60.
[4] *Die Gedichte*, p. 15.
[5] *Gedichte*, p. 148.

> Ratten! Fresset meine Eingeweide!
> Zerspell mich, Fels, ertränk mich Furt!
> Was starb ich nicht vor der Geburt?
> Aufstrahlt mir nie das Land der Freude.

Introspection, which will suffer no idea to sink tranquilly to rest but must pursue each one into consciousness, only itself to become an idea, in turn to be pursued by renewed introspection.

This pursuit, originating in the midst of men, carries one in a direction away from them. . . . Where is it leading? The strongest likelihood is that it may lead to madness.[6]

This statement of Kafka makes responsible for his isolation his introverted, excessively cerebral personality, which has drawn him away from his fellows, created a vacuum around him, and finally threatens his sanity. An overdeveloped intellect may, furthermore, preclude the kind of practical intelligence and adaptability on which success and happiness in the world are based. Kafka recalls that, in his youth, he was expert in abstract theological discussions; but it never occurred to him that his awkward looks, which disturbed him, were caused by ill-fitting, badly tailored clothes.[7] The clothes, of course, were a symptom and not a cause of Kafka's unhappiness. His type of mind, which liked to delve into depths and complexities but did not grasp a simple empirical connection of cause and effect, caused his unhappiness. Thus, instead of changing his tailor, Kafka ascribed his unsatisfactory looks to a cruel fate, a special curse that forbade him to be happy; here we can easily see at least one cause of the peculiar metaphysical pessimism that inspires and characterizes his work. The whole direction of his life, so Kafka demonstrates to himself with logical acuity, was determined by this failure of his abstract, introspective mind to explain the obvious.

There is in Expressionism a feeling of the poet's inadequacy and isolation more intense and desperate even than that which torments the heroes of Thomas Mann's early works. Many Expressionists consider themselves cerebral monsters, unable to relate themselves to ordinary humanity. A hypertrophied brain has usurped and destroyed in them the practical and vital traits of personality, the capacity for action and feeling; it inhibits normal functioning and tends to lead to the total disintegration of personality, or, in the words of Kafka, to "madness." These Expressionists look with a furious or yearning envy upon the untroubled simplicity of the average man. The young Franz Werfel's cry, "My only wish is to be related to you, O Man!" and the wide echo which it found are symptomatic

---

[6] *The Diaries of Franz Kafka, 1914–23*, ed. by Max Brod, tr. by Martin Greenberg, with the cooperation of Hannah Arendt, p. 202.

[7] *The Diaries of Franz Kafka, 1910–13*, ed. by Max Brod, tr. by Joseph Kresh, pp. 205 ff. Hereafter this volume will be referred to as *Diaries I*, the later volume as *Diaries II*.

of a generation of authors who felt remote from humanity and desperately attempted to bridge the abyss between themselves and "men." The pathological instability and self-hatred of the cerebral, underemotional personality lie at the bottom of two apparently antithetical Expressionist tendencies: the cry for the dominance of brute life, life unencumbered by intellect and reason; and, second, its apparent opposite, abstractionism, which banishes the personal and emotional element, which is painful and humiliating to the Expressionist, from the new purely formal art which he proclaims and practices. The abstractionist worship of the intellect, while apparently predicated on the intellectual's self-esteem, is, as will be shown, intimately connected with his self-contempt, nihilism, and despair.

At the outset of the Expressionist movement, Max Brod's Walder Nornepygge, the hero of his first novel *Schloss Nornepygge* (*Nornepygge Castle*) (1908)—which Kurt Hiller hailed as the *Faust* of the new generation—envies ordinary people because they live in a fool's paradise which his own acid intellect has "pierced through" and thus made uninhabitable for him. It is the human atmosphere of habits, actions, convictions, and idiosyncracies—the irrational element in people—which gives all others their clearly defined individuality; but his own overdeveloped consciousness has destroyed this atmosphere around himself, leaving him naked, defenseless, without character or personality:

O my ancient experience: all human beings around me, all except myself, have a style. They are fenced in by certain habits, hobbies, instincts, prejudices, they live happily, they operate a firmly defined individuality. And it surrounds them like a wall, gives them strength and courage, helps them across contradictions, dims their consciousness so that they never learn of their lack of freedom. Style hides for them the strings on which necessity pulls them. . . . They live. . . . But I . . . alas, am weary, my logic is prompt and neat. . . . I am nothing but consciousness, I control myself always, I know at every hour of my life that everything I do and think happens by necessity.[8]

Walder's introspective intellect, which recognizes the equal value and justification of all courses of conduct, leads to a total ambivalence which makes any action extremely difficult, indeed absurd, cancels out value, and undermines the will to live. Like a certain common type of neurotic described by Karen Horney,[9] Walder never finds his real self in a succession of "new selves"; each "new self" is only a role assigned to him by his despair, and he discards it. Apart from his changing roles—decadent sybarite, devoted husband, Don Juan, political revolutionary, and others—he is

---

[8] *Schloss Nornepygge: Der Roman des Indifferenten*, pp. 104–5.
[9] *Neurosis and Human Growth: The Struggle toward Self-Realization*, p. 165.

nothing. This forerunner of Musil's *Man without Qualities* knows he can-not have a character. Though he desperately craves to acquire a personality, or, as he expresses it, a style of his own, he knows that his innermost "character is lack of character": "I float along with the wind, I am transparent, I am nothing at all but a warm breeze, a questioning intonation, an un-aspirated H."[10]

Since in all his activities he himself is never really present, Walder is, of course, incapable of genuine feeling, unable to love. His body makes the gestures of love; his curiosity pursues women; his mind stands aside and observes. But he himself? There is no self. The integration of feeling, thought, and action which constitutes the self is unknown to Walder; and this breakdown of his human function isolates him more thoroughly and hopelessly than social ostracism. What emotion he has is concentrated in a single bitter craving to have emotions, to be authentic. He aims at a re-duction of consciousness, at a more primitive but vital way of life. He admires the Philistine and the slow-witted person, he longs to be like the insipid and the foolish:

O Polledi, you clown . . . what would I not give in exchange for one single night of your childish, genuine, unself-conscious laughter! How I desire to be naïve, simple, irresponsibly alive! (p. 140)

The longing to be fully and "irresponsibly" alive marks that tendency in Expressionism which we shall call vitalism. The vitalist philosophies of the turn of the century, above all Henri Bergson's theory of the *élan vital*, postulated a dichotomy between the unconscious flow of life and the ossi-fying, categorizing intellect that is very similar to the conflict postulated in Expressionism. However, Bergson saw in a mental faculty—memory—a means of comprehending the irrational stream of life; his is a serene and Gallicized version of Nietzsche's Dionysian principle. In Expressionism the Dionysian roots of vitalism remain much more evident. The Expres-sionist experiences the problem of vitalism more dynamically and with greater immediacy than did such French and Anglo-American authors as Proust, Valéry, T. E. Hulme, and T. S. Eliot, who were deeply influenced by Bergson. Expressionist vitalism is an extreme and violent reaction to an extreme form of cerebralism. Unlike Proust and T. S. Eliot, the Expres-sionists—in their early phase, at any rate—did not seek to recapture the time-less reality of flowing life through the mental act of memory and artistic recreation. Instead they reacted against all mental activity with a wild, anarchic yearning for "irresponsible life" and "pure sensation."

[10] *Schloss Nornepygge*, p. 468.

Expressionist vitalism reacts against an excessive cerebralism, and its intensity is proportionate to the degree to which the intellect is felt as an inhibitive and disintegrating force in personality. Walder Nornepygge's vitalism is comparatively moderate and subdued; but when the intellect assumes even more destructive proportions than it does in Brod's early hero,[11] vitalism too appears in a more extreme form. "Am I not alive— am I not life?" cries the protagonist of one of Georg Kaiser's earliest plays, *Rektor Kleist* (1905), a misshapen, impotent, acidly intellectual school principal, who has to turn to the intellect because he can find no solace in life. "But my mind is the dead thing inside me which draws me away from life to the flight toward death—to eternity. . . ." (p. 74) The hyperintellectual hero of Gustav Sack's novel *Ein verbummelter Student* goes to work in a mine. He wants to be an animal, hard working during the week and content with gin and women on Sundays, "looking for rescue from himself in the pleasures and the filth of the gutter." "Now," he prays to the stars, "leave me this! Let me remain an animal and stop enticing me with your glittering magic and infernal enigmas—do not let me go mad, eternal gods!" (pp. 247-48) He craves to be a mere cog in the industrial machine, hardened and insensitive, like the iron on which he works.

One cog in a wheel of this . . . infernal clock . . . is worth more than the most iridescent idea and the most profound insight. Strike! Become iron . . . ! Iron, that's it; unfeeling, unscrupulous . . . ! (p. 233)

But he does not succeed in ridding himself of his intellect; he does not give up his futile brooding. "Where is a meaning? Where is a purpose? Where is a reason?—No knowledge, no meaning, no purpose, no reason, no goal, no escape—damnation!" (p. 299) These are his last words before he kills himself.

The escape which the Perennial Student seeks in manual labor, the Nameless Man, the hero of Sack's second novel, looks for in sex. The hyperintellectual goes to the least intellectual, the uneducated, superficial, promiscuous pretty girl and, with the frenzy of a drowning man clutching at a straw, enthrones her in place of his lost God. He comes to her not with love, but for salvation. He has no ambition left, no hope. He wants only to bury his head in her lap, to shut his eyes, and to forget. A man so deeply unhappy, so thoroughly impoverished, cannot, of course, succeed. The girl leaves him for another man. He wishes that, like any normal man, he could challenge his competitor for the girl's affection, and knock him out.

---

[11] Brod himself offers an even more extreme example of the Walder type in the hero of his *Ein tschechisches Dienstmädchen* of 1911.

That would be a solution. But of course he cannot do that. He has been paralyzed by "the thorn of intellect." He does not defend himself, but merely marvels at the incomprehensible, yet long-expected, fact. He realizes that "as I am not fit for knowledge, I am not fit for love nor pleasure, either." " 'Keep your hands off love, if you can't love as the crowd loves, with rage and jealousy!' So pattered the rain on his window, so scoffed the stormy night."[12]

The most extreme example of "the thorn of the intellect" is found in the early work of Gottfried Benn, next to Kafka probably the greatest and most influential Expressionist. It is not merely emotion or action but any kind of social contact and communication at all that presents a staggering problem to Benn's Dr. Rönne, in whom we see a stage in the Berlin physician-poet's development. His purely theoretical mentality cannot achieve the spontaneity required for communication with his fellow-men. When he is required to address a remark to someone, he nearly collapses. Terror grips him as he lunches with colleagues. How can he narrow his intellect sufficiently to participate in a conversation, take sides, form opinions, express requests? He can see everything from so many angles, can think of so many possible remarks he *might* make, that he can make none. In Rönne, says his author, we see

a man who no longer possesses a continuous personality. His existence . . . is indeed a single wound of craving for such a continuous personality, the personality of the "gentleman," who "does not say no to a little drink after his meal and imbibes it with a little joke," but because of his constitution he cannot find his way back to this mode of life. . . . The dissolution of natural vitality in him has taken on forms which look like decadence.[13]

Philistinism appears as unattainable bliss to Benn-Rönne. He yearns for the solidity and rootedness of the ordinary citizen, the *Herr* resting in the enormous self-assurance a thick skin and uncomplicated mind can provide. Benn-Rönne cannot be a *Herr* except in rare moments when, by a colossal effort of mental concentration, he succeeds, for the duration of a luncheon, in participating in the conversation. Then the effect on him is as exhilarating as though he had performed a world-shaking deed:

Jubilation erupted. Chants of triumph. Answer resounded . . . and that for him . . . other remarks joined his, he joined groups of men beneath a vaulted roof of great bliss; he even made an appointment for the afternoon. . . . Rönne tasted his triumph to the full. . . . He deeply experienced the happiness arising

---

[12] *Werke,* I, 339 and 392.
[13] Benn, "Lebensweg eines Intellektualisten" in *Doppelleben: Zwei Selbstdarstellungen,* p. 31.

from the fact that from each of his fellow-lunchers the address "Sir" ascended to him. . . . He gave the impression of solidity and ability to stand up for his convictions; but also of well-bred tolerance of other views. He felt his features smoothed, and a cool self-possession, an even steadiness triumphant on his face; and he retained it until he left the room and closed the door behind him.[14]

But when he leaves the room, he turns once more into the unassertive "junction of wave-systems" he was before. He despairs of ever becoming like those "men of brass" around whom "the objects surge." Wherever he turns he sees peace, unity-in-the-self, identity, blissful limitation, the joy of unself-conscious life. Only he, the intellectual, is excluded; he can only think, he cannot be:

> I only, with censor between blood and paw,
> a brain-devoured corpse, trans-yelling
> curses in the void, with words bespattered,
> the fool of light.[15]

Between his blood, which is part of nature, and his "paw," the tool of action which should be motivated by the blood, lies the guard, the "Wächter" (the "censor"), thinking, reflecting, ambivalent, and hesitating self-awareness.

Because Benn's cerebralism is more extreme and his self-hatred more furious than that of Brod's hero, his reaction to it is more violent and radical. Brod's Walder longed to sink merely to the level of the simpleminded average man of today; Benn-Rönne wants to sink much lower. His ultimate ideal is not the robust Philistine, the *Herr,* though he admires him; it is not even woman, although he speaks of her with envy, since by reason of her physiology she will always stay closer to nature than will man. *Herr,* woman, and savage are only stages on the way to a more remote and primitive ideal, the subhuman and animal, and even further away, the protozoic, the vegetative, and the inert. At the dawn of conscious life there were planted the seeds of the debacle which at the other end of the proud arch of evolution has overtaken the intellectual of our time, who finds himself cut off from all creation and steeped in his sterility. Benn wishes his eyes could partake of the primeval light ("guten frühen Voraugenlichts") which in the form of warmth caressed some lowly creature's skin before the

---

[14] "Die Reise," *Die weissen Blätter,* III/3 (June 1916), 247.
[15] "Ikarus," in *Die gesammelten Schriften,* pp. 37–38.
> Nur ich, mit Wächter zwischen Blut und Pranke,
> ein hirnzerfressnes Aas, mit Flüchen
> im Nichts zergellend, bespien mit Worten,
> veräfft vom Licht.

I have tried to render the typically Expressionist "zergellend" by an equally bold word coinage in English—"trans-yelling."

eye, the pioneer of the hated intellect, began to divide the world into objects seen and a self that sees. Then all was feeling, touching, sensing, a blissful slumber in unity with all nature:

> O that we might be our ancestors' ancestors.
> A little ball of slime in a tepid moor.[16]

With the hopeless longing of the condemned prisoner for his irretrievable freedom Benn exclaims:

O to be like these again: meadow, sand . . . a broad expanse. Earth would nourish me in cool and tepid waves. No more forehead. I would *be* lived.[17]

Retrogression thus becomes the self-hating intellectual's ideal. By universalizing his own cerebralism as the sad fate of modern man, or Homo sapiens as such, Benn-Rönne is enabled to act. He rises up in arms against the scientific century, which has dissolved the blooming world of phenomena into abstractions of mass, space, and energy.[18] Benn-Rönne's rebellion against science is at the same time a revolt against humanitarianism which science serves. What kind of humanitarianism is this, he asks indignantly, that would foist on the human mind the burden of a universe without a meaning; that has no room for God, but only for numbers; no room for completeness, but only for fragmentariness; that knows no end, but only means; and leaves nothing finally, neither color nor shape, neither love nor desire, neither nobility nor enthusiasm, neither unity nor faith, neither the self nor God—only abstractions, only "words and the brain"? Science has ruined its faithful devotee. He would have been happier as a jellyfish.

By universalizing his personal plight into the plight of mankind and postulating retrogression as an absolute ideal, the poet is not merely enabled to act in revolt, but to establish contact with a deeper layer of life, which corresponds closely to Bergson's vitalist Reality and to Jung's concept of the "collective unconscious." A spontaneous feeling wells up, breaking the crust of a cerebralized self, and beckons like the mirage of the blue ocean in desert wastes. "Südlichkeit" ("Southernness") is the leitmotiv of these visions. It is associated with a tropical bliss of inactivity and

---

[16] "Gesänge," in *Schriften*, p. 19.

> O dass wir unsere Ururahnen wären.
> Ein Klümpchen Schleim in einem warmen Moor.

[17] *Schriften*, p. 127.

[18] See also Picasso's reproaches to Pameelens' father for having let his son study instead of protecting the boy's tender senses from the poisonous acid of twentieth-century science. *Schriften*, p. 142.

sensual release; with the serenity of a flight of white marble steps beneath
a hot sun, which promises a kind of religious salvation to the brain-monster
Pameelen, the *Vermessungsdirigent*; with the color and warmth of the
Mediterranean, exemplified by the rhapsodic vision of Van Gogh splash-
ing ecstasies of color on a canvas in a lush garden in Provence; or simply
by the single word "Ithaca," which surges up from the subconscious, a
magic word, rich with associations of sunlight, repose, lushness, and a
primitive, ecstatic way of life:

O it flutters like a dove to my heart: laughing—laughing—laughing—Ithaca!
—Ithaca! O stay! Stay! Do not forsake me yet! O such striding, to have found
home, amidst the falling blossoms of all the worlds, sweet and drowsy.[19]

The capture of supreme moments, the formulation of the ineffable, the
expression of subconscious reality—the implicit goal of art through the
ages—are the avowed goals of modernism. Rimbaud's *Illuminations* and
Mallarmé's evocation of rich associations through single words pointed the
way. But whereas Rimbaud, the Surrealists, and Expressionists like Trakl,
Heym, Kafka emphasize the image or dreamlike scene as the building stone
of their compositions, Mallarmé, Valéry, T. S. Eliot, Benn, and the Expressionists of the *Sturm* circle make the single word (in Benn's case a noun
like "Ithaca," for example), and the universe of associations buried in its
sound effects and multiple meanings, the basic unit of their "magic." We
see an analogous contrast between the dream play of Strindberg, with its
reliance on visual effects, apparitions, lighting, dreamlike entrances and
exits, on the one hand, and, on the other, the drama of Wedekind, Sternheim, and Kaiser, with its emphasis on linguistic effects, epigrammatic
concentration of dialogue, and aggressive formulations. The sardonic Expressionism of Wedekind, Sternheim, and their novelistic counterpart
Heinrich Mann greatly influenced Benn's "word magic." Benn cites Sternheim and Heinrich Mann, next to Nietzsche, as the chief influences on
him. In Benn's poetry the *parole essentielle* of Mallarmé assumes the place
of the *image essentielle* of the visionary Expressionists. As Edgar Lohner,
in his excellent analyses of Benn's poetry, has made clear, Benn's finest
poems, like "Die Dänin" ("The Danish Girl") or "Das verlorene Ich"
("The Lost Self") consist of strategic nouns (not strategic metaphors as in
the visionary poetry of Trakl and Kafka), strung together in musical compositions. The basic chords of these compositions are cultural associations
and evocations rather than dreamlike metaphors. This method connects

---

[19] *Schriften*, p. 128.

Benn with T. S. Eliot. Both produce poetic effects by means of a highly Alexandrian learning, an Alexandrianism that the title of Benn's chief prose work, *The Ptolemaic,* deliberately underlines. Benn's word "Ithaca" is an early example of his method. This single noun evokes, like Eliot's quotations and allusions, a whole world of cultural, historical, mythological, and literary associations for poet and reader. Yet despite its learned connotations, it is a "magic word," a *parole essentielle* in Mallarmé's sense. It achieves the same kind of hypnotic and concentrated effect as the dream-like metaphoric visualizations of Kafka or Trakl. Its use and effect are musical. It evokes a magic contrast, a counterpoint of bliss and freedom to the main theme, the wretchedness and frustration of the "brain-eaten" modern self. If properly used, the single noun acts like an incantation. It enables the poet to conjure an atavistic surreality which redeems him from his monstrous modernity.

Benn's experience of spontaneity and paradisiacal bliss arising from these word-inspired visions is precarious and short-lived. The poignancy of the visions comes from the desperate and nostalgic urgency with which they are entertained. A cold, deadly reality closes in on Benn's visions from all sides and threatens the poet with final sterility:

> See the last blue fragrance of this summer
> on seas of asters float to distant
> tree-brown shores; see
> this last counterfeit-bliss hour
> of our Southernness
> dawn
> vaulted high.[20]

It is the terror of losing this last autumnal illusion of spontaneity, this "counterfeit-bliss hour" ("Glück-Lügenstunde"), that prompts Benn-Rönne, in the little drama *Ithaka,* to murder his old professor who sees in scientific knowledge the supreme value of life. In his trancelike state, Rönne steps up to the scientist and scholar, seizes him by the throat, and incites his fellow students to kill him:

[20] *Schriften,* p. 20.

> Sieh dieses Sommers letzten blauen Hauch
> auf Astermeeren an die fernen
> baumbraunen Ufer treiben; tagen
> sieh diese letzte Glück-Lügenstunde
> unserer Südlichkeit
> hochgewölbt.

We are the youth. Our blood cries out for heaven and earth, and not for cells and worms. . . . Soul, spread your wings; yes, soul! soul! We want to dream. We want ecstasy. We call on Dionysus and Ithaca![21]

Around the same time as Benn's esoteric *Ithaca*, a more sensational Expressionist drama was written and became a stage success, Hanns Johst's *The Young Man* (1916), in language and structure one of the most typically Expressionist plays. Johst's drama likewise shows the revolt of a young student against a hated teacher, Professor Moralclean. The Young Man shouts at his teacher to "shut up." This unheard-of breach of discipline, which leaves the professors gasping, is followed by a ringing denunciation of the school system and a paean on youth and life.

We are young, young! . . . We are blossom! . . . Nothing but color and cry!! . . . Nothing but fragrance! . . . Nothing but joy! . . . . . . Life! . . . Life! . . . Is yearning! . . . . . . And action drops from the hand! . . . Thunder and lightning! . . . Above all and again and again: Long live life!!! . . .

Professor Moralclean:
You'd do better to study your grammar than declaim a misunderstood Nietzsche! . . .
The Young Man:
(*steps up to him, solemnly, festively; all eyes are wide, fixed upon him*) You deserve worse, much worse! . . . But I will only slap an exclamation point in your face! . . . This shall be the dirge for my brother Euphorion Jubeljung![22]

This passage in Johst's drama is the naïve and rhetorical-Expressionist counterpart to Benn's scene of revolt. The spirit of the two works is the same. We confront the same kind of revolt on two different levels: one, Johst's, on the naïve and personal level; the other one—Benn's—on a more philosophical and abstract level. Johst's hero avenges his schoolmate whom the crowded school curriculum of the traditional German high-school system has ruined; Benn's hero avenges the self that the excessive burden of knowledge has destroyed. Style and vocabulary are nearly identical; a hectic explosive rhythm is common to both passages.

Both passages exhibit certain key words flung at the aged representatives of learning with deadly provocation: Youth, blood, soul, life! Their conjunction with "Dionysus" in Benn's passage betrays immediately the Nietzschean heritage. The new image of Greece proclaimed by Nietzsche in the work of his own youth, *The Birth of Tragedy*, also underlies Benn's

---

[21] *Schriften*, p. 129.
[22] *Der junge Mensch: Ein ekstatisches Szenarium*, p. 16.

magic "Ithaca." But Nietzsche likewise made the key words of German vitalism "life" and "youth" fashionable in Wilhelminian and post-Wilhelminian Germany. In his second "Thought Out of Season," *Of the Use and Abuse of History for Life*, as its full title runs, Nietzsche condemns the German educational ideals and pillories the memorization of factual knowledge as detrimental to a wholesome, active, and truly cultured life. He finds excessive knowledge and vitality incompatible, and thus raises an issue which assumes in German vitalism a much more formidable role than in the French vitalism of Bergson. Nietzsche concludes his eloquent denunciation of the German *Bildungsideal* with a ringing address to German *youth* whom he encourages to unburden themselves of the dead weight of knowledge for the sake of knowledge. With this work, Nietzsche gives voice to a Storm and Stress which was to prove more powerful and lasting even than the original Storm and Stress initiated by Rousseau one century earlier. The irrational Youth movement, founded in the 1890's, vitalist Expressionism, the whole accent on youth, vitality, and irrationality, and the glorification of instinct, which characterized an important segment of German intellectual life from the Wilhelminian to the Hitler period, found their first inspiration in Nietzsche's brilliant attack on the overburdened educational tradition of Germany. It was not Nietzsche's fault that this "vitalism" was greatly favored by the ruling class of the Prussianized Germany whose barracks could, of course, thrive better on vitality and instinct than on excessive doses of intellectuality.

Benn's key word "soul" relates to the Expressionists' own contemporary climate of thought. A decade after Benn's *Ithaca* and Johst's *The Young Man* were written, a work appeared that expressed in extreme form the philosophy of German vitalism: Ludwig Klages' *The Mind as the Adversary of the Soul*. The ex-disciple of the poet Stefan George postulates the inevitable conflict between reason and instinctive vitality—or between "mind" and "soul"—as the catastrophic fate of Western man. He voices the same desperate hostility to the mind and the same desperate yearning for a primitive, instinctive, "soulful" life which we find in the Expressionists. Expressionism and Klages' vitalism are both extreme symptoms of the same cultural discontent; and Klages' style, too, shows a significant similarity to the dithyrambic prose of Expressionism.

Ludwig Klages' dithyrambic glorification of "the soul" turned into the Nazis' still more vitalist glorification of "the blood," the final key term resounding in Benn's outcry against science. There is an unmistakable proto-Nazi sentiment in Benn-Rönne's violent rebellion against modern science and humanitarianism, in this invocation of a primitive way of life for which the "blood" of "youth" cries out;[23] and like Johst, Bronnen, Klemm, and other Expressionists, Benn joined the Nazi movement. Nevertheless, this step surprised many in view of the modernist and experimental form of his work. In a letter to Klaus Mann, however, Benn explained that what attracted him to Nazism had also inspired the central theme of his work—the longing for retrogression and liberation from intellect:

Metropolis, industrialism, intellectualism, all these shadows which the age cast over my thoughts, all these powers of the century which I took issue with in my work—there are moments when this whole tortured life vanishes and nothing remains but the wide plains, the seasons, the earth, simple words—: folk. This is the reason why I placed myself at the disposal of those to whom Europe . . . denies recognition.[24]

Madness, in the sense of Benn's "counterfeit-bliss hour," an escape into retrogression from an inner complexity too difficult to bear, was for most Expressionists (though rarely as extremely stated as in Benn's case) a consummation devoutly to be wished. Surfeited with his ivory-tower intellectualism, Wedekind's Alwa Schön extols the life of criminals and athletes, of people "who have never read a book,"[25] and emulates them though it ruins him. Despairing over the falsification of reality inherent in the act of mental creation, Sorge's Beggar pines for escape into pure physical sensation. Edschmid and Klabund celebrate heroes who leave mind and conscience behind them and plunge into careers of furious and insane activity. "I'd rather be a brute than spiritualized" (Lieber verroht als vergeistigt") is Sack's motto, and the hero of his autobiographical novel A Nameless Man envies flowers and vegetables their unconscious existence. Kaiser's Billionaire in the first drama of his Gas trilogy, The Coral, exalts the coral, the symbol of primitive, vegetative life, over the cross, the symbol of the spirit. Paradise lies behind us, says Kaiser's Billionaire, and the way to happiness is a way of retrogression. Like Benn's Dr. Rönne, he yearns for the security of the prehuman paradise and commits murder to attain it. The impersonator Oliver in Kaiser's drama Twice Oliver shuts his eyes to a deeply unsatisfying reality and, in order to keep his illusion and make his "counterfeit-bliss hour" permanent, actually goes mad. He finds his paradise, his literal fool's paradise, in the insane asylum.

The same longing for retrogression to a simpler, less inhibited way of life is found in other modernist literature. Eliot's Prufrock wishes he could be "a pair of ragged claws / Scuttling across the floors of silent seas." In

---

[23] The parallelism to Nazism is also clear in Benn's lecture to German First World War veterans, "Das moderne Ich," in Schriften, pp. 192 ff.

[24] "Doppelleben," in Doppelleben, p. 90.

[25] Wedekind, "Die Büchse der Pandora," in Gesammelte Werke, III, 125.

Valéry's "Cimetière marin," the sea exerts the same fascination as the symbol of unconscious life that the coral has for Kaiser and the amoeba for Benn. André Gide's *Nourritures terrestres* and his *Caves du Vatican* (*Lafcadio's Adventures*) picture the same mirage of irresponsible vitality, the same Nietzschean Rousseauism, that beckon the Expressionists. Yet Gide's revolt against Victorian inhibitions and useless learning is idyllic compared to the violence of the Expressionists. This infinitely greater violence in both content and tone of the Expressionist revolt can be attributed to the traditional peripheral social existence of the German intellectual, which, as we have noted, tends to incline him toward a greater subjectivism and rebelliousness than his more integrated Western colleagues.

There is a definite interrelation between the frustrations and humiliations under which German youth had to grow up in family and school and the violence of the Expressionist and vitalist outburst. Yet families and schools in Germany were probably not more authoritarian than in France, perhaps less so. But while the French high-school student already tended to look on himself as a part of society, and on his misery as something in the nature of things, a necessary passing phase, the German adolescent did not see himself as part of society and was more prone to resort to violent anarchic rebellion in his daydreams and fantasies. At any rate, it is easy to trace the close connection between the repression exercised by the German family and school and the rise of the Expressionist movement. The two works which, in the drama and in the novel, first reveal Expressionist tendencies—Wedekind's *Frühlingserwachen* (*Spring's Awakening*) (1891) and Heinrich Mann's *Professor Unrat* (1905) (the latter world-famous in its film version, "The Blue Angel")—contain violent caricatures of the German school system. In Wedekind's play the school system is seen resting firmly on the tyrannical authority of the father; it is characterized by the puritanical suppression of the adolescents' sexual instinct. Kaiser, too, whose *From Morn to Midnight* is the classic treatment of the favorite Expressionist idea of a "breakthrough" into "life," starts his dramatic career with plays about adolescents and school tyrants (*Rektor Kleist*; *Pupil Vehgesack's Case*). Wedekind anticipates the Expressionists proper when he puts "life" in glamorous contrast to the martyrdom of adolescence. Melchior Gabor, expelled from school and condemned by his parents, contemplates suicide at the grave of his schoolmate Moritz Stiefel. The symbol of Life, the "Masked Gentleman," appears to him; he looks significantly like a fashionable roué, a man of the world who probably frequents the fanciest night clubs. He dissuades Melchior from heeding his dead friend's ghostly call and leads him into the "world."

The world beckons as a vision of triumph to the youthful poet Georg

Heym, whose apocalyptic visions belong to the most striking work of the Expressionist revolution. Heym rebelled furiously against the compulsions and restrictions which family and school imposed on him. One of his schoolmates committed suicide, and Heym envied him the courage for a deed which he himself continuously contemplated. Heym's fascinated preoccupation with death, a conspicuous element in his work, can be traced partially to his early wretchedness and isolation. A skull decorated with vine leaves graced his desk as a constant memento.

Heym's somber meditations on death provide the foil to his yearning for glory, enjoyment, and triumph, his dream of a wild exuberant life in years to come. This brooding introvert is at the same time possessed by a fierce vitality, a hunger for love, experience, physical and emotional fulfillment. He has the reputation of being a wild student, an instigator of "orgies" in outlawed fraternities, a leader among his classmates, and a horror to his teachers. The impression he makes on the Berlin Bohemians among whom he later moves is that of "life itself. . . . He was the boldest, sunniest, least self-conscious [of us]: his vitality broke through all barriers of convention."[26] It strikes his literary friends as incongruous that this sports-lover and "nature boy" should be the poet of the most macabre visions and miasmic scenes. The strange combination of melancholy pessimism and exuberant extroversion, of *Weltschmerz* and *Kraftnatur*, is strongly reminiscent of Storm and Stress; it suggests that similar forces of repression caused similar reactions of anarchic individualism in the late eighteenth and early twentieth centuries. In a diary entry Heym analyzes the relationship between his melancholy death-bound self and his restlessly ambitious life-bound self.

The strangest thing is that no one has yet noticed that I am the most delicate . . . but I have carefully concealed it *because I have always been ashamed of it.*[27]

This conflict between a surface brutality and an inner delicacy which the surface brutality covers is symptomatic of Expressionist vitalism.

Like Heym, young Hans Werner in Hanns Johst's autobiographical novel *Der Anfang* (*The Beginning*) (1917) is poised between the lure of early death and the fascinating vista of adventurous life. Two of his friends have killed themselves during the final year of the hated Gymnasium. The day after commencement, Hans himself stands in the ceme-

[26] Helmut Greulich, *Georg Heym (1887–1912) Leben und Werk*, in *Germanische Studien*, VIII (1931), 33. See also Seelig, "Leben und Sterben von Georg Heym," in *Georg Heym, Gesammelte Gedichte*, pp. 215–16.

[27] Greulich, *Georg Heym*, p. 29. (My italics.)

tery, having "soberly decided" to put a bullet through his brain; but he decides to experiment with life for a little while and reserve suicide for later.

This impulse to suicide stems from a terror of his own grandiose expectations of adult life after the long purgatory of his school years, which assails the adolescent when he stands at last face to face with this "fabled" life—his sustaining hope throughout his long, tortured school years.[28] Shut off from significant experience during their formative years, the young idealists in Johst's novel vowed to change the world and "start an absolute reformation" as soon as they had gained their freedom. But when the hour strikes, they are terrified. They have anticipated adult life so intensely that its actuality can only be anticlimactic.

The Son in Walter Hasenclever's programmatic drama Der Sohn, which was the first genuinely Expressionist play ever performed (1916), refuses to pass the baccalaureate examination because he is too afraid to venture into life. The horror of school life produces in its victims a will to fail which often ends in suicide even when success is in the student's power.

Hanns Johst dedicates his "ecstatic scenario" The Young Man, "a hymn to life, youth, and ecstasy," to "the shades of [his] first friends" who died as high-school students by their own hands. Beneath this dedication he writes: "It is a frenzied pleasure to be young and to know of the enchantment of death." A strong death-wish presupposes the ecstatic embrace of life. The two cults which dominate German youth in the early twentieth century, the cult of suicide and the cult of passionate irrationalism, are complementary. This combination explains the paradox that vitalists like Sack, Kaiser, and Benn should long for the lowest and least conscious forms of life, and indeed for the inanimate. Their cult of "life" is a longing for the cessation of individualized existence, a craving for a kind of sensate death or sleep.

Even as Johst's Young Man, after avenging himself on his hated teachers, strides forth into life, Hasenclever's Son steps into freedom literally over his father's corpse. The Son, a high-school student of twenty who has failed his baccalaureate examination, is a virtual prisoner of his father, who forbids him to go out, supervises his homework with a whip, and keeps a governess to watch over the boy when he himself has to be away. From his window at dusk the Son looks out over the city, where the first

[28] About the waves of suicides which swept through German youth shortly before 1914, see the highly interesting article by Landauer, "Selbstmord der Jugend," in Der werdende Mensch: Aufsätze über Leben und Schrifttum, ed. by Martin Buber, pp. 68–72.

lights of the restaurants and night clubs sparkle, as remote and unattainable as the stars. The forbidden night life of the city is a magic legend and the rumors that come from the forbidden paradise are as fabulous as tales from Arabian nights. The dreams which they engender in the lonely youth are of a fearful intensity. The women, whom he can see only from afar, are goddesses; the desires they arouse in him, which, of course, cannot be fulfilled, throw him into terrible depressions. Since experience is denied him, he has an abnormal lust for it, and an unconquerable sadness overcomes him on Sundays, when "every housemaid can go to a dance," and he may not leave the house. The "obligatory student suicide" again presents itself as the way out. But again the balance between death-wish and hunger for life tips in favor of life. The Son's vitality is greater than his morbidity, although both are facets of the same emotional instability which finds reality only in moments of ecstasy.

One only lives in ecstasy; reality would embarrass one. How beautiful it is to experience again and again that one is the most important thing in the world.[29]

In Arnolt Bronnen's fierce drama *Vatermord* (*Parricide*), a fifteen-year-old youth kills his father (significantly, a Social Democrat), pushes his lecherous mother aside, and strides out to embrace his liberty. The parricide's deed has no social or constructive motives whatsoever. It is pure, almost mythical, self-exaltation. The murderer revels in his vitalist, godlike power and freedom. When we consider the even more sadistic outburst in the sequel to this drama, *Die Geburt der Jugend* (*The Birth of Youth*), it will not appear as mere coincidence that the author was to become a Nazi fanatic. Roving bands of boys and girls on horseback gallop over the aged, trample them to dust, and shout that they are God.

There is, of course, a deeper reason for the violence and retrograde longings of German Expressionism. It is the spiritual despair which Nietzsche's message "God is dead!" formulated, which is not limited to Germany but blights the whole outlook of the Western world. "God is dead!" His mind forces this difficult truth upon modern man. Eternal death, so his mind informs him, is the fate of all existence. But man's narcissism longs for immortality. Therefore, he is tempted to turn against his mind. But while Eliot recommends deliberate return to tradition and traditional faith as the exit from the "waste land," and Valéry concludes his "Cimetière marin" with the cautiously experimental motto "il faut tenter de vivre," the German intellectuals cannot so easily accept either solution; they have never known a central social-cultural tradition capable of affording them a spirit-

---

[29] Hasenclever, *Der Sohn*, p. 7.

ual home; and emotional revolt has been a chief stimulant to the flowering of their literature. The greatest work of German literature begins with a powerful protest against the very same frustrations and alienations with which the twentieth-century poets still deal; and the antithesis between thought and feeling has informed this literature ever since Goethe's Faust and the whole Storm and Stress rebelled against an Enlightenment which deprived man of the comforts of religion—his only solace in social isolation—and in addition came to the German from an envied and hated neighbor.

Nostalgia for a vanished, idealized era rather than affirmation of a living tradition in continuous growth emerged as the keynote of German thought. One of the most remarkable documents of the Storm and Stress, Herder's *Auch eine Philosophie der Geschichte (Another Philosophy of History)* (1774), contrasted the virtues of earlier periods, especially the Middle Ages, with the decadence and melancholy which hyperintellectualism had injected into the modern age. Thus, Herder reversed the customary view of history held by the Enlightenment. He diagnosed the modern age as sick and decadent but found vigor and greatness in a period which all enlightened men despised. Herder glorified earlier ages because in them he saw life still unspoilt by intellect, strong, clear, and generous in its emotional responses, undivided in its will.[30] While the Romantics continued Herder's idealization of the Middle Ages, Winckelmann, Goethe, and Schiller yearned for "the noble simplicity (actually 'simple-mindedness'— 'Einfalt') and tranquil greatness" of an idealized Greece. Both the *Klassiker* and the Romantics emphasized the simplicity and vitality of their idealized historical periods as a deliberate and polemical foil to the debilitating sophistication and one-sided intellectualism of their own age. The more extreme the plight of the German intellectual became, the more remote, paradoxical, and retrogressive his idealizations turned out to be. In the opening paragraph of his *Use and Abuse of History*, Nietzsche dwells on the impression of "noble simple-mindedness and tranquil greatness" created in us by the sight of grazing mammals. With serene artistry Nietzsche evokes the idyllic bliss of the herd. He contrasts the animals' enviable ability to forget from one moment to the next with the curse of

[30] Of course, Herder also championed the French Revolution to his dying breath. To represent him as purely backward-looking would be decidedly unfair. In many ways he himself was one of the great representatives of the Enlightenment. Like Diderot, Rousseau, Lessing, and most other men of the Enlightenment, Herder sought to balance and harmonize reason and feeling. His backward-looking antirational extremism was only a phase of his youth. Yet it was this side of Herder upon which the Romantics of the next generation concentrated exclusively and which they developed into a militant irrationalism.

excessive memories which prevent the Gymnasium-trained German from ever attaining the happiness and fulfillment of a harmonious existence. Nietzsche's image of the animal herd passing by us with the tranquil serenity of total forgetfulness became a leitmotiv theme of modern German literature. Kaiser's envied coral and Benn's protozoic idyll in the primeval "tepid moor" are extreme variations of Nietzsche's grazing herd. But distant echoes of the Hellenism of Weimar can also be perceived in Benn's longing for "southernness," the magic word "Ithaca," his evocations of the azure sea and marble steps basking in Mediterranean sunlight.

These bizarre idealizations of low forms of consciousness arise from the cerebral man's desperate desire to escape the inhibiting and disenchanting consequences of his intellect. The intellect, as Nietzsche pointed out, not only deprives us of our cherished illusions, but it also undermines our ambitions, our sense of values, and finally our will to live. "Life must be saved from intellect!" became the watchword of too many German intellectuals after Nietzsche. They ignored Nietzsche's passion for truth and analysis and his supreme respect for intellectual honesty. They overlooked the subtle and melancholy irony contained in his image of the herd and in similar ideals of retrogression found in his works. By taking him literally and reading him partially, they misunderstood him totally, as Walter Kaufmann's study of Nietzsche has made abundantly clear.

Unfaithful to Nietzsche but desperate in their need, his German successors indicted "the mind" as such as the deadly and deadening enemy of "the soul." Intellect was identified with "Jewish intellect." The self-hatred of the German outcast-intellectual turned into hatred of his Jewish fellow-intellectual in whom he could despise a still more extreme form, indeed a caricature, of his own alienation from the ruling type of his society, the Prussian officer and the captain of industry who together had created the glory, wealth, and power of the new German *Reich*. As Fritz Stern in his study of the "Germanic Ideologues" has shown, the men who provided Nazism with its ideological armor—Paul de Lagarde, Langbehn, Moeller van den Bruck—were all disgruntled, unhappy, rootless, and thoroughly isolated intellectuals who turned a pathological insecurity into pathological hatred of the intellect and of Jews. It was the sensitive editor of Dostoevski's collected works in German, Moeller van den Bruck, who before he ended his nomadic and Bohemian existence by suicide turned out the tract that gave Nazism its slogan—*The Third Reich*; and this spiritual godfather of Nazism was a close friend of the Expressionist poet Theodor Däubler, who collaborated with him on the Dostoevski edition. A displaced professor, who hated professors with the ardor of the Expressionists,

Eugen Dühring, famous for Engels' polemics against him, was the first man to suggest the mass extermination of all Jews as a solution to the cultural crisis of modern Germany. The wave of violent irrationalism that swept through the ranks of the German intellectuals after the First World War had its roots in much earlier phases of German history. This irrationalism enabled men of great intellect such as Oswald Spengler and Ernst Jünger not only to condone but to foster the Nazi spirit, and thus to commit the worst *trahison des clercs*. Thereby, however, they betrayed Germany's basic tradition, which had never been pure anti-intellectualism but rather a combination of extreme intellectuality and extreme concern over its debilitating consequences. Not only Faust's disgust with the intellect but also the fact of his being an intellectual hero in the first place is of significance. The proto-Nazi intellectuals ignored one half of the German tradition and thereby falsified the whole. They were forced to strike off the lists of "true Germans" not only Heine, but also Kant, Lessing, Herder, Goethe, Schiller—and a correctly understood Nietzsche as well.

The greatest Expressionists could never be true prophets of Nazism because they embodied the traditional German tension between intellect and anti-intellectualism rather than the pure anti-intellectualism of the Nazis. Intellect was too deeply ingrained in them. No matter how desperately they wanted to, they could not rid themselves of it. No matter how they hated it, intellect made them what they were. It was the essential condition of their existence as well as of their art. Intellect formed their style as it had formed Schiller's and Nietzsche's. Even if Benn deceived himself when he joined the Nazi movement, the Nazis on their part could not be deceived for long. They refused to tolerate a "decadent" and "Judaized" modernist in their ranks and cast him out into the isolation that had always been his true home. Rhetorical Expressionists like Johst and Klemm, in whom modernism had not deeply taken root, could divest themselves of their Expressionist past and become Nazis in good standing. Intellect had not become their style. But Benn's flirtation with Nazism had been, as he saw by 1936, a double failure of judgment. He had misjudged the nature of the Nazi movement when he believed that it could ever make concessions to intellect; and he had misjudged the nature of his own genius when he believed that simple retrogression could ever save it from itself.

The Expressionist attitude toward the intellect is not entirely negative; it is ambiguous. Though the Expressionist hates and rebels against his intellect and feels it as a lacerating thorn in his flesh, a painful wound that prevents him from participating in ordinary life, he also considers the intellect his strength, the only source of his creativeness. Thought, though an ailment, is also a refuge for the ailing; it is the activity that transmutes deficiency into creativeness, weakness into strength. It is, to employ Edmund Wilson's terms, the link that connects the "wound" with the "bow," and embraces both the negative and the positive aspects of the artist's personality. But beyond playing an ambiguous role in the poet's personal life, the intellect has also an ambiguous role in social and cultural terms. On the one hand, intellect shatters the illusions of the average man and reveals a universe without purpose and ruled by absurdity; on the other hand, mind transcends the nihilism implied in its own discoveries and constructs a new universe of eternal ideas, pure forms, abstract and unchanging beauty. "The artifice of eternity," as W. B. Yeats called this "unnatural" world that the human mind erects as a consoling refuge above the quicksands of natural existence, beckons the Expressionist as enticingly as does the retrogressive ideal of unconscious animal or vegetative vitality. This "abstractionism," as we might call this worship of the abstract intellect, is not unrelated to "vitalist" contempt of the mind; both tendencies exist in the same authors and even at the same time. Abstractionism and vitalism form two aspects of the hypercerebral personality. Vitalism corresponds to the hyperintellectual's self-hatred, abstractionism to his self-glorification or self-justification; and the two alternate, intertwine, and combine. While the Expressionist intellectual sees himself as an outcast and inhuman monster, he likewise views himself as a martyr, a pioneer, and a savior of his fellow men. The work in which this ambivalence receives its most consummate treatment is Kaiser's Socrates drama, *Der gerettete Alkibiades* (*Alcibiades Saved*) (1920), a masterpiece of tragic irony.

Kaiser's hero Socrates, a sculptor—a character based on the historical Socrates—is a wretched hunchback who compensates for his physical deformity by developing his reflectiveness. (Fifteen years earlier, in one of his first works, *Rektor Kleist*, Kaiser had defined the intellect as the sublimation of physical shortcomings; and *Rektor Kleist* foreshadows the contrast between the extrovert physical hero Alcibiades and the deformed intellectual Socrates in the coach Kornmüller and the classical-humanist school principal Kleist. In an argument with Kornmüller about the principles of education Rektor Kleist exclaims, "The greatest Greek was Socrates!") "My hump," Socrates says, "is a detour for my blood so that it cannot rush to the head too fast and flood my reason."[31] He is an intellectual artist, a *Denkspieler,* who works in stone as his creator works with words. For Socrates, as for Kaiser, the head, not the heart, is the guide

[31] *Der gerettete Alkibiades,* p. 49.

in art, the creative principle. "Writing a drama amounts to thinking out a thought to its conclusions," says Kaiser.[32] His Socrates makes hermae, images of heads resting on stone pillars. His art is "head-art," a metaphoric visualization of Kaiser's own art. Socrates' images lack a body. As the work is, so is the artist. Alcibiades compares him to a herma "with a head that is alive over the foundation of dead stone!" (p. 76) A chill emanates from Socrates and no one feels at ease with him. His probing mind disturbs good fellowship and upsets the carefree spirit of Athenian society. At his appearance, a novel shadow seems to fall over the habitual games of poetry and love. However, the decisive fact about Socrates' startling intellectuality is not an external but an invisible infirmity. A secret debility sets him completely apart from all other men and forces him to adopt a unique and revolutionary behavior. This secret wound is a symbol of the inhibiting, isolating, and revolutionary nature of the intellect; it opens Socrates' eyes to the meaninglessness of the world and the absurdity of human destiny; it compels him to develop a behavior monstrously different from the mores of his society; and finally it enables him to transcend his nihilism and isolation and to evolve new values which save his society from disintegration and despair. The same infirmity which reduces Socrates to a cripple and a monster also permits him to become a hero.

Socrates once served as a reluctant private in a military campaign of his native republic; during the army's retreat he stepped on a thorn which became lodged in the sole of his foot. The pain prevented Socrates from keeping pace with the retreat. He sat down on the road and, enraged with pain, beat around him with his sword so furiously that the foe retreated. Thereby, quite accidentally, he saved Athens' idol, Alcibiades, from capture and death and was acclaimed by the grateful republic. The triumph is based on a profound misunderstanding of which only Socrates himself is aware:

Who am I?—A severely wounded man who has a cactus thorn lodged in his foot . . . to whom neither friend nor foe mattered—: who only wanted to sit down so that by walking he wouldn't push the thorn deeper into his foot!— [My heroism] doesn't exist! I did not want to save Alcibiades. (p. 39)

Socrates cannot reveal his secret and have his thorn removed, without making Alcibiades and Athens appear ridiculous.

[The doctor] would pull it out—and more would come to the light of day [than my thorn]:—the immense fraud that will make Alcibiades ridiculous

---

[32] "Der Dichter und das Drama," quoted by Bernhard Diebold in *Der Denkspieler Georg Kaiser*, p. 15.

to the end of time!—The doctor will make me well in no time—but he will make Alcibiades sick to the core! (p. 40)

On the other hand, since his sore foot prevents him from doing what is expected of him, he deliberately casts doubts upon conventional behavior and substitutes for an extrovert culture "the pale cast of thought."

Socrates refuses the laurel wreath which the grateful city wants to bestow on him because he cannot ascend the high stairs to the Acropolis to receive it. To his fellow-citizens, ignorant of the secret reason, this disdain of public honor appears as a most remarkable example of humility and sets a revolutionary precedent in glory-loving Athens. Socrates braves Alcibiades' dagger with a calm smile because to a sick and suffering man death comes as a release. But Alcibiades, who does not know the real reason for Socrates' stoicism, is astounded by what appears to be the philosophical contempt of life by which the intellectual shames the physical hero.

Fearing the pain in his foot, Socrates, at the banquet in honor of the Poet, refuses to rise to crown the Poet with laurels; instead he invents a new theory of art. The person of the artist, so Socrates rationalizes, is nothing but an empty shell. The body which was host to the spirit when the work of art was created has lost its importance after the work is done. To crown the person is absurd. The wreath should be put, if anywhere, on the bust, the herma, which will outlast the body.

Socrates' aesthetics, so contemptuous of the personality of the artist, so exclusively concerned with the work, is Kaiser's own:

This is the duty of the creator: to turn away from each of his works and to go into the desert; if he reappears he must bring a lot with him—but to build himself a villa with garage in the shade of his sycamores: that simply will not do.[33]

What is the dramatist's attitude to his finished work? ... He turns his back on it the instant the last word is written—and resolutely forces himself to submit to a new dramatic labor. ... We have to utilize the time which brain and blood are granted in this place. ... *The purpose of existence is to establish records.*[34]

Both the humility and the functionalism of these views reveal the modernist's contempt for himself as a personality, as a growing and living human being. The continuous personality of the artist, his experiences, his individuality, his "soul" command no interest. The artist is to be nothing more than an executive organ for the record production of works. His greatness

---

[33] "Der Mensch im Tunnel," quoted by Eric A. Fivian in *Georg Kaiser und seine Stellung im Expressionismus,* p. 268.

[34] "Der Dichter und das Drama," quoted by Diebold in *Der Denkspieler Georg Kaiser,* pp. 15 ff. Italics mine.

is measured by the quantity of his achievements. The writing of a drama is "a geometric problem."[35] It has nothing to do with the writer's character. This production engineer's view of the creative process derives from the Expressionist's self-hatred. What this view implies is something like this: "My personality is hateful and unendurable, if it can be said to exist at all. The less said about it the better. Fortunately there exists an escape from my humanity (or rather lack of it) into a world of pure forms and abstract ideas. When I write I escape into this world, which is as pleasantly impersonal as mathematics." Kaiser's reduction of literature to a geometry of ideas is the exact opposite of the view of Goethe, who regarded the work of art as part of his personal growth, and who viewed personality as of supreme importance, as "the highest bliss of earth's children." The impersonal, self-hating Expressionist is opposed to Goethe, the genius of life, as the coldly ironical thinker Socrates in Kaiser's play, from whom everyone shies away, is opposed to the Poet, whom his grateful people feasts. In Kaiser's antipersonal functionalism we see another aspect of the "musicalization" of the arts, which replaces the ideal of character portrait by the ideal of composition. We also recognize now beneath this fundamental principle of modernism a certain self-hatred, a vengeance, as it were, on those who still possess a definite individuality, a character, and believe in its value. We encounter in it an example of the strong anti-Goethean strain in Expressionism which in several respects sought to accomplish a radical break with the Goethean-Romantic individualism in German literature and civilization. Expressionism sides with Kant (and Schiller) against Goethe.[36] Both in their abstractionist and, as we shall see, in their ethical phase, the Expressionists rejected Goethe, although for different reasons.[37]

Kaiser's dramatic practice closely conforms to his theory. Like Strindberg, he does not write dramas of character, but dramas of ideas. But in contrast to Strindberg's, Kaiser's drama is not patterned on the existential journey and the splitting of the self into leitmotiv aspects. It is not a "musicalization" of the miracle play. Neither is it based on dream and visualization. It grows out of aphorism, anecdote, and debate. Kaiser's model dramatist was Plato. It is also a further development of Wedekind's and Sternheim's aphoristic, epigrammatic dialogue. Kafka's stories are extended metaphors; Kaiser's dramas are extended aphorisms. The aphoristic

---

[35] See Fivian, *Georg Kaiser*, p. 225.

[36] See Georg Simmel, *Kant und Goethe*, for an excellent discussion of these two opposed strains in the German intellectual tradition.

[37] Oskar Walzel sees in Goethe the supreme embodiment of the "impressionist" artist against whom the Expressionists revolted. "Eindruckskunst und Ausdruckskunst in der Dichtung," in Max Deri *et al., Einführung in die Kunst der Gegenwart*, pp. 26–46.

parable, the anecdote with a sharply formulated twist, form the basis and strength of Kaiser's dramas. Early works like *The Jewish Widow* (1911), a parodistic version of the Old Testament subject treated by Hebbel, show this tendency very clearly. Judith kills Holophernes and liberates the Jewish people accidentally, motivated not by heroism but by sexual frustration. She wants to sleep with the Babylonian king, the first potent man she has met; when the general Holophernes interferes with her lustful desire for the king, she simply slays the famous general and thus liberates the besieged Jewish town. Babylonian king and army flee in panic. The disappointed heroine is brought back to her people in triumph and finally satisfied by the potent High Priest sent from Jerusalem. We note the parodistic irony as in Wedekind. The parodistic idea determines the plot. The characters are neither personalities in the traditional sense nor Strindbergian projections of subconscious states; they are carriers of the "joke," the ironic trick effect of the work.

The kinship between Wedekind, Sternheim, and Kaiser lies in their tendency to unmask "the essence" of social reality not by naturalistic imitation, which would still lull us in illusions, but by crass and shocking formulations. Their drama seeks to demonstrate in pure and, therefore, necessarily abstract and distorted conditions (in the experimental laboratory, as it were) the true nature of existential or social problems. In *The Jewish Widow,* for instance, Kaiser unmasks by his "joke" the true nature of heroism as frustration. In his *Burghers of Calais,* probably his greatest work, he demonstrates by two highly dramatic surprise effects the true nature of heroism as pacifism and self-sacrifice. In his *Alcibiades Saved* he demonstrates by a highly ironic tour de force the true nature of the intellect as both a wound and a heroic fraud. Here the trick, Kaiser's basic dramatic form, merges with the dramatic content and idea. *Alcibiades Saved* is the dramatic formulation of its author's form of existence.

Bert Brecht's post-Expressionist, anti-illusionistic "epic theater" is deeply indebted to Kaiser's method and represents a further development of it. Continuing Wedekind's and Kaiser's basic form, Brecht in his *Three Penny Opera* demonstrates the true nature of capitalism by showing its pure form in Mackie Messer's gang and Mr. Peachum's financial investment in human misery. In *Mahagonny* he constructs for us the "dream city" of capitalist society in which lack of money is the only crime. Brecht paid his tribute to Kaiser when he transformed Kaiser's *Alcibiades Saved* into one of his *Calendar Stories;* and Brecht's great collaborator Kurt Weill wrote his first opera to the text of Kaiser's drama *The Protagonist.*

The depersonalizing, deadening cleverness in Socrates' pain-inspired views outrages Alcibiades, the hero of physical vitality and *joie de vivre,* even as Kaiser's, Sternheim's, Brecht's, and George Grosz' provocative, unmasking "cleverness" outraged and infuriated the German "romantic" *bourgeoisie.* Alcibiades' last weapon against Socrates is Woman. The charms of the beautiful courtesan Phryne will surely undo the cold reasoner. But the intellectual cannot love. The thorn in Socrates' flesh prevents him from approaching Phryne and making love to her. Pain has destroyed desire in him. His aloofness, on the other hand, converts Phryne to asceticism. The first man to disdain her impresses her as the true human being, the godlike man. Like everyone else, she mistakes Socrates' infirmity for strength. His incapacity for love raises him to the level of the gods.

Nietzsche saw the historical Socrates as the initiator of Greek decadence and the pioneer of the Christian "slave revolt"; Kaiser sees in Socrates the fateful innovator who ends the age of naïve self-assurance and ushers in a self-conscious, i.e., guilt-ridden, civilization. The mind replaces the muscles. Reflection drives out spontaneity. The cripple wins out over the athlete. But Socrates' revolutionary philosophy does not result from the cripple's resentment of the strong and healthy; it results from his compassion for them. Although it was necessary, Socrates regrets his victory:

I had to invent what should have remained uninvented!!—I had to blanket the sky—and wither the earth—!![88]

He takes Alcibiades' guilt for overturning the sacred hermae upon himself and suffers the death penalty in his stead.

Kaiser-Socrates' intellectualism reveals itself as a protective barrier against nihilism. Only Socrates, the intellectual, knows the trivial accident to which the hero Alcibiades owes his life; if he had disclosed it, Alcibiades would have become a laughingstock, Greek faith would have been shattered, and the *meaninglessness of greatness* would have been brutally obvious. Civilization could not have withstood such a shock. Better to interpose new values between the traditional hero worship and the banal truth than to allow the truth to destroy all values. Chilling and subversive as these new values of abstract intellect may be, they still serve as a screen between man and the devastating insight into the absurdity of the universe and human existence. Thus Socrates suffers his thorn and sacrifices his life to save Alcibiades, and with him Greece, from the despair of nihilism.

Kaiser's Socrates drama symbolizes in a subtle and ingenious way the cultural situation of Europe and the intellectual's role in it. The Athenians in the play would, if not saved by Socrates, face the same spiritual bleakness

[88] *Alkibiades,* p. 47.

which, as a result of the disenchantment of the world through mechanistic science, confronted European man in the late nineteenth and twentieth centuries, a spiritual prison from which Expressionism strained to break loose. The curse of the intellectual, the curse of too much knowledge, now threatens even the average man. But the intellectual wishes to spare his fellow men the agony that has been his own lot. This he cannot accomplish by a selfish escape into the vitalist dream of retrogression, but only by a feat of reinterpretation and re-evaluation of intellect. The intellect which cripples man and undermines his will to live can, if reinterpreted, become the very power that enhances and liberates the human will.

This is the message of abstractionism. Abstractionism ranges human intelligence resolutely against what is "given" by nature and insists on the autonomous and creative power of the mind. It views man as *homo faber* who tames nature and imposes order upon chaos. Thus, man becomes a partner in the creation of the world as distinguished from chaos. History, too, is in Kaiser's view a jumble of accidents, brutalities, and meaningless events; but human intelligence, embodied in the poet as "a maker," interprets the facts and gives them a meaning. It is the poet who creates the only history meaningful to man: "He orders the confusion. He draws a line through the hubbub. He constructs the law. He holds the filter. He justifies man."[39]

Werfel hails the poet as the name-giver who, by the act of expressing what was unexpressed, lifts the world out of the night of the unconscious and thus creates the cosmos once more.[40] Werfel rejects the German-Romantic view of the poet as a simple dreamer and naïve child of nature, calling this view "dishonoring loss of status and reduction to the visionary cretin," and insists on the primary role of mental discipline in the creative process. Inspiration for him is intellectual insight, *Erkenntnis*. The poet's intellectual insight differs from that of the scientist only by the method with which he arrives at his findings. "Only the method of arriving at it distinguishes this [poetic] knowledge from everyday empirical and scientific knowledge. The logic of the poet is called symbolism."[41] The glorification of the intellect reaches its apogee with the political and social claims which Heinrich Mann and the activists staked out for the intellectual. They rebelled against the traditional German reverence for what is "given" in nature and history and demanded that the intellectual re-create the social

[39] Kaiser, "Historientreue," *Berliner Tageblatt*, September 4, 1923.
[40] "Der Weltfreund singt," in *Der Weltfreund*, p. 88; *Die Versuchung: Ein Gespräch des Dichters mit dem Erzengel und Luzifer*, I, 30. The world lies mute and despairing; it is the poet who makes it conscious and aware of itself, and thus enriches and saves it.
[41] Werfel, "Brief an Georg Davidsohn," *Die Aktion*, VII/11–12 (1917), 152–54.

world according to his ideals of justice and absolute reason. They transferred the basic Expressionist principle of vision and visualization of inner or mental states to the ethical and utopian-political sphere.

As long as Expressionism ruled as a fashion, this wave of ethical and utopian-political sentiment partly concealed the abstractionist ingredient of the movement. The social and moral claims of mind overshadowed the much more fundamental and permanent aesthetic application of intellect to the creation of works of art. Only the periodical *Der Sturm* and the circle associated with its editor Herwarth Walden consciously promoted a pure abstractionism, free of ethical and political or religious elements. The formal experiments of the *Sturm* poets transferred the extreme concentration of Wedekind's, Sternheim's, and Kaiser's dialogue style to poetry and developed the possibilities of linguistic condensation and abstraction to startling—and at times highly effective—extremes. By stripping language of its syntactical structure and reducing it to its essential elements—verb and noun—the *Sturm* Expressionists expressed the "essence" of their age. They created a spare, telling, and breathless medium shed of the values of *Gemüt,* warmth, and atmosphere, liberated from all circumlocution, description, and diffuseness, and shorn of any element, such as conjunctions or inflected word endings, that fails to serve directly the purpose of expression.

Their language differs essentially from the rhetorical Expressionism of such poets as Klemm, Otten, Johst, Rubiner, Ehrenstein, and others. The rhetorical Expressionist spouts out a cataract of highly charged emotional words and allows this verbal cataract to carry him away to empty theatricality and pose and to unintended inaccuracies and absurdities. A good example of this rhetorical Expressionism is offered by Albert Ehrenstein's lines: "Ratten! Fresset meine Eingeweide! / Zerspell mich, Fels, ertränk mich Furt!" Ehrenstein starts out by screaming out his raw emotion of desperate self-hatred. He calls on the rats to eat his bowels—an invocation powerful enough to be considered rhetorical in the best sense. But then he goes on to call on the river ford to drown him. The ford, however, is the place in a river least suitable for drowning; in the shallows of the ford drowning is almost impossible. Thus, in only the second line of his poem, Ehrenstein succumbs to empty rhetoric. The *Sturm* poets aim at the opposite of such rhetorical inaccuracy. Their linguistic experiments and distortions are dictated by the wish to achieve a degree of poetic precision and expressiveness which the existing linguistic structure with its worn and standardized words and word forms cannot attain. While the rhetorical Expressionist in his nebulous emotionalism falls to a level of precision far below that of conventional speech, the *Sturm* poet seeks to rise to a level of precision far above that of the existing language. By different means, the *Sturm* poets pursue the same goals as Kafka, Trakl, and Barlach. The goal of these Expressionists is the disruption and dissolution of the habitual, indeed habit-created, and conventional texture of thought and feeling, and the expression of a "translogical" reality which art alone can communicate. They differ in their means. Kafka and Trakl seek to express "translogical" reality by the "pictorial idea," by means of visualization, metaphor, image, and gesture. Benn seeks to create it by the "magic pronunciation" of certain nouns able to evoke a wealth of buried racial memories. The *Sturm* poets seek to express "translogical" reality by means of linguistic compression. August Stramm, an obscure postal clerk and later an army captain killed in the First World War who had originated the *Sturm* method, also achieved its finest results.

Stramm frequently reduces sentences to single words. Words in turn often lose their familiar features, prefixes, suffixes, grammatical endings. Above all, by inventing new words which by their derivation from or similarity to one or several existing words convey strong connotative without any definite denotative significance, Stramm transforms words into "pure aesthetic attributes." In his poem "Wunder," for instance, he coins a verb "ich winge." This word has no dictionary meaning but suggests echoes of the existing German words "ich schwinge" (I swing or wing) and "ich winke" (I wave)—both of which are also suggested by the context of the poem. In addition, the English word "wing" is suggested by both sound and context of the newly coined word.[42] These multiple associations in conjunction produce a certain emotional effect; they convey the experience of flight, lightness, elation ("I wing," "I swing") as well as of closeness and approach ("ich winke") between the "Ich" and the "Du" mentioned in the poem. Barred from a definite intellectual comprehension, the reader of Stramm's poem experiences an emotional reaction which lies somewhere between the effects produced by musical chords and those caused by words with established conceptual meanings. Stramm's poetry—and that of the *Sturm* circle in general—anticipates the great classic of "non-objective" literature, Joyce's *Finnegan's Wake,* which consists entirely of "aesthetic attributes" and aesthetic ideas, based not on metaphors and dreamlike images, but on word fragments and word deformations.

After the Messianic enthusiasm of the Expressionist movement had ebbed away, this highly disciplined and intellectual linguistic abstraction-

---

[42] On account of both his educational training and his geographical residence we can assume that Stramm had at least some familiarity with English.

ism emerged clearly as the permanent core of Expressionism. *Der Sturm,* under Herwarth Walden's editorship, continued to publish "Expressionist" poetry until the advent of Hitlerism; and the only Expressionist who considered himself one until his death in 1956, and whose work exerts a living and growing influence today, is a spokesman and supreme practitioner of pure abstractionism. It is not a fortuitous paradox but rather a symptom of the Expressionist's ambivalence toward his intellect that this spokesman of abstractionism should be the same Benn who was once the most extreme spokesman of vitalism. The Expressionist intellectual vacillates between extremes—extremes of self-rejection and self-glorification. If he rejects himself as a vitalist, he justifies himself as an abstractionist. Benn, who, as we have seen, suffered the personality crisis of the cerebral man most acutely, went to the extreme in either direction. His abstractionism, practiced in his poetry of the 1920's, -30's, and -40's, and expressed in his essays of the same period and in his essayistic novel *The Ptolemaic,* is particularly instructive for our discussion since it is presented as a solution to the problem of nihilism. Benn practices in his poetry and formulates in his essays what Kaiser represented symbolically in his Socrates drama.

His method of evoking a magic surreality by richly connotative words like "Ithaca," although already encompassing a much greater range of cultural-social reality than the private dreamlike images of Trakl and Kafka, evolved in his later period much further in the direction of an Alexandrian poetry of learned allusions and so arrived, completely independent of them, at the kind of intellectual poetry practiced by Eliot and Pound. However, in a manner reminiscent of Brecht's and Weill's collaboration, Benn ironically offsets, and thereby underscores, with the lilting melody of his verse, the harsh and bitter dissonances produced by the cultural-historical contrasts which he evokes in his poems. Although Benn created this kind of poetry after Expressionism as a fashion was over, it is a logical development of his early work written in the Expressionist decade.

In his earliest volume, *Morgue* (1912), Benn, practicing a poetic collage technique, lets reality provide the dissonances which he selects and presents to an outraged public. What distinguishes this poetry from Naturalism is its jaundiced selectivity, the deliberate achievement of cruel and shocking dissonance. Benn arranges observed facts of hospital and morgue in combinations which reflect dissonance as the fundamental law of being. In his poem "Aster," Benn tells us that he found the aster stuck between the lips of a drowned beer-truck driver. As he performed the autopsy, the flower slipped into the dead man's brain. Finally Benn sewed it into the thorax of the corpse, which has now become the flower's "vase," and he concludes with a cynically elegiac epitaph. In the poem "Happy Youth," the hole under the diaphragm of a drowned girl serves as an "arbor" in which a brood of water rats have spent their "happy youth." Here nature is reflected through more than a temperament. It is reconstructed by the will to demonstrate its hidden essence—total indifference to human values and universal death. Benn refined this technique in his maturity and broadened its range enormously; the whole history of civilization serves him now as hospital and morgue had served him in the beginning. Spirit and form have remained the same: the evocation of the fundamental dissonance of existence witnessed and recorded by an agonized, impotent, and cynical consciousness. This poetry is at once ironic and elegiac; and this combination, plus Alexandrian learning and musical artistry, relates Benn to Eliot, a kinship which Eliot acknowledged when he paraphrased Benn at length in his "Three Voices of Poetry." Like Eliot, Benn looks at the cultural-social reality of Western man in his period of decline and contemplates the constancies and contrasts, the eternal pattern of myth and the sterilized vulgarity of the technological era side by side. "Charon or the Hermae / or the Daimler flight," Benn begins one of his finest poems, "The Danish Girl," summing up in these three symbols of locomotion ("the Hermae" are dedicated to Hermes, god of travelers, merchants, and thieves) the constancy and the change, eternity and transitoriness, theme and counterpoint, that have produced and will destroy the splendid tennis-playing girl of today, even as they have produced and destroyed her prefiguration, Dido of Carthage. But within and beneath everything, Benn sees the waves of emergence and passing, of birth and destruction, rolling on in ever-meaningless monotony—the world as Will beneath all Ideas. Yet Benn transfigures this vision of disintegration, ruin, and meaninglessness and redeems it in the euphony and rhythmic beauty of his form. Formulation is here more than ironical contrast to the desolate content expressed. Formulation becomes its transcendence. Benn, who, unlike Eliot, cannot find his way back to tradition of Church and country, raises his own "pure form," his own process of formulation and expression, to the Absolute and source of salvation.

Creation, according to Benn, is nothing but the concentrated effort to conceal one's despair. "It is evident that all the great minds of the Caucasion peoples have perceived only one single task for themselves, that of concealing their nihilism by creation."[43] The intellectuals and creative

---

[43] *Der Ptolemäer*, p. 28.

spirits have always known nihilism in themselves. Degenerates, pathologi-cal types, emotional cripples without warmth of feeling, they saved them-selves from inner paralysis—from the "frigidization of the self"[44]—by the discipline of creation. What in the past was the problem of isolated spirits now faces mankind as a whole. Thanks to "progressive cerebration," the average man also has lost his human warmth and capacity for spontaneous action and now shares the "nausea" of the intellectual, a nausea which Benn calls "nihilism." Retrogression, such as he himself had once advocated, Benn now sees as impossible; hope lies only in the opposite direction. Only the mind can provide the cure for the spiritual devastation which the mind has wrought. Mankind must learn the trick which the creative intellectual has always used in his long agony: mankind must learn to see destructive intellect as "constructive mind" ("konstruktiver Geist"). The intellect has to shake itself out of its sentimental attitude toward life, become aware of its creative capacity, and assert its autonomy and its superiority to "natural life":

[We] see it [the mind] not involved in an eternally languishing tragic love affair with life, but we assume it as superior to life, constructively superior, as a forming and formal principle: Intensification and condensation—these appear to be the fundamental laws of the mind. From this completely trans-cendental view a possible transcendence . . . of nihilism might result.[45]

The concept of "constructive mind" with which Benn seeks to overcome nihilism is nothing else but the principle of artistic creation. However, Benn's concept of art has nothing in common with the traditional view of art as representation of reality or as a confession of experience. Like Kaiser, Benn is not interested in the personality of the artist; nor is he concerned with the raw material of art nor with the psychological effect of the finished work. Indeed his poetry is addressed "to no one." He is solely interested in the *method* of artistic creation, in the sifting, organizing, condensing activity of the mind in the process of creating. The constructive mind, as Benn understands it, is not a "what" but a "how"; it is a method of or-ganizing data into significant patterns. It is "style."[46] The type of art of which Benn thinks is not the psychological novel or the drama of individual characters; he rejects "psychological complications, causality, milieu-trac-ing."[47] The ideal art which he envisions has no content; it is nothing but form. It is to embody the complete triumph of mental organization over

---

[44] *Nach dem Nihilismus*, p. 9.
[45] *Nihilismus*, p. 20.
[46] "Dorische Welt," in *Essays*, pp. 43–47.
[47] *Nihilismus*, p. 21.

the resistance of matter. The raw material, the "data" given by nature—and nature includes human nature—should be sucked up and made to disappear in the formal structure of the work. Benn's "constructive mind" is the spirit that rules modern technology and functional design:

Switch from the inward to the outward, transmission of the last bit of substance into forming processes, transformation of forces into structures. Modern technology and modern architecture point in the same direction. (p. 21)

The "constructive mind" thinks only in functional terms. Facts, things, feelings, and persons do not exist for it in their own right, but only as parts in a working relationship to other parts. Even as content gives way to form, the concept of "being" yields to the concept of "functioning." This is the Expressionist ideal of the "desubstantivation of the world" ("Entsubstantivierung der Welt"), which Werfel demanded in 1917 and which Benn formulated and elaborated with a consistency and tenacity lacking in the other Expressionists. Substance is transferred into process and function; the noun bows to the verb; content becomes method; active *expression* replaces passive *experience*. With these ideas, German Expressionism is completely at one with European modernism. The theories of Kaiser, the *Sturm* poets, Werfel (for a short period of his life), and especially Benn cannot be distinguished from those of Kandinsky or Valéry. This kinship allows us to see the modernist "musicalization of the arts" in a new light.

Modernism is not entirely opposed to the technological century, but on the contrary extremely consistent with it. The transformation of the ancient concept of substance into the modern concept of function is probably the single most important philosophical revolution wrought by modern physics in which matter is defined as energy. In modern psychology behavior replaces character as the fundamental concept. Here, too, we see activity, method, process, *expression* or form—behavior is the *expression* or form in which the psyche manifests itself—supersede the older idea of a permanent personal substance, called character or "soul." Even as the idea of expressive form supersedes the idea of content in modernist aesthetics, behavior, the "form" or "expression" of the psyche, takes the place of the psyche in modern psychology. The core of personality is no longer assumed to exist; only the processes, the "pure form" of its manifestation, are granted a degree of reality.

Substance always implies permanence and "givenness," the given world of nature surrounding man. The technological age has been losing the experience of both. Breath-taking change has shattered the idea of permanence, and the rapidly increasing control and transformation of nature have destroyed the ancient conviction that a given external creation, a cosmos, exists outside man. Technology has made our world conform ever more closely to Kant's philosophy in the *Critique of Pure Reason:* each day the world resembles a little more a construct created by our mind in a chaos of meaningless phenomena. These trends of our century agree well with Benn's concept of the "constructive mind." We discern in them a striving to transcend the "givenness" of nature by asserting the autonomous and creative potentiality of the mind. Through his mind, modern man regains the possibility of free will and action, of which the mechanistic determinism of the nineteenth century, by making him the puppet of blind forces, had robbed him.

The "constructive mind" enables the cerebral man to create despite the "frigidization of the self." It allows him to act. In that respect abstractionism represents a solution to the problem of the Expressionist intellectual, while vitalism remained an impossible dream. However, the inability to act was only a subsidiary problem. The cerebral man's basic problem was how to become a fully integrated human being—in other words, a real person in whom feeling, thought, and action are integrated. Does the "constructive mind" solve this life-and-death problem of the Expressionist?

To begin with, we notice a strong antipersonalism in the very concept of "constructive mind." The "constructive mind" substitutes function for substance. A substance exists in and for itself; it can be considered an individual. A function, on the other hand, has no existence in isolation; it acquires meaning in relation to a totality. The idea of individual personality has meaning in a world of substances; it is meaningless in a universe of pure function and process. Personality, in the Goethean sense, exists in and for itself; it exercises no function beyond that of being itself. It is, furthermore, rooted in a given physiological and biological constitution and cultural environment. It is this static "givenness," this "innerness" of personality, which Benn's "metaphysical anti-individualism" cannot accept. The cerebral man who suffers from the "frigidization of the self" denies the existence of the self. The hypercerebral man who sadly knows the lack of substance in himself decides at last that substance is a false concept. By disputing the legitimacy of individuality and denying the necessity for feeling, the abstractionist shirks the problem of attaining an individuality and acquiring the ability to feel. He repeats the trick of Kaiser's Socrates; he proclaims his deficiency a virtue and starts a philosophical revolution to prove what he proclaims.

Thus, we find that neither vitalism nor abstractionism solves the Expressionist intellectual's basic problem of becoming a human being. As a vitalist he tries to sink below the human level and act as a beast; as an abstractionist he tries to rise above the human level and act as disembodied intelligence. In either guise the Expressionist escapes the responsibility of being human. For most Expressionists, however, this responsibility was their prime concern. Their chief problem was not only cerebral but also emotional, and a purely intellectual solution was inadequate. The inability to relate themselves to others, the inability to love, formed their existential "wound," for which a "bow" had to be found that neither vitalism nor abstractionism could provide.

CHAPTER FIVE

The Impotence of the Heart

ALMOST TWO DECADES BEFORE THE EXPRESSIONIST MOVEMENT BEGAN, THE YOUTH-ful Neo-Romantic Hugo von Hofmannsthal wrote a verse play called *Der Tor und der Tod* (*Death and the Fool*). It is the tragedy of a narcissist-aesthete who, in the hour of his death, comes to realize that he has not really lived because he has never truly loved. This theme of the auto-emotional man, the highly cultivated narcissist who, unrelated to all human community, builds a universe out of his sensations, perceptions, and dreams, and whom in consequence "life" passes by, is a development of the ivory-tower attitude which poets and artists began to adopt when the emerging bourgeois society left them without a function to perform. Faust in his cloistered study and Manfred in his mountain wilderness are proud and manly forerunners of Hofmannsthal's aesthete Fool who has to wait for death to open his eyes to life. Rilke's Malte Laurids Brigge, Proust's Marcel, T. S. Eliot's Prufrock, and the heroes of André Gide's and Thomas Mann's early works are such auto-emotional men, enriched by the sophistication and burdened by the hesitancies of a sunset age. None of them can love except from the distance, in dreams, or, as in Marcel's case, in doomed unhappy possessiveness. Aesthetic cognition, the universe of memories and irony, saves them. But love tantalizes them with a continuous lure and a continuous reproach. Impotence of the heart, first the unwillingness and then the inability to relate oneself to others, is an important facet of the subjectivism and withdrawal from the world that began in late-eighteenth-century pre-Romanticism and climaxes in twentieth-century modernism.

The Expressionists suffered still more intensely from this "impotence of the heart" than the Neo-Romantic aestheticist generation that immediately preceded them. Indeed the urgency of the Expressionist cult of love is directly proportionate to the intensity with which the Expressionists experienced the inability to love. Although closely related to it, this emotional defect must be distinguished from the hypercerebralism which we have just discussed. If cerebralism rather than the deadness of the heart is singled out as the chief existential problem of the writer, as it is in Sack's and Benn's case, for instance, a mental act can solve the problem; the vitalist's repudiation of intellect is as much an intellectual act as the abstractionist's deification of intellect. Both take place in the sphere of thought and action and do not essentially concern themselves with still deeper layers of the personality. The problem of the auto-emotional aesthete, however, is his inability to feel, to relate to others. Thus a situation arises for which neither vitalism nor abstractionism is appropriate.

The best example of the close link between the narcissistic Neo-Romantic aestheticism of the turn of the century and the genesis of Expressionism is Thomas Mann's elder brother Heinrich Mann, who embodies this link in his career. Even in his early, Neo-Romantic period Heinrich Mann wrote "Pippo Spano," the story of an artist, which, though typically Neo-Romantic, is at the same time highly significant for the psychological genesis of Expressionism. It is the story of Mario Malvolto, a modern poet, who is unable to love because he is unable to evince real interest in anything except himself. He is "forever incapable of a genuine emotion, a sincere attachment." Art for him is an asylum from a reality which he distrusts and fears.

This weak man with inauthentic emotions admires the *"condottieri* of life," the strong and passionate, "who consume their whole life in a single hour and die happy." He keeps the portait of a Renaissance *condottiere,* Pippo Spano, in his study to remind him of the strong and full life to which he aspires. Gemma Cantoggi, a passionate girl, is deceived by the strong characters that people Malvolto's books. Mistaking the author for the dream, which he has put down on paper precisely because he feels so remote from it in life, she falls in love with him.

Malvolto is afraid of the emotional commitment for which he feels neither sufficient strength nor sincerity in himself. But his "superego," as Freud would call it, Pippo Spano's portrait, challenges him to plunge into this frighteningly real experience. Now that Gemma has entered his life, he faces the obligation to be "like a strong man," to identify himself with Pippo Spano, who constantly watches him with his cruel, scornful smile.

Their love affair having been discovered and turned into a scandal, Gemma tells her lover that they must die together to avoid separation. Her faith infects him and they decide to commit suicide together. But his faith in the reality of his love is only sufficiently strong to make him kill her; when it is his turn to kill himself, his strength for action is gone. "It is not simply cowardice," he explains his failure to follow her into death, "it is just that one does not kill oneself really at the end of a comedy." He will live and turn his affair with Gemma into a literary masterpiece.

But the dying girl whom he has sacrificed cries out at him: "Murderer!" And he agrees; he has failed the test of love.

We shall now trace the theme of "Pippo Spano" in a number of Expressionist works, particularly works of early Expressionism. Two facets of this Neo-Romantic theme are especially relevant for the understanding of the genesis of the Expressionist cult of love and vitality. One is the emotional impotence of the artist and his longing to be different, to be his opposite, the strong simple man of action who is fully alive to the world around him and, therefore, capable of genuine feelings and love. The second, closely related to and a direct consequence of the first, is the desperate need of the artist for someone stronger and healthier than himself to whom he can cling; he exploits "the other," appropriates his vitality, and finally destroys him, as Malvolto destroyed Gemma, either in order to create a work of art, or simply in order to save himself from emotional starvation by feeding on "the other's" powerful experience. We shall call these two related aspects of personality impotence and vampirism.[1] But before we set out to follow the theme of "Pippo Spano" in Expressionism, one important variation has to be pointed out. The envied antagonist and counterpart of the artist, his "superego," is no longer the Renaissance superman but the average man, the bourgeois, of today. We can observe this shift in one of the earliest works of Expressionism, Carl Sternheim's comedy *Die Hose* (*The Bloomers*) (1911).

Theobald Maske, in Sternheim's comedy, is the common man who in the beginning of the common man's century is proud and sure in his commonness. Exaltation, eccentricity, and greatness of any kind are incomprehensible to him. His motto is "What is comfortable is right."[2] He is ignorant of Shakespeare and has only vaguely heard of Goethe. His principle is not to read books, "because I am not interested in the opinions of other people." He is perfectly satisfied with the ideas formed in his own brain; reading would only interfere with his originality. He has not the least interest in politics or philosophy, nor in any issue outside his personal well-being. Maske's smug ignorance shocks the intellectual poet Scarron, who has always lived for ideas and ideals.

Scarron:
How can one not view such a completely empty life as yours tragically?

[1] Sexual impotence is a leitmotiv in the early work of Georg Kaiser, e.g., in *Rektor Kleist, Die jüdische Witwe, Der Zentaur*. Konstantin Strobel in *Der Zentaur* has to prove to himself that he is able to beget a child. He wants on a physical plane what Heinrich Mann's Malvolto aspires to on an emotional plane: the proof that he can love.

[2] "Ist bequem nicht recht?" Sternheim, *Die Hose: Ein bürgerliches Lustspiel*, p. 117.

Theobald:

Listen: Making a living gives it some content, after all. As I was saying, for seven hours a day.

Scarron:

Seventeen remain.

Theobald:

Eight for sleep, two for meals, one for getting dressed and getting undressed. There remain only six, from which travel to and from the office has to be deducted. (p. 115)

Frau Luise Maske, the young wife of the typical Philistine Theobald Maske, is attracted to the poet Scarron, who has rented a room in her apartment because he is in love with her. She makes only the slightest pretense of resistance to the romantic cavalier. The conventional development of this situation would show romantic young people getting together and putting horns on the bourgeois husband. But in the Expressionist comedy the reverse occurs. The bourgeois is the successful rival in love; the poet loses by default.

The poet's passion is verbal, not real. He is in love with the idea of being in love, not with a woman of flesh and blood. When Luise, slightly impatient with his ineffectual enthusiasm, expects him to make love to her, he rushes off to write about her. The artist's absorption in work is an effectual device for keeping him pure and untainted by life. It is the alibi of the man who cannot feel deeply and genuinely enough to engage in a human relationship. Afraid of real emotions, Scarron escapes to idealization and art. Like Mann's Malvolto, Sternheim's Scarron is unable to fulfill the romantic expectations which he has aroused; like Malvolto, he is a cheat.

When Luise's amorous and unhappy manner reminds him of his failure, he shifts his interest from the wife to the husband. For all his vulgarity, the solid bourgeois acts like a magnet on the weak and fickle intellectual. Scarron senses that this smug "little man," who is so proud of his littleness, is actually the great man to whom the future belongs. The poet is on the defensive, no longer believes in his romantic values; the bourgeois, perfectly at peace with himself, is on the offensive, cannot conceive of any values other than his own.

Theobald (grinning):

My insignificance is a cloak which allows me to indulge without inhibitions in my inclinations, my innermost nature.

Scarron:

I'm more confused than I can express. For the first time I'm confronted with such a view of life as a conviction.

Theobald:

Of a little man.

Scarron:

At any rate of a man. (p. 134)

It is the prosaic Maske who proves superior to the poet in everything, even in the poet's special domain: awareness. He knows Scarron better than Scarron knows himself.

Theobald:

This man is a strange hothouse flower. For all his colorful appearance he has no roots. . . . As he never fully possesses himself, he can never possess anyone else. (p. 154)

Maske is also victorious in that other human realm traditionally associated with the poet: love. Crude and egotistical though he is, Maske can love. In contrast to the poet, who promises so much and gives so little, the bourgeois promises little but accomplishes much. He may not speak of love with Scarron's eloquence but, on the most primitive and basic level, he loves and satisfies the women he desires. While his wife is in church seeking consolation for her disappointment in Scarron, Theobald Maske makes love to a spinster into whose lonely life he brings a ray of affection. And the rent money received from the unstable poet (who has paid a year's rent in advance for a room of which he tires after one day) enables Maske to afford to give his wife a child. Whereas Scarron will soon be nothing but a faded memory to a woman whose life has found a meaning in domesticity, Maske founds a powerful dynasty which is destined to rise to a ruling position in business and industry. The "heroic life of the *bourgeoisie*," as Sternheim calls his cycle of middle-class comedies, has begun with Theobald Maske's total victory over the ephemeral values of literature and the intellect. The commonly held view that sees in Sternheim, and the Expressionists generally, mere rebels against the bourgeois way of life is likely to obscure the fascination which the ruthless self-confidence and vitality of the bourgeois hold for the early Expressionist, who keenly feels these qualities lacking in himself. The modern bourgeois passes the test of love which the modern poet fails. Sternheim's style demonizes the speech of the German *bourgeoisie*. Its effect is ambiguous. It is an aggressive parody of the bourgeois, to be sure; but, at the same time, it flatters him by exaggerating his ruthless forcefulness and cynical virility. It raises the bourgeois to the rank of a "blond beast." Thus, Sternheim's "telegram-style" dialogue expresses the typical Expressionist's ambivalence toward the bourgeois: he secretly admires him while overtly attacking him.

In an early dramatic sketch of Franz Werfel's, called *Versuchung* (*Temptation*) (1913), the poet puts to himself the question of why he has lost his girl to a prosaic Philistine, and he finds as his answer his inability to love. Love is not with the sensitive introvert but—and here we observe at the roots of Expressionism the heritage of Thomas and Heinrich Mann— with the practical man, the bourgeois, the "statistician." Vitality, sincerity, enjoyment of the moment "sparkle behind [the bourgeois's] pince-nez." Warmth and sympathy reign in his heart, which is untroubled by the poet's diffidence. The poet understands the girl, but he does not love her. Thus, he can no longer maintain his traditional contempt of the bourgeois. At bottom he admires him. The common men are "great lords, sufficient unto themselves, full of calm and composure, and they possess a center. They ... are human beings!" But he, the poet, has "never been a human being!"

Like Faust contemplating the havoc which he has wrought on Gretchen's life, the Expressionist poet feels like an *Unmensch* whom a terrible chasm separates from the enviable sheltered world of ordinary men. In one of his poems, Werfel admits that his incessant call for love ascends from a heart that does not love anyone; he ends the poem that he calls "Despair" with this lament:

> And everything craves love.
> I too for love have cried.
> But haven't loved a soul![8]

From this terrible conviction of being "inhuman" and monstrous there arises the desperate yearning to be united to the human race, to feel akin to "the others" and belong to mankind. "My only wish is to be related to you, O Man," Werfel concludes his first volume of poetry, *Der Weltfreund* (*The World's Friend*). The Expressionist cult of "man" and "mankind" (of which Werfel is one of the most eloquent and persistent spokesmen) is to be understood as a consequence of the feeling of being sadly different from all men.

In Alfred Wolfenstein's drama *Besuch der Zeit* (*Visit of the Times*), the poet is reminded that the "higher love" found in literature is a rationalization of those who are impotent in the "lower love" of real life. The poet, because of his neuroticism, feels the need to reach for the unattainable and change the solid world of facts into the kingdom of his dreams. His ac-

---

[8] Werfel, *Wir sind*, p. 54.

> Und alles rauscht nach Liebe.
> Ich auch nach Liebe weine.
> Und hab doch keinen gern.

tivity is not only superfluous but also antisocial, since it irritates his fellow men and makes their happiness suspect to themselves. But the poet's ambition to elevate mankind, his dissatisfaction with the flatness of life as it is, are only the results of his misanthropic disposition. The poet's visitor, who is the embodied spirit of the modern age and spokesman of the masses, brings the poet's secret weakness out into the open.

In the past, the Visitor says, people revered the poet because they took him at his word and believed that the love of which he sang was in himself.

Oh, we thought a poet was synonymous with love. We were afraid that there was a world high above us like Heaven. That would have been more dangerous to us than a country stocked with the most terrible secret weapons. But fortunately I am finding out that you yourself are without love. Kneel down. Kneel down before me. . . . You realize, thanks to my visit, that your pure world, your artificial word, your ivory-tower poetry are: Absence of love! Incomplete humanity![4]

If anywhere, it is out there, in the bustling crowd, not at the poet's desk, that love and complete humanity can be found. Wolfenstein's poet draws the consequences; he leaves his desk and becomes a farmer, and later a stockbroker; finally he befriends a sick and friendless prostitute and, toiling to earn money for her cure and restitution, he achieves his own salvation.

The guilt feelings that his emotional shortcomings arouse in the writer of the Expressionist generation find their most poignant and significant expression in Franz Kafka. He understands that the reasons for his constant rejection in love lie within himself, that indeed it is not the others who reject him but he who rejects them. He is "forsaken not by people (that would not be the worst thing, I could run after them as long as I was alive), but rather by myself vis-à-vis people . . . I am fond of lovers but I cannot love, I am too far away, am banished."[5]

His will to fail not only in love but in all social relationships is evident to himself; and as the fundamental cause of his failure to be loved he sees his own failure to love.

The gesture of rejection with which I was forever met did not mean: "I do not love you," but: "You cannot love me, much as you would like; you are unhappily in love with your love for me, but your love for me is not in love with you." It is consequently incorrect to say that I have known the words, "I love

[4] Wolfenstein, "Besuch der Zeit," in *Mörder und Träumer: Dreiszenische Dichtungen,* p. 27.

[5] *Diaries* II, p. 215.

you"; I have known only the expectant stillness that should have been broken by my "I love you"; that is all I have known, nothing more.[6]

Kafka's own life, which he interpreted in terms and raised to the level of myth,[7] provides a striking analogy to the fictional characters we have just discussed. These weak, unstable artists always posit a counterpart-image of great solidity acting both as a stinging challenge and as a threat to themselves. Mann's Malvolto looks up to Pippo Spano, the Renaissance *condottiere;* Sternheim's Scarron to the smug Philistine Maske; the poet in Werfel's *Temptation* to the "statistician," the "Kerl wie Weissbier," to whom he loses his girl; the poet in Wolfenstein's *Visit of the Times* to the Visitor; Franz Kafka to the image of his father that he had formed in his mind. Kafka's feeling of guilt is founded on his conviction of falling short of the parental example of robustness, energy, and success. Above all, Kafka realizes that at the basis of his father's success lies a fund of emotional substance, an emotional reality and authenticity that he feels wanting in himself. What overawed Kafka in his father was, according to Max Brod, the self-assurance of the "naïve, nonreflective, 'nonconscious' man who follows only his instinct in questions of principle."[8] And in his famous letter to his father, Kafka says to him admiringly: "You possessed for me that enigmatic quality of all tyrants who are right on the basis of their personality, not their thinking."[9]

This was precisely the quality that overawed and shamed Mario Malvolto when he contemplated the powerful figure of the *condottiere;* and even as Pippo Spano's portrait impels Malvolto to plunge into his disastrous love affair in order to prove himself, so Kafka follows the example of the normal productive life, life *dans le vrai,* which his father set him, into his catastrophic engagements. Like Malvolto, he fails. Bachelorhood is the inevitable fate of the man who cannot love. And Kafka knows very well that he cannot love; he confesses that he "should have to look for a year before finding a true emotion" in himself.[10]

This emotional impotence causes Kafka to see himself as a parasite and vampire. The vampire has to suck the blood of others because it does not possess blood of its own. Similarly, Kafka, who feels that his "body is too

---

[6] *Ibid.,* p. 221.

[7] See Politzer, "Franz Kafka's Letter to His Father," *Germanic Review,* XXVIII/3 (1953), for an excellent discussion of this process.

[8] Brod, "Commentary on Extracts from Franz Kafka's Letter to My Father," tr. by Sophie Prombaum, in *A Franz Kafka Miscellany: Pre-fascist Exile,* ed. by Harry Slochower *et al.,* p. 40.

[9] Kafka, "Brief an den Vater," *Die Neue Rundschau,* LXIII/2 (1952), 196.

[10] *Diaries I,* p. 42.

long for its weakness . . . hasn't the least bit of fat to engender a blessed warmth, to preserve an inner fire,"[11] experiences a humiliating need of dependency, of clinging to others and exploiting them. He is convinced that he must, therefore, inspire disgust in everyone, particularly in women. It is in this connection that the fascinating and horrible insect story *Metamorphosis* receives its proper setting as a metaphoric portrait of the artist. In the letter to his father, Kafka combines the metaphor of the insect with the concept of the exploiting vampire which, too helpless to live independently, must prey on stronger individuals.

Kafka sees his "vampirism" as the inevitable consequence of his preoccupation with artistic creation. The exclusiveness with which he follows his mission does not leave room for life. He calls literature "my only desire and my only calling. . . . I hate everything that does not relate to literature."[12] He hates the details of everyday life because they distract him from his sole concern. He shuns marital happiness, which means to him earthly salvation, because it would tend to deprive him of time and opportunity for writing. His art has flourished only in loneliness, he remarks; it draws him away from humanity. The demands of literature are the true vampire, sucking away his lifeblood.

This concept of art as feeding on life and destroying it like a dangerous parasite haunts the Expressionists. It is highly interesting to observe that Kaiser, who was obsessed with the idea of sexual impotence in his early "comedies of the flesh," alternates in his mature period themes of pacifist heroism and altruistic self-sacrifice with vampirism and insane narcissism. George Sand, the heroine of Kaiser's drama *Flucht nach Venedig* (*Flight to Venice*) (1922), says that "literature kills life!" Like Mann's Malvolto, Kaiser's George Sand is a "comedian" in life. In everything she does a part of herself is detached, watching, taking mental notes, gathering material for future works, and polluting the "purity of experience." The ardor of her lovers is for her merely subject matter for her books; their most intimate secrets will be exhibited on the stage or at the bookstalls.

"A vampire sucks our veins," says Musset of George Sand, "we give our heartbeat to her—and turn into bloodless shades!"[13] But in this, as another character in the drama observes, "she merely obeys . . . the great law of art." (p. 15) Too weak and empty to live by himself, the artist slips, as it were, under the skin of his fellows, exploits their feelings, lives on their emotions, and utilizes these for his work; having accomplished his purpose, he leaves his victims behind, drained of their vitality, husks of their former

[11] *Ibid.*, p. 160.
[12] *Ibid.*, p. 292.
[13] Kaiser, *Flucht nach Venedig*, p. 15.

selves, while he himself moves on to new adventures. Thus, the artist is
the parasite par excellence. His career proceeds over human ruins, and the
beauty of his work is like the iridescent effects of putrefaction. "Who is
this woman?" asks one of George Sand's lovers at the end of the play, and
Musset answers him: "The inhuman human being!"

But the artist cannot help the destruction he causes. He is his own
victim, "deceiver and deceived all at once." "I am not a murderess!"
George Sand cries out; but Musset tells her: "You cannot live." (p. 30)
The artist's constitutional deficiency, which lies at the basis of his vampirism, is likewise the reason why he has to be an artist. In art he has found
the only refuge from the poverty and agony of his life. His work does not
grow out of strength. Creative joy, the outpouring of a rich exuberant heart,
are not what Kafka, for instance, finds in his writing. Writing for him is
the only possibility of survival, the only state in which he can live without
fear. It is his attempt to flee unbearable suffering, the only justification of
his "monotonous, empty, mad bachelor's life."[14]

The inhuman exclusiveness of art, which in turn is the consequence of
escape from a "monotonous, empty, mad bachelor's life," may lead to actual
murder. This is the theme of Kaiser's one-act play *Der Protagonist,* which
served Kurt Weill as a libretto for an opera. The "protagonist," an actor,
lives so completely in his stage world that he has lost all sense of reality and
identifies himself with whatever role he happens to play. Yet his loss of a
stable, authentic personality is accompanied by a desperate need to cling
to his sister, a normal healthy girl, who represents the actor's only link to
reality. "I would not find the way back to myself," he says to her, "if you
did not call out 'brother.' "[15]

One day she informs him that she has become engaged. He receives the
news with outward calm. But later in the day the theater program is
changed; instead of a comedy a tragedy will be performed, in which the
actor is to play the part of a jealous man. Carried away by his role, he kills
his sister as she approaches him with her betrothed. The schizophrenic
suppression of reality that the artist practices enables him to commit the
murder from which his normal consciousness would recoil. Art, while it
affords the artist escape from his own loveless and meaningless "bachelor's
life," also demands the clinging exploitation and finally the literal sacrifice
of other life. In Kaiser's *Protagonist* the emotional vampirism of which
George Sand is accused—and of which Kafka accused himself—has turned
into actual murder.

[14] *Diaries II,* p. 79.
[15] Kaiser, *Der Protagonist,* p. 9.

Art, while it affords the artist escape from a loveless and meaningless reality, also demands the literal sacrifice of human life. A very similar identification with the part he plays allows the unhappy impersonator Oliver in Kaiser's *Twice Oliver* to kill the man who is his double and his happy rival in love.

In both dramas the artist's link to reality and the object of his desperate attachment is a close member of his family, in the one case his sister, in the other his daughter. Incestuous love, which we have already observed as a powerful motif in the life and poetry of Trakl, is an obvious correlative of the narcissistic element in much of Expressionism.[16] The connection between narcissism and incestuous passion is pointed out clearly in René Schickele's autobiographical novel *Der Fremde* (*The Stranger*). Paul, the hero of that novel, desires his mother sexually because her beauty confirms "the happiness in his own beauty, which was his mother's rejuvenated image." (p. 45)

Paul is, like so many Expressionist characters, a "stranger" among his fellow men. Though his alienation has an apparent external reason in the fact that he is the child of a French woman living in Prussian-occupied Alsace, his position in a no man's land between two hostile cultures only symbolizes his inner loneliness. Prussians, Alsatians, and French alike sicken him at times and he flees from them to Pan in the woods, where the eyes of the deer console him.[17] He feels close only to his mother, who in the end also rejects him.

The aim of his incestuous passion is not simply possession of his mother's body; he wants to see in her eyes his triumph over her and to hear her lips admit her surrender. To the weak and lonely boy who has been denied love, happiness can come only from the proof that he is lovable.

One single 'Yes' spoken with veiled eyes, and nothing more. He would take it with him into life; *he had to have one security* . . . He collapsed and clung to her spasmodically . . . "No one troubles himself about me. I'm an outcast," and then he blurted out: "But I want you to love me, I want it, I want it!"[18]

---

[16] The incest motif fascinates some Expressionist writers even after they have passed through the Expressionist phase. Incest is the theme of Kaiser's late novel *Es ist genug* (1932) and Leonhard Frank's *Bruder und Schwester* (1929).

[17] For the deeply romantic nature of the Expressionist Schickele the motto of his drama *Hans im Schnakenloch* is most significant:

> Der Hans im Schnakenloch hat alles, was er will.
> Und was er hat,
> das will er nicht,
> und was er will,
> das hat er nicht,
> Der Hans im Schnakenloch hat alles, was er will.

[18] *Der Fremde*, p. 84. Italics mine.

Paul's love is not outgoing; it will not enwrap the beloved, it will not protect her and give her joy. His love is a furious craving to escape his insecurity. For that reason it is bound to fail and be rejected. An excellent example of this Expressionist flight from insecurity is Kaiser's play *The Coral.*

The Billionaire, the hero of *Die Koralle,* is, in a way, a Faust in reverse, Whereas Faust lusts after the universe of experience out of insatiable desire, the Billionaire garners the riches of this world out of frantic fear. What looks in him like will to power is in reality dread of impotence. The Billionaire's Horatio Alger career has been a continuous breathless flight from the traumatic experience of childhood poverty. He has hoped, by amassing a fortune, to shut out the trauma. But external goods cannot give security to him who lacks security in himself. His children turn against him and disdain the fortune which he has won for them by the ruthless exploitation of his fellow men. When his children reject him, he faces once more the abyss which he has tried to escape all his life.

At this crucial moment, his secretary, who is his double in appearance and whom the Billionaire has hired to deceive would-be assassins, chances to remark upon the secure happy childhood which he enjoyed. The Billionaire now realizes that security and happiness cannot be acquired. Like the elect of Calvinism, one is born into blessedness. The only salvation (it seems to the Billionaire) is an exchange of identities, the casting off of one's own damned self and the permanent appropriation of another's secure and blessed self. To this end, the Billionaire kills his double and lives on as the secretary, the man who has enjoyed a sunny childhood. In exchange for the contentment his new identity gives him, the Billionaire gladly accepts the death penalty as the convicted murderer of his old Billionaire self.

The psychological process to be observed in the development of vampirism is this: flight from an unendurable reality engenders a feeling of unreality, of lack of substance, of inner emptiness; this in turn produces the desperate need for someone strong, real, and substantial, on whom the empty man can lean, whom he can exploit, whose strength and vitality he can appropriate; eventually he destroys him in order to insure his own survival.

Perhaps the crassest example of the vampire-like personality in Expressionism appears in Klabund's tale *Der Mann mit der Maske.* The central figure of this tale becomes a writer when a disease disfigures him so that he is forced to wear a mask and avoid his former social contacts. Like a spider in his web, the Masked Man sits in the café waiting for naïve victims whose lives can serve him as raw material for his fiction. He has to glean the experience of others, for if reduced to his own inner experience he would have nothing to say. This empty man who wears a romantic mask over his disease-eaten face and uses art to make the void in which he lives tolerable is a perfect symbol of the Neo-Romantic and early Expressionist (and, we might add, Freudian) view of art as compensation for constitutional inferiority.[19]

A romantic young girl falls in love with his mysterious mask. Tantalized by curiosity, she has herself invited to his house and permits him to make love to her. She begs him to lift his mask and let her see his secret. When he complies, she is deeply shocked; soon afterward she kills herself. The experience that has destroyed her serves him as material for a story.

Art, a product of disease and inferiority, makes life its victim. The artist uses a mask, the "romantic fraud," to hide the horror of his real self. The naïve whom his mask fascinates feed with their happiness, eventually with their lives, the infernal beauty of his creations. The same formula, which we have observed in Heinrich Mann's Neo-Romanticism, continues into Expressionism.

In the end, however, the artist is his own victim, as is shown by the fate of the sculptor Benkal in Schickele's novel *Benkal der Frauentröster* (*Benkal the Consoler of Women*), who exploits and ruins the life of his mistress only to undo himself eventually. Benkal's vampirism, too, has its roots in a constitutional weakness, helplessness, and deficiency. In his youth no man would take him seriously, but women, whom his soft lyrical nature attracted, helped him to become aware of his gifts and nourished his faith in his art. In time Benkal became a great sculptor.

At the height of his career he meets Ij, a celebrated dancer and a great lady. Her arrogance bewitches the artist, whose apparent self-confidence rests on most unsure foundations. His love is not free of cruelty, first toward himself, then toward her. He compares her to a voracious, beautiful insect, "hypnotizing by the terror of its unleashed beauty.... Then it kills." (p. 136) His love is not so much love as triumph over his own weakness and self-distrust. As he holds Ij's proud body in his arms, he feels that he who was once despised by all has mastered life at last.

But since he does not love Ij as a person but as a prop to his self-assurance, he cannot accept the fact of her aging. There is another, closely connected, reason for Benkal's callousness to the woman whom he thinks he

---

[19] This view of art and the artist is most explicit in Gustav Sack's novel "Ein Namenloser," in *Gesammelte Werke*, I, 305–26.

loves. It is his obsession with his art. His triumph over life, necessitated by his inner insecurity, is symbolized better by timeless sculptures than by a living woman subject to decay. He has immortalized in sculpture Ij's beauty at the moment of her highest bloom, and the figure of marble, so triumphant, so eternally intriguing, takes for him the place of the aging woman of flesh and blood. Benkal considers the living person the mere shell of the work of art. Love demands more attention than Benkal can afford to spare; love would distract him from art. Ij, who loves him, understands this and sacrifices herself to his art; she takes herself out of his life and disappears in order to avoid further interference with his work.

But with her departure, Benkal's art becomes meaningless to himself. He realizes with horror the boundless cruelty at the basis of his art and, like Hofmannsthal's Claudio, feels that he has been left empty and self-defeated in the end. He conceives an intense hatred for his own work and secretly defaces and destroys the masterpieces for which he once sacrificed a life of love and happiness. On the ruins of his lifework he drinks a toast to life.

... I knelt before the stone; I crawled around it on hands and knees; I embraced it, naked, for hours. The stone, the devil, refused to grow warm, but I—I froze; my blood froze all around my warm heart, which pulled and chafed and wished to get away. . . . Yes, the devil is wherever there is a heart not filled with love. (pp. 185–86)

In this conclusion of Schickele's *Benkal,* we encounter the message of love which is so significant of Expressionism. This message is, in a number of Expressionists, the observable result of the agony which inability to love has inflicted on the narcissistic writers and poets. Devotion to the Neo-Romantic, *fin de siècle* cult of Art and its further development in Abstractionism no longer represents a solution to this new generation, because, in their experience, aestheticism, instead of serving the emotional life from which art grows, stifles and kills it; and thereby it destroys art itself.

The emotional sterility of Kafka's life, which made him escape to literature, becomes in turn a fetter on his art. "I see how narrow my limits are in everything, and consequently in my writing too."[20] Despite references to euphoric states which writing inspires in him ("it is a leap out of murderer's row; it is a seeing of what is really taking place"), doubt and depression prevail in his diaries after the great breakthrough of creativeness in the autumn of 1912 (when he wrote *The Judgment* at one sitting). He feels he lacks the long breath and energy necessary for extended works. He

[20] *Diaries II,* p. 108.

constantly wavers, revises, deletes.[21] Could he blame his inability to write except in fits and starts on his hated office work, he would be happy. But when he does not have the office as an excuse, he comes face to face with literary sterility, which of all his failures is the one most horrifying to him.

I can't write any more. I've come up against the last boundary, before which I shall in all likelihood again sit down for years, and then in all likelihood begin another story all over again that will again remain unfinished. This fate pursues me. And I have become cold again, and insensible; nothing is left but a senile love for unbroken calm. And like some kind of beast at the farthest pole from man, I shift my neck from side to side again.[22]

We have in these frequent spells of lethargy and despair a powerful reason why Kafka put up with his job for the larger part of his adult life, even though he complained bitterly of the degree to which it interfered with his creative work. A writer so dangerously poised over the abyss of sterility would be afraid of plunging into free-lance writing. The job, hateful though it was, provided a bulwark against the responsibility of continuous creation. Kafka doubted his ability to devote all his time to literature. Even the additional work that he took on in his father's factory appeared at times as a positive boon, and a sensation almost of relief filled him at the thought of his escape from writing.

Artistic crises similar to Kafka's are related by Ernst Barlach in his autobiography, *Ein selbsterzähltes Leben*. At thirty-four, an age when other artists have often done their best work, Barlach had not even begun to feel the slightest assurance about his attempts at art. Without accomplishments, without faith in himself, he returned to Berlin from a position as ceramics teacher in the Rhineland.

A plague hit my confidence, I had to break with self-satisfaction ("Behagen"), and confidence in life became a doubtful thing which had to keep silent. . . . I knew I was in hell and sat in it struggling, day in day out, to overcome the consciousness of being utterly superfluous. (pp. 38, 39)

He hides in the darkest corners of coffeehouses, wishing to be invisible, "worthy of no attention and hardly in need of it." (p. 39) He is disgusted with the work so far accomplished, and his self-respect evaporates together with his courage. No sooner does he rise than he wants to creep back to

---

[21] *Diaries I*, p. 35. Actually Kafka labored for years over his novels *The Trial* and *Amerika* and finally left them both in a fragmentary state in order to start *The Castle*, which also remained a fragment.

[22] *Diaries II*, p. 98.

bed. He views his life as futile and doomed and himself as a mere encumbrance in the world.

Barlach's and Kafka's examples show how misleading it is to think of Expressionism (and modernism in general) as merely a reckless revolt of Bohemian youth, wilfully bent on upsetting traditional concepts of art. Some of the most significant "revolutionaries" of the "young generation," men like Kaiser, Stramm, Frank, Benn, as well as Kafka and Barlach, were mature men when they first appeared on the scene. The violence of their new forms and themes was the result of a desperate struggle to wrest some land from the ocean of doubt and fear which threatened to submerge them.

It is symptomatic of the Expressionist's concern with creative sterility that Werfel chose the crisis in Verdi's life, the years of silence between *Aïda* and *Otello*, as the theme of his "novel of the opera." Werfel's *Verdi* can be considered the great epic of his Expressionist period. Conceived at the outset of the author's poetic career, the ripening of this work spans the entire period of Expressionism; even though it was not actually written until the end of the Expressionist phase, it analyzes and sums up, so to speak, some of the fundamental problems of the Expressionist.[23] It is then of great significance that his book about the artist is at the same time a book about the artist-in-crisis. It approaches the problem of creativeness by exploring the failure of creativeness. It deals with the artist's agony when the wells of his inspiration seem to have dried up permanently. Verdi, having failed for decades to complete a work and trying his waning powers in vain on the subject of *King Lear* (even the choice of this theme of abdication and old age indicates the composer's state of mind), comes to a point where, outdone and overshadowed by Wagner's triumph, he is ready to surrender. From the nadir of his life he looks back upon its peaks. His whole life, as he sees it now, has been unrelenting drudgery in the services of that "accursed and affected fraud called Art." Art was the lifelong fever that left no time for the simple pleasures that make life worth living. And this intoxication with creation had not been happiness. "He had never permitted himself to rock peacefully on the easy wave of the moment." As with Kaiser's Billionaire, the constant fear of failure prevented him from relaxing and enjoying the moment without pangs of conscience over neglected work. He hurried from social gatherings back to his lonely desk. He did not permit himself to read, because reading would take precious minutes from his never-ending task, which was joy and satisfaction "only

[23] In his preface to *Verdi*, Werfel writes that the plan of the novel was conceived around 1911, the year his *Weltfreund* was ready for publication. *Verdi: Roman der Oper*, p. 7. *Verdi* was completed in 1922, first published in 1923.

in the rarest moments, but mostly pain, wrestling, overexertion of the will, to the point of perspiration and near faintness." (p. 506)

And in the end came the agony of sterility. The creative machine, overworked, refused to give further service. Worse than the tension of creation was the humiliating stillness of creative impotence. From the depth of Verdi's desperate sterility emerges the suicidal thought of modern art:

And for what purpose this drudgery of a whole lifetime? Do men need art? Without hesitation he gave answer: The nations of today do not, in the least, need any higher form of art.... Thus the dreadful tension of his life had merely served a delusion.... (pp. 506–7)

All the strain and the exertion, all the deprivations and self-denials had been merely a spectacle for a few aesthetes, "the neurotic spawn of certain well-to-do strata." At what seems to him the end of his creative life, Werfel's Verdi considers himself the fool who has bartered his God-given life for less than baubles—for vanity.

There goes, then, through Expressionist literature the thought that "art hath grown too heavy," and that the sacrifices made for its cause are a suicidal crime against life and happiness. This notion is closely connected with the Expressionist's hatred of, or at least indifference to, his own work. Gottfried Benn stopped writing at the age of thirty-five (although years later he was to resume on a different basis) and concluded the slim volume of his collected works with a self-deprecation the desperate sincerity of which is hardly matched elsewhere in literature.

Here they are, these collected works, one volume, two hundred pages, very meager; one would have to be ashamed of them if one were still alive. Not a remarkable document; I would be surprised if it found readers; it is already very remote from me, I cast it behind me as Deucalion his stones; perchance human beings may come of these distortions, but whatever may come of them: I do not love them.[24]

Franz Kafka, like Benn, was utterly uninterested in the public reception of his work and considered the author's pride in reading his manuscripts with an eye to publication ridiculous and harmful. He had to be coaxed to hand over some of his works to his publisher. When an actress requested permission to give a public reading of some of his stories, he refused. In his will (as is well known) he requested Max Brod to burn all his manuscripts.

Albert Ehrenstein's mouthpiece Tubutsch stops writing one day when

[24] Benn, *Schriften*, p. 214.

he observes two dead flies in his ink bottle. This sight makes the word "fame" "explode in his face." For a while he decides to write in pencil, to make what he writes "still more transitory." Then he gives up writing altogether.

The Poet in Wolfenstein's *Visit of the Times* abandons literature and goes out into life. He watches farmers at work; their labors have a concreteness which he has always missed in his literary toils. The results of their efforts can be measured in bushels and pounds. The earthiness of this new life refreshes and converts him. "Now I, too, till the soil. That is less, but also more, than creating a world in fiction." (p. 27)

This self-hatred, rarely paralleled in older literature, links the Expressionist to the Dadaist, who takes the next logical step and destroys himself as an artist. But this Dadaist suicide of art, which is associated with the breakdown of Europe at the end of the First World War, has antecedents long before the World War. We find a "Dadaist" manifesto in one of the earliest works of Max Brod, the weird story bearing the significant title *Tod den Toten! (Death to the Dead!)*, which was written perhaps as early as 1902, and not later than 1906.[25] "The dead" are art and the artists. The romantic glorification of genius (so runs the philosophy of the hero of that story) has to be discredited once and for all. The dogma of the importance of art is merely a remnant of mysticism and superstition. Modern man has made the great artist, the genius, a substitute for the God in whom he can no longer believe. But this outdated idolatry blocks the way to a healthier and more progressive life on earth. The cult of art perpetuates the vicious reflexes of religion. It substitutes emotion and authority for reason, and with its worship of the great individual it is inimical to democracy. The reputation of a "genius" depends upon accidental factors and, once established, on habit and authority. A commonplace or an absurdity is considered a profound insight if Shakespeare uttered it.

Mankind has to take three steps. The first led it past the flames of Sinai into religion; the second through the stakes of the Reformation and away from religion into art; the third will lead through the burning of the storehouses of art—the time has come! We are preparing for the third step. The last epoch, the golden age, has dawned. A hot haze will lift from over the world! All fancy, all art, all imagination will vanish! Truth will make its entrance! We will love the earth once more, and life; we will no longer disdain anything; day and night the torches of labor and sweet voluptuousness will be lit; no one, no one must be allowed to withdraw from his fellows, no one must be unhappy. (p. 35)

[25] This tale is contained in the collection "Novellen des Indifferenten" for which the dates 1902–1906 are given. Cf. *Die Einsamen.*

The artist's guilt from his isolation, his "withdrawal," is the clue to his despair in art. In Wolfenstein's *Visit of the Times,* the Visitor appeals to the social conscience of the Poet: "We need you, but the witch, the blood-sucker . . . your poetry . . . takes you away from us." (p. 24) The author of Brod's "Dadaist" manifesto realized, too late for his own happiness, that art only distracted men from leading a full and happy life. He himself was too old to re-establish contact with the raw bustling life which he scorned in his youth. But at least he could point the way for others and warn them against wasting their lives for the sake of the moribund "anachronism." He used his fortune to buy up as many masterpieces, rare books, etc., as he could obtain and withdrew them from public use. Then one day, when his sprawling house was filled with art, he dynamited it. "Since I have recognized the truth I must reveal it to the world by this enormous act."[26]

With this flaming finale of art, the inner development that leads from the artist's withdrawal and self-absorption to his self-destruction is complete. In dynamiting his temple of the muses, Brod's hero merely draws the consequences of the bitter disappointment in art which we have found voiced or suggested by all the authors discussed in this chapter. Art kills life: so runs the theme. The logical conclusion of this realization is that life, in self-defense, must kill art.

The way out of this dilemma is an inner regeneration, a *Wandlung* (a favorite term in Expressionism). Only if the self-absorbed, narcissistic artist learns to identify himself with others, share their sufferings, serve and love them, can he save himself, and become a true poet, a seer, and a healer of mankind. The painful feeling of "unrelatedness," the sense of one's own inhumanity, was an important reason for the deification of humanity, the demand for embracing all mankind in one grand gesture, which the Expressionist generation postulated.

[26] Brod, *Die Einsamen,* p. 40.

PART TWO

The New Man

CHAPTER SIX

Anti-Zarathustra

ART AT PEACE WITH SOCIETY AND THE ARTIST AT ONE WITH HIS FELLOW MEN
was the goal of a large segment of Expressionist literature from its inception. "My only wish is to be related to you, O Man!" cried the twenty-
year-old Werfel; and this cry found an enthusiastic echo among German
intellectuals.[1] But the Expressionist's goal of integration in the human community, on which recovery and survival of his art depend, finds its greatest
obstacle in his own character. The delusion of grandeur, the self-deification
of genius, stand in the way of the artist's regeneration. "There is a difference between the creative man and all others," says the composer Daniel
Nothafft in Jakob Wassermann's Dostoevskian and semi-Expressionist
novel *The Gooseman,* in which the isolation, catastrophe, and regeneration
of the modern artist are most beautifully told; "genius," Daniel claims, "is
nearest to God." "But his downfall," he is answered, "starts one step from
God's throne, and he falls deep."[2]

Although Daniel scorns all efforts to appeal to an audience, secretly he
hopes that his bold *avant-garde* compositions will one day bridge the gap
between him and mankind. He guards them as his most precious possession and sacrifices the joys of a normal life to his work. He exploits and
ruins the few who love him and, to be rid of responsibilities, entrusts the
care of his child and household to a vicious semi-idiot. This creature sets
fire to his house, and all the artist's unpublished works are destroyed.

In this crisis, the thought dawns on Daniel that the loss of his manuscript was the outcome of his failure to exercise his responsibilities as a
human being. His sin had been life in the "ivory tower": "What is human
guilt? Failure to feel, failure to act. . . . What is greatness? Nothing but

---

[1] Kurt Pinthus, in a conversation with the author, dated the beginning of literary Expressionism in Germany from Max Brod's reading of Werfel's poem "An den Leser" to a group
of Berlin students and *literati* in 1910; the immediate effect of Werfel's poem was enormous.

[2] Wassermann, *Gänsemännchen,* p. 589.

the fulfillment of an infinite number of small duties." Daniel had never fulfilled "the small duties" of life. He had demanded all, given nothing. With Luciferian pride he had thought that he, a genius, could dispense with the "small duties" to his fellow men and be a "monster," a "noncitizen." His downfall had been contained in this pride.

But in the lowest depth of despair there is hope for the humbled artist. His work, doomed because it grew on self-love and coldness, has been destroyed; the page is blank for a new beginning.

> There is a regeneration, and through it one attains absolution. Turn your eyes from the phantom and become first a human being, then you can be a creator. Once you are a human being, truly a human being, you won't perhaps even need to create . . . strength and glory will radiate from *you* yourself. Are not works, after all, merely detours of man, merely imperfect attempts at his revelation? . . . How can he who shortens and deceives what is human in himself be a creator? It's not a matter of craftsmanship, Daniel, it's a matter of being. . . . Your music can't give anything to people as long as you are imprisoned in yourself. Feel their anguish! Feel their boundless loneliness! See them! See them! (pp. 595–96)

The voice that brings Daniel this message of hope and cure through self-knowledge and knowledge of others is that of the Gooseman, a small bronze statue on the fountain in the market square of Nuremberg. The Gooseman is to the self-centered and wretched artist a symbol of what the artist should be. An unpretentious figure, he stands in the busy market, in the center of life, lending an unobtrusive dignity to the work-a-day affairs that take place around him. When the citizens look up at him from their haggling and bargaining, he helps them to remember that they are part of a great community. He suggests to them that there is a beauty and an order in the universe which both contain and transcend their shrewd and anxious lives. Yet his important function is never dictatorial and forbidding. Despite his exalted station, the citizens look upon the Gooseman as upon a cousin, one of their own.

The saving discovery that Daniel makes in his contact with the Gooseman is that all these ordinary human beings whom he was wont to fear or to despise are at heart not very different from himself, the superman, who had thought he was almost God. He looks into their eyes and finds "the same ardor, the same anxiety, the same suppliance, the same loneliness, the same death, in all of them . . . God's soul." (p. 599) With this insight into the essential oneness of all men, Daniel feels no longer alone. As his eyes open to the suffering of others and as he understands that he is not unique in his isolation, he is healed. The wall between the misunderstood genius and mankind has fallen.[3]

The old conflict between artist and bourgeois fades as a consequence of the artist's new outlook and gives way to the concept of the fellow man, a suffering creature in need of sympathy and love. After his regeneration,[4] the Expressionist no longer sees the world filled with smug Philistines, strong men, and proud, beautiful women, a glittering ballroom from which he alone, by his fatal gifts of intellect, is excluded; now he sees the world filled with suffering, a vale of tears waiting for salvation. Johannes Becher sees armies of joyless workers trudging to the factory day in and day out;[5] Albert Ehrenstein sees scrofulous children of the slums playing "telephone" by shouting down into a sewer hole; piece-time workers who dare not take time out on Sundays impress Rubiner; abandoned young women with illegitimate babies play vital roles in Sorge's *Beggar* and Johst's *Young Man*; a diseased prostitute brings happiness to Wolfenstein's Poet in *Visit of the Times*; old housemaids who have spent their lives in unceasing drudgery are by their very existence a flaming accusation of the middle-class poet Werfel, who is allowed to live a life of comfort and leisure. The world is a great hospital and poorhouse, and even those who appear happy are frightened and pained at heart.[6] In such a world the lonely and neurotic artist-intellectual is no longer an exception. His personal tragedy may be unique in its particular manifestation, but at the same time it is merely part of the "human condition." Thus, the Expressionist finds that he is related to man through his suffering.

[3] Daniel's experience of regeneration, which is typical of many Expressionist experiences, is similar to the profound changes of heart found in the lives of religious leaders such as St. Paul; but it is also similar or, at least, parallel to the changes of personality and outlook brought about in an individual by psychoanalytic treatment. Significantly, those works of Hermann Hesse which show some Expressionist features, *Demian* and *Steppenwolf*, were preceded by the author's psychoanalysis. See Ball, *Hermann Hesse: Sein Leben und sein Werk*, pp. 151–60. "The Expressionist is not psychological but he is psychoanalytical," says Max Picard ("Expressionismus," *Die Erhebung* I (1919), 329 ff.).

[4] The term "regeneration" applies to many Expressionists but not to all. Some, like Edschmid and Benn, never underwent a regeneration—Benn merely underwent a shift of point of view—while others, like Werfel, seem to have possessed the "regenerate" outlook from the beginning. Moreover, reversals and relapses are frequent; constant vacillation is, for instance, a prominent feature in Kaiser, who changes his outlook from play to play.

[5] Becher, "Abschiednehmen," *Ein Mensch unserer Zeit*, p. 167. This poem is an autobiographical confession, explaining Becher's shift from his middle-class background to the proletarian movement. In view of Becher's political importance as literary dictator of Communist East Germany, this poem is of special interest since it shows that the roots of left-wing terrorism lie in an awakened humanitarian conscience.

[6] Cf. the lines "Weiss nicht die Qual, wenn Kaiserinnen nicken," and "Kenn ich der Mädchen stolz und falsches Plauschen?/ Und weiss ich, ach, wie weh ein Schmeicheln tut?" in Werfel's "Ich bin ja noch ein Kind" (*Wir sind*, p. 92).

But his guilt remains. It merely takes on a different aspect. He is no longer "guilty" because he is rejected and miserable in a world of contented Philistines. Now he is guilty because he is privileged to write and create in a world in which millions go hungry and are racked by pain and disease. Even in the presence of the beloved woman, Werfel feels a profound sense of guilt, remembering that on this very day, which he is allowed to spend in the rapture of love, laborers have to toil in factories, clerks sit crouched in gloomy offices, and sick men breathe their last.[7] Does art have a right to exist in such a world, is it not an unforgivable luxury in a universe where the most crying need is for immediate help and relief?

The answers to this question and encouraging examples come to the German Expressionist from national traditions alien to his own. They come from the Latin south and west—Italy and France; from the Russian east; and from the Judaic element within the Christian tradition. The saving experience of regeneration involves a repudiation of the chief tradition by which the German intellectual had lived since the Storm and Stress, and especially since the ascendancy of Bismarck's *Reich*.

In the same year, 1910, in which the public reading of Werfel's still-unpublished poem "An den Leser" ignited a spark of enthusiasm, Heinrich Mann published two brief essays, *Geist und Tat* (*Spirit and Action*) and *Voltaire-Goethe* (*Voltaire and Goethe*), which attempted to answer this question. In Italy, Heinrich Mann had been impressed with a pattern of life in which the fateful opposition between artist and bourgeois did not exist. His novel *Die kleine Stadt* (*The Small Town*) (1910) is a monument to that harmonious relationship between the artist and society, which also inspired Wassermann's *Gooseman*.[8] But in his essays, Mann went a step further and attempted to create a new vision of the writer's role in German society.

The isolation of the German intellectuals, Mann claims, has been for the largest part of their own making. The German intellectuals have done nothing to lessen the distance between themselves and the people. They have indulged narcissistically in their personal experiences, cultivated fine emotions, nurtured private melancholies, and forgotten the poverty and backwardness of their people. It is obvious that with this condemnation of

---

[7] See his poem "Als mich dein Wandeln an den Tod verzückte," in *Menschheitsdämmerung*, p. 107.

[8] According to the former Expressionist critic and scholar Rudolf Kayser in his moving memorial address *In Memoriam Heinrich Mann* (at the MLA convention in New York, 1950), *The Small Town* exerted a profound influence on the Expressionist generation. Its effect was parallel to that of Werfel's "An den Leser"; a state of affairs was shown in which the artist-intellectual lived at peace with the people.

the Romantic tradition, Heinrich Mann sits in judgment over his own past. The aesthete who admired the "strong man," the Renaissance condottiere, has reversed himself.

In contrast to the German intellectuals, Latin men of letters, particularly in France, have always been in the center of political life and wielded a powerful influence on the everyday affairs of their people. Voltaire and Rousseau, according to Mann, were the architects of the French Revolution; Voltaire rehabilitated Calas; Zola saved Dreyfus; and Victor Hugo was the great antagonist of Emperor Napoleon III. In all these men a restless, critical, humane, and compassionate intellect was at work: "They all have known the happiness of . . . seeing their word move things, of seeing the spirit transformed into reality and action."[9]

The German man of letters has never known such happiness because he has never wanted to know it. While Voltaire and the French writers allied themselves with the human spirit and progress, Goethe and the German poets allied themselves with nature and the *status quo*. While Voltaire helped to shape the fate of Europe,

[Goethe's] work, his memory, his name have changed nothing in Germany; they have not eradicated a single barbarity, they have not cleared a single inch of the road toward a better future. There were no grateful relatives of a Calas to walk in Goethe's funeral procession. . . . Man involved in the dusty struggle for existence squints up amazed at him—and goes on toiling. . . . Idle hedonists cover their empty existence with his name as the emblem of their "culture," as if culture were possible without humanitarianism. Voltaire, on the other hand, the hope of humanitarianism, is at home among the lowest of his nation. . . . Freedom: that is the totality of all goals of the spirit, of all human ideals. Freedom is movement, emancipation from the soil, and elevation over the beast: progress and humanity. . . . Yes, freedom is equality. Inequality makes unfree even him for whose benefit it exists. (pp. 14–16)

The adulation of its great men has cost Germany her greatness as a civilized nation. The "great man" is great only in those moments in which he creates great works. To venerate him as a person intrinsically different from other men, a kind of superman, is to insult and deny human dignity in his fellow men. The myth of the superman, moreover, deprives the work of genius of any real effectiveness, since what is true of the superman cannot be true of the lowly crowd, and his thoughts can have no real relevance to ordinary men.

The last person, however, to whom this aberration [the myth of the superman] . . . should be permitted, is the man of the intellect, the man of letters: Yet it

[9] Heinrich Mann, "Voltaire-Goethe," in *Macht und Mensch*, p. 12.

was he who had consecrated and propagated [this myth]. . . . He had been especially active in Germany . . . in the cause of anti-intellectualism, rationalizing social injustice to the advantage of his archenemy—authority. What strange perversion caused him to do this?[10]

Mann concludes the essay *Spirit and Action* with a rousing formulation of what was to become the program of German activism.

The time demands . . . that they [the German writers] . . . become agitators, that they ally themselves with the people against authority, that they devote to this people's struggle all their eloquence. . . . The enemy must be the man of the fist, the authoritarian. An intellectual who offers his services to the ruling caste commits treason against the spirit. For the spirit is not a conservative force and does not grant privileges. The spirit dissolves; it is egalitarian.

In some discussions of Expressionism the tendency has been to belittle and even deny the political-activist element. This attitude, which would draw a sharp dividing line between religious *Expressionism* and political *activism,* overlooks the deeply spiritual nature of activism on the one hand, and, on the other, the revolutionary and social-minded element in religious Expressionism. Walter Hasenclever in his activist drama *Der Retter* (*The Savior*) (1915), which is deeply influenced by Heinrich Mann, finds his inspiration in the prophets and apostles of the Judaeo-Christian tradition. The hero of this drama, an activist poet, kneels and prays to God to show him the way to save the world. It is significant that Saint Paul, whose life affords the supreme example of conversion or *Wandlung* and subsequent *propaganda fidei,* appears to the Poet and proclaims him as his successor. Because Paul's spirit passes into the Poet, he gains the courage to challenge the powers that be. Ernst Toller refuses to distinguish between the political and the religious writer: "The basic prerequisite of the political writer (*who is somehow always a religious writer*) is this: to feel responsible for himself and everyone of his brethren in the human community. To repeat: he must be a human being who feels responsible."[11] Ernst Toller's definition of the common denominator of activist-political and religious Expressionism might serve us too. The common denominator is ethical responsibility.

The Expressionist is an ethical idealist. This distinguishes him radically from the Marxist. His goal is spiritual, not material. It is the rule of the

---

[10] "Geist und Tat," *ibid.,* p. 8.

[11] Toller, "Bemerkungen zu meinem Drama *Die Wandlung,*" *Tribüne der Kunst und Zeit,* XIII, 46 ff. (Italics mine.)

spirit on earth. The Marxist bows to history and the iron laws of necessity even as Goethe bowed to nature. Thus Marxism, in the Expressionist view, does not constitute a break with the German tradition, which is what the Expressionist demands for his own salvation and the salvation of his people. Marxism with its doctrinaire masses is merely the reverse of the Prussian military state. Marxism does not include the inner spiritual regeneration, the *Wandlung*; it has no room for ethical absolutes and the free will of man to choose the good. It was the explosive idealistic French Revolution, not the well-organized German Social Democracy, which Heinrich Mann held up as the inspiration for the revolutionary writer.[12] Expressionism culminates, according to Kurt Pinthus, in "political poetry," but a "political poetry of a higher order, which does not aim at the overthrow or victory of certain political parties and personalities, but at the politics of humanity and humanitarianism from which alone, after the present chaos, the necessary reconstruction can result in art as well as in statesmanship."[13] When we keep these facts in mind, the essentially spiritual and humanist nature of German activism will be clear.

From France came to the Expressionists not only the vitalist modernism of Rimbaud and Apollinaire, the abstractionist modernism of Mallarmé, and the political-activist inspiration of Voltaire, Hugo, and Zola, but also the Christian poetry of Charles Péguy and the Christian modernism of Paul Claudel. Both, especially Claudel, influenced the Expressionists in their search for regeneration. The exalted goal which Fritz von Unruh was to set for Expressionist art was inspired by the role of Holy Communion in Claudel's drama. "Yes, we are communionists," Unruh says, "because we communicate to all men the one great holy vision of their deification."[14] This view of art had informed the first German work in which Strindberg's dramatic Expressionism is fully applied—Reinhard Sorge's *The Beggar*.

Sorge's Beggar-Poet writes experimental dramas which no existing stage will perform; but when a patron of the arts, impressed by his talent, offers him a ten-year annuity to develop his gifts, the Beggar rejects it. He is not interested in perfecting himself in a life of luxury and leisure. He desires to be effective and help humanity by means of his drama, and he demands a stage on which to have his plays performed. His new drama is a communal drama. It is not to be read by isolated individuals in their private

---

[12] See Heinrich Mann's drama *Madame Legros*.

[13] Pinthus, "Zur jüngsten Dichtung," *Die weissen Blätter*, II/12 (December 1915), 1509.

[14] *Flügel der Nike: Buch einer Reise*, p. 123. Although Unruh's book was written at the close of the Expressionist period, it echoes a good deal of the early Expressionist message and mood.

rooms. It is to be acted in front of hundreds and thousands. His theater is
to be a place of pilgrimage where the sick of heart will find a cure, the
desperate gain new hope, and the broken in spirit be comforted. Workers
will stream to it in great masses, since they will see in it their souls rise.
Starving girls with illegitimate babies will find in it solace and "bread," and
cripples will learn in it to love life.

The Beggar's new theater has, of course, nothing in common with the
conventional theater. It is not a place of entertainment, but a place of worship and salvation, more like a church, a school, a political or revivalist
meeting than the traditional stage.[15] Its inspiration is the Greek theater. It
is a communal affair, not an affair of individuals who pay to be amused.

Although Sorge's Beggar fails to find the patron for his experimental
theater, and so fails to reach the masses, the idea of his new drama has,
nevertheless, fulfilled its communionist mission: it has saved at least one
human being from despair. A girl with an illegitimate child, abandoned by
her lover, has overheard the Beggar's impassioned explanation of his new
drama; aroused by his vision she, who was on the point of committing
suicide, has gained new courage.

"Poets are lovers," says the First Critic at the beginning of the play,
"lovers of the world and limitlessly addicted to their love." But this love is
quite different from the sexual frenzy of the vitalist. It is free of sensuous
self-gratification, so free that it almost ceases to be physical. M. S. Humfeld
in her book on Sorge relates that Sorge had no sexual relations with his
wife during the first nine months of their marriage;[16] they read, worked,
prayed together in a harmonious intimacy of the spirit. The Beggar in his
relationship with the Girl repeats in some measure Sorge's (strangely chaste
and spiritual) life with his wife Susanne. The main problem facing the
Beggar and the Girl, who have become lovers, is this: should the Girl keep
or give away her child by another man? The Girl would give the child
away to devote herself entirely to her lover, but the Beggar insists that she
think of her child first. The welfare of another human being takes preced-
ence over their own self-indulgent love; no happiness can grow from
selfish passion. The Girl resists his wish for a long time but finally glad-
dens him with the news that she has resolved to keep her child.

> You have found the way to yourself, beloved,
> Vanity has gone, humility has come.

---

[15] This idea of the "new theater" is also developed by Rudolf Leonhard, "Das lebendige
Theater," *Die Erhebung*, II (1920), 258 ff.

[16] Humfeld, *Reinhard Johannes Sorge: Ein Gralsucher unserer Tage*, pp. 154–55.

And the Girl answers him:

Never yet
Have I seen the sun so glorious. . . .

The same "humility" that makes the Girl finally keep her child, instead of sacrificing it to passion, makes the Beggar take a job in a factory. These two decisions are announced simultaneously, and thus their unity is emphasized. Both actions represent the repudiation of selfish vanity, the arch-sin in the communionist's world.

Yet the ambivalence of this transitional play is such that Nietzschean self-aggrandizement and humanist communionism mingle even in the same plots and subplots. At the end of the drama, the Girl, now pregnant with the Beggar's child, revokes her former decision and sends her child by her former lover away, and the Beggar consents. He now expects her to devote herself entirely to him. His decision to go to work in a factory also has a Nietzschean aspect. His pride demands that he make it hard for himself. Toil and self-imposed suffering are the crucible of the "superior man." The Nietzschean aspect, moreover, is forcefully emphasized by the fact that the Beggar soon leaves the job, realizing that his special mission as an artist exempts him from menial labor to which the majority of men are subject. The "superior man" is a law unto himself.

The communionist-artist's task is to change the world and save and transfigure his suffering fellow men (and thereby save and integrate himself). Unlike the Marxist or purely political writer, he aims to bring succor not only to the socially underprivileged; he also wants to help and comfort those whom even the most perfect social order cannot help—the under-privileged by nature, the ugly, the lonely, the aging, and the unloved. The artist assumes the role of the healer of the injured and the physician of broken souls. René Schickele calls his novel about an artist *Benkal, Comforter of Women.*

Benkal's greatest work is a group of "Mothers," aging and ungainly bodies done with compassionate attention to detail. The effect of this work is enormous. Women crowd around these statues, shocked at first by this unprecedented rejection of female beauty. Only gradually dare they admit to themselves that this public glorification of woman as she is, not as man desires her, gives them a sense of infinite relief.

Those who thought themselves ugly no longer feel ashamed when their beautiful and elegant sisters look at them; now they can stand next to them with heads unbowed. Those who have been happy lose their aggressiveness of bearing, their boundless desire to dominate, their eternal defensiveness. They may now, without fear or bad conscience or the fretting thought of their decline, deem themselves more beautiful than they had ever known. . . . An epidemic of comfort erupts among women. They raise their heads and know that all has not been in vain, that they will live, that all women are one, and will not perish. (pp. 62–63)

This is the loftiest effect the ethical Expressionist can hope to achieve in his work.

For the communionist, to love is to comfort the miserable and the despised. Schickele's Benkal loves women with blemishes, women whose hands are calloused from heavy chores and whose breasts are not those "full and firm bosoms which painters and sculptors like to depict." He kisses the disfiguring mole his mistress tries to hide from him. He points out to her certain fine qualities of her husband, teaches her to love her children with greater devotion and to give more thought to their education. He brings a "clear and ardent atmosphere" into the life of this woman who had thought herself unattractive and neglected. Even in his illicit love affairs, the communionist artist seeks to help and to reform. Love is charity. Through Benkal's love, Hahna blooms forth into a new and fuller life. "Somehow Benkal felt responsible for Hahna's well-being . . . responsible to the world-spirit, to love, to the love of all mankind. . . . The gravest, the only sin was to deny love." (p. 49)

Yet the same Benkal who brings happiness and love to the unloved Hahna and other women later displays thoughtless selfishness in his affair with the proud dancer Ij. It seems as though the Expressionist could be kind only to the underprivileged who have always, like himself, lived in the shadows, and as if he resented those who have always lived on the sunny heights of life. About this mixture of charity and *ressentiment* in the Expressionist, we shall have to say more later. Whatever the ultimate motivations that distinguish Benkal's behavior toward the proud, glamorous Ij from his behavior toward the humble, unhappy Hahna, Benkal betrays his ideal of responsibility and succumbs to ambition; thereby, he ruins both his love and himself. He commits the "one sin"; he "denies love."[17]

Conversely, Werfel's Verdi finds not only his personal happiness but also the resurrection of his long-dead inspiration by his renunciation of ambition and his rebirth as a humbled "new man." In the depths of the crisis that threatens his life as well as his art, Werfel's Verdi realizes his guilt. He has

[17] See Fritz von Unruh's remark, upon seeing the sad look of D'Annunzio's neglected wife, that all his glory as a poet would be meaningless if he found a similar look in the eyes of his loved one. *Flügel der Nike*, p. 116.

succumbed to a neurotic hunger to be greater than his fellow man, to out-shine him and have no gods beside himself. He is saved as soon as he can feel indifferent to the eclipse of his fame and resign his compulsive am-bition to outdo Wagner. He decides to retire to his estate and live out his days as a simple farmer. The hostility to Wagner, which had poisoned him, leaves him now: "Let the world place him as far beneath Wagner as it pleased, his mind . . . would not be deceived: Richard Wagner was his comrade on earth!" (p. 519) As Verdi changes from a machine of creative-ness to a simple human being who can live without greatness, the dried-up wells of his creativeness flow again, and his art becomes greater than it ever was. During the night of Verdi's regeneration Wagner died. The over-whelming feeling of human solidarity in the face of death seizes and fills Verdi. All thoughts of rivalry are past and forgotten.

. . . and suddenly this cry escapes from his lips in a brief, hoarse, senseless melody: "Vendetta!"
. . . .
Vendetta is not a word. Vendetta is strength lost. And more. Vendetta is the magic moment of that love which is born to last only for a second and, even so, is not born often in life. (pp. 570–71)

Vendetta is the deepest inspiration of the communionist artist. His art is not the affirmation of a grandiose ego; but neither is it routine technique. It is the protest of man, the outcry of his heart at suffering and finiteness, the ejaculation of his compassionate grief, and also the shout of his hope and his joy over having found the gate out of his loneliness and the access to his fellow men.

The Poet in Wolfenstein's *Visit of the Times* finds in compassion not only the meaning of his life but also a new access to his artistic creation. He takes a diseased prostitute into his home and resolves to earn money for her cure. With this decision to live and work for another human being in direst need, he regains justification for his writing, which the guilt feeling of isolation had made him abandon. Johst's Young Man finds the meaning of life in compassion. A friend of his wants to rid himself of his pregnant girl friend; the Young Man receives her with a tenderness to which she has never been accustomed. He provides food and shelter and, although he does not possess her, assumes all the obligations of a husband toward her.

The glorification of the prostitute in communionist Expressionism be-trays the unmistakable influence of Dostoevski's Sonya. The prostitute, to be sure, had become an important figure in European literature with the so-cially conscious proto-Naturalism of Dumas *fils,* and *La Traviata* made the

Western world weep over the courtesan, sinned against more than sinning. Still, despite nobility and self-sacrifice, the prostitute remained an object of compassion rather than of admiration. With Zola's *Nana* and full-fledged Naturalism, she became the accusing symbol of social corruption, the embodied indictment of a social system which coupled economic exploitation with moral hypocrisy and thus allowed the self-destructive destroyer of society to emerge from the gutter and prey on the physical and moral health of mankind. In the *fin de siècle* aestheticism of Pierre Louys, the courtesan, perfumed and elegant, became the symbol of antibourgeois and anti-Christian defiance, a glorious goddess of beauty to be opposed to the sordid worship of money. The attitude is carried over into vitalist Expressionism. Wedekind's Lulu, the "earth spirit," embodies the untrammeled dominance of sex over money, respectability, and power; she is the life-force and rules tyrannically over all men. For the vitalist, the prostitute is a variant of Dionysian self-exaltation and ecstatic affirmation of the omnipotence of unconscious vitality. Under Dostoevski's influence, the communionist Expressionist (who frequently was the vitalist in a different phase of his life), however, considered the prostitute in an entirely new light, which differed from the sentimental pity of proto-Naturalism, the sociological accusation of full-fledged Naturalism, and the immoral idealization of aestheticism and vitalism. To be sure, for Dostoevski and communionist Expressionism, as for Dumas, Sue, and Verdi, the prostitute was still the pathetic victim of a callous and brutal society; but since Dostoevski (and the communionist Expressionists) viewed victimization from a Christian rather than a social point of view, its meaning underwent a profound change.

Suffering, for Dostoevski, was not an evil to be ameliorated or abolished by social reform; it was a gate to salvation. It was the imitation of Christ. The martyred scapegoats of society, the Marmeladovs and Sonyas, became the true successors of Christ on earth. The degradation to which Sonya submitted in order to save her family resembled the self-sacrifice of the Savior. For her act of love, mankind ostracizes and crucifies her on the cross of shame and insult. But a healing power radiates from her and nurses Raskolnikov from spiritual sickness slowly back to spiritual health and rebirth. The prostitute heals and regenerates those whom intellectual arrogance has inwardly petrified and robbed of their ability to love. Throughout Expressionism the Sonya-Raskolnikov relationship is repeated in many variations. In the prostitute the Expressionist hails and glorifies the saving power of love which he himself desperately yearns to learn and to experience. The poet in Johst's novel *The Beginning* celebrates the prostitute as the savioress of her brothers, the whole male sex. She is the universal victim, representing human suffering and degradation at their most intense. Her sacrifice insures the well-being of men and the respectability of "good" women. Her position as the martyred scapegoat of society is like Christ's. She rises to redeem her denigrators and persecutors. To the humiliation which others inflict upon her she responds with indefatigable and saving love.

In Paul Kornfeld's drama *Himmel und Hölle* (*Heaven and Hell*), in its extreme form an unintentional caricature of communionist Expressionism, the savioress is a poor streetwalker, aging and fading, and a Lesbian to boot. Passers-by make the sign of the cross when they see her and mothers tell their youngsters to look away. "I am a cast-off thing, a worn-out beast!" she says. "A thing, a beast!" This woman—Maria—is on many counts the lowest, most wretched creature imaginable. Yet through her, as through her namesake Mary, salvation comes to this earth.

The protagonist of the drama, Count Umgeheuer, the "near-monster" or "momster" as his name implies, represents man in his God-forsakenness. An inner block of shame and pride keeps him from expressing the affection which he knows his wife craves. Mortified by his emotional inability, he has come to hate himself, and therefore he inflicts injury where he would love. He expresses the insight of so many Expressionist heroes: "I hate myself and so I hate the world!"

Oh, this ragout of embarrassment and shame! This knowledge: you have beaten others and are beaten yourself! You have made victims and are a victim yourself![18]

To hurt his wife and thus to be enabled to despise himself still more, he takes the ugly prostitute Maria into their house although she is repulsive to him.

Kornfeld's Maria embodies the communionist ideal in its most extreme and bizarre form. She relates herself to humanity, which has cast her out, by sacrificing herself for the happiness of others. She wants to restore the Count's foundered marriage and be "the bridge on which the two can meet." She assumes responsibility for a murder which the Countess has committed and accepts the punishment. Maria's decision to die for the Countess redeems all persons around her. She teaches the Countess to believe in her husband's buried love. The impact of her sacrifice breaks the shell of the Count's soul. He overcomes his inner barriers, breaks down with emotion, and confesses his abiding love to his wife. Maria's Lesbian friend Johanna, pining to die with Maria, commits a crime so that she can be executed

---

[18] Kornfeld, "Himmel und Hölle: Eine Tragödie in fünf Akten und einem Epilog," *Die Erhebung,* I (1919), 118.

together with her. The two women stride to the block as though to a love feast. They have attained the joyful, indomitable heroism of early Christian martyrs. In the moment of Maria's execution the Countess, too, fulfills her desire and enters eternal life. In the operatic epilogue the three women float down on a cloud, lift up the Count, and take him with them to Heaven. Thus, the ugly Lesbian prostitute enables God to justify His ways to men. She offers abundant proof of the communionist thesis that "one ascends to Heaven through martyrdom incurred for the sake of one's fellow men." She saves herself by saving others.

Although the rediscovery of *Barock* literature, and the influence of Strindberg, Claudel, and Péguy must not be discounted, it was in several ways a Russian Christianity which the Expressionists discovered. Dostoevski more than any other writer led the Expressionists to the ethics and outlook of apostolic Christianity. The cult of Dostoevski in Germany, initiated by the complete German edition of his works before the First World War, reached its apogee in the late teens and early twenties when Hermann Hesse, in his semi-Expressionist period, raised the Russian writer to the rank of a prophet. The twisted intellectuals and passionate-vitalist saints, the conversions and spiritual regenerations which people Dostoevski's pages, the violent intensity of his style, the Naturalistic surface appearance and the deeply probing visionary essence of his form, left a lasting imprint on German Expressionism. Dostoevski influenced the German Expressionists more than any other writer except Strindberg. Wassermann, Kornfeld, Kafka, Trakl, Däubler, Werfel, Wolfenstein, and Leonhard Frank show his influence in their works or attest directly to the fascination he exerted over them.

Tolstoy, too, exerted a powerful influence on the rise of the ethical-communionist aspect of Expressionism. The great Russian's self-repudiation and spectacular conversion to an apostolic way of life form the archetype of the numerous regenerations and repudiations of one's past which characterize the lives and works of the Expressionists. The repudiation of the Goethean tradition in German letters and the German past in general that Heinrich Mann and Carl Sternheim undertook from a Latin, especially French, point of view, other Expressionists, such as the Russian-speaking Ludwig Rubiner, undertook with Russian traditions in general and Tolstoy's example in particular in mind. Rubiner hails in Tolstoy the prototype of the "responsible," "ethical" artist and puts him in sharp contrast to the aristocratic German poet Stefan George. Tolstoy, the prophet of a primitive-Christian way of life, replaces Zarathustra, the prophet of self-exultation and anti-Christ, as the Expressionist ideal. Even as Italy and France became for Heinrich Mann (and Italy for Werfel) idealized counterimages to a Germany in which the artist was able to survive only as a lonely demigod, the Russian village community, to which Tolstoy directed their attention, fulfilled a very similar function for other Expressionists. At the turn of the century, the experience of the Russian peasant — mediated through Tolstoy's influence—had caused a decisive spiritual liberation in Rainer Maria Rilke's life. A few years later, it liberated Barlach from artistic sterility and caused him to find his Expressionist style.

The *Wandlung* which Barlach experienced on a trip to Russia was for him a liberation and assertion of religious feelings and creative powers in one. Russia gave him the courage to acknowledge and express the stresses and ecstasies of his deepest self. "This breakthrough of religious feeling" released his long-suppressed artistic energy. For this German from the soberly reticent Protestant North, Russia was a revelation of terror and riches, a world of stark forms, shrill emotions, and extreme attitudes, an archaic battlefield on which angels and demons waged war for possession of the human soul.

There dawned in me this enormous thought: "You may without shame reveal everything within you, the most extreme, the inmost gesture of piety, and excess of rage—because everything, paradisical infernos and infernal paradises, is expressible; Russia has taught you this. . . ."[19]

For Barlach, as for Trakl, Kafka, and Kornfeld, it is the mythical-demonic Russia of Dostoevski; for Rubiner, Goll, Becher, and Frank, the Russia of Tolstoy and the village mir (and a few years later, the Bolshevik Revolution) that appear as liberator. But within and beyond the Russian experience in either form lay that which both Dostoevski and Tolstoy proclaimed and the village community represented—the image of the fraternal way of life of apostolic Christianity. For the German Expressionists, Russia pointed back to Christ.

The idea of regeneration which forms the core of communionist Expressionism is a Christian idea, and the form of the Expressionist drama, in which the experience of regeneration is usually presented, the Strindbergian *Ich-drama,* descends ultimately from the Christian Passion and morality play. Strindberg's *To Damascus* deals with the problem of regeneration. The haughty, stubborn, passionate, and isolated self of the Unknown Man must be broken to be reborn in humility and love. The title of this first Expressionist drama points to the prototype of spiritual rebirth and the first German Expressionist dramatist, Reinhard Sorge, repeated Saint Paul's

[19] *Ein selbsterzähltes Leben,* p. 41.

example in his own life when a sudden illumination in the winter of 1912 converted him from Nietzsche to Christ.

Sorge's conversion constitutes a mystic-religious parallel to Heinrich Mann's conversion from romantic aestheticism to social democracy. Mann's activism has a spiritual basis; Sorge's Christianity has an activist character. For Mann, after his regeneration, art is to be propaganda for social democracy. For Sorge, after his conversion, art is to be *propaganda fidei*: "Thenceforth my pen has been and forever will be only Christ's stylus—until my death."[20] But not only the missionary concept of literature is common to Mann and Sorge after their respective conversions; the enemy against whom they revolt is also the same—the German tradition which culminates in Nietzsche's doctrine of the superman.

Sorge's first work after his conversion is a work of agitation against the myth of the superman. He tried to publicize his repudiation of Nietzsche by means of personal letters but, finding that the audience thus reached was all too small, he decided upon his *Gericht über Zarathustra: Vision (Judgment upon Zarathustra: A Vision)* (1912). The intensity of Nietzsche's superman cult is here redirected toward a "radicalism of brotherly love";[21] that is, the fervor of life which Nietzsche advocates is to be the same, but its direction and purpose are reversed. Sorge considered the *Judgment* one of his most important works.

Like Heinrich Mann's condemnation of Goethe, Sorge's condemnation of Nietzsche is also a rejection of the poet's own past.

> Do you know who that boy is? Look, Zarathustra, he loved you, he was your disciple. Your ardor seized his, and he squandered all for your sake. Because his ardor was such that he loved you above everything. . . . Your spirit was turned earthward, my spirit allowed itself to be deceived. For the sake of your ardor it deceived itself.
>
> Then came the hour when it turned upward, do not ask how, the spirit is its own answer . . . the command came from above to be a fighter against the brother-spirit (Zarathustra), to judge him by the authority of Heaven.[22]

According to Sorge, Nietzsche's cult of strength, his vision of a mortal superman, his proclamation of a reign of pitiless force, were the compensation for his physical inferiority:

> A raving hunchback runs through the streets: "Wipe out the cripples! Long live straight limbs!"
>
> Oh, your male dignity, Zarathustra! (pp. 10–11)

---

[20] Quoted by Susanne M. Sorge in *Reinhard Johannes Sorge: Unser Weg*, p. 46.
[21] Cysarz, *Geistesgeschichte des Weltkrieges*, p. 83.
[22] *Gericht über Zarathustra*, p. 7.

He who partakes of the spirit has no need to boast of his body. He understands the oneness of mankind and knows that athlete and cripple, king and beggar, are brothers because God is their father.

For the Spirit erects a very firm bridge between man and man. . . .
The Spirit sees and testifies:

"*One* Spirit in truth. They who labor toward Me also labor toward each other, and he who rests in Me rests with many." (pp. 14–15)

This community of all men, which is clear to him who has found God, is the most compelling answer to the wretched isolation of the Nietzschean who has only himself and who cries out for a single friend in the desert of his loneliness. To have disregarded the basic oneness of all men is the tragic aberration of Nietzsche. His excellent mind, which was so close to the Spirit, turned upon itself and, madly glorifying life, destroyed itself.

The drama *Guntwar,* written later the same year (1912), is an elaboration of the ideas of the *Judgment.* Christianity has given content and meaning to the vague, aimless mission of the Beggar, which has been changed into the concrete mission of the Christian "prophet" and apostle who wins souls for God. Specifically, the drama deals with the recently converted poet Guntwar's efforts to save his unregenerate friend, the painter Peter, and lead him to grace. This difficult conversion is Guntwar's apprenticeship for his world-wide mission which, he tells his maternal friend Mirjam, Peter's wife, must start with his nearest friends.

Even as, in the main plot of the drama, Guntwar saves one fellow human being by his relentless pursuit, he rebuilds, in the Second Interlude, the modern world after its destruction. The new world is to be built on truly Christian foundations. Through Christ men will be united. The anguish of the One — Christ — truly relived and experienced makes each man a brother of all others. "He who dips [into the grief of Christ] becomes truly common ['wahrhaft-allgemein']."[23]

The regenerate Expressionist, whether converted to Christ or to activism, tries to become "truly *common*"; i.e., he tries to wipe out in himself whatever separates him from his fellow men. He completely rejects the Goethean-Nietzschean cult of personality and pride of individuality, which informed the greatest part of the German cultural tradition in the nineteenth and early twentieth centuries, and culminated in the cult of the "great man" or superman. With this tradition, the Expressionist rejects the aristocratic outlook of Stefan George and his circle. The Expressionist combats the Nietzschean aristocratic Neo-Romanticism so fiercely because he himself, as

[23] Sorge, *Guntwar: Die Schule eines Propheten,* p. 80.

we have seen, grew up in it and suffered under its impact. Because he is much closer to its "agony," Neo-Romanticism is a more vicious enemy to him than Naturalism. Wolfenstein, for instance, distinguishes the "new art" from Romanticism rather than from Naturalism.

. . . the new art is *no longer selfishly romantic*. Its tone and content know of human suffering. It does not aim at charming confusion but at the essential. It is not akin to ironical detachment but to a virile embrace. . . . Instead of the romantic self-perfection of the artist its message is the elevation of man.[24]

By "romanticism" the Expressionist understands certain elements in cultural life which were particularly marked in Wilhelminian Germany and against which he rebelled as violently as the vitalist sought to embody and surpass them: priority of the aesthetic over the ethical or the vital over the moral; the worship of the amoral "great man" simply because he is successful and strong; the adoration of irrational force in nature as well as in man; the pride of a sharply defined personality; the aristocratic contempt of the masses.

In the year of Sorge's *Judgment upon Zarathustra,* there appeared a magazine, *Der lose Vogel (The Loose Bird),* all of whose contributors were anonymous. The activist Rubiner hailed its appearance as "the German revolution of 1912."[25] Anonymity, Rubiner argued, abolishes vanity and implies responsibility. The publication of an anonymous magazine amounts to a repudiation of Nietzsche and George. The cause, the subject to be expressed, triumphs over the personality of the writer. Similarly, the "new man" of Kaiser "wants to be dissolved in humanity; he does not want to outstrip the collectivity in any respect."[26] The "new man" cares nothing for name or fame because these erect barriers between man and man, and no one can be human in isolation. Through anonymity and self-effacement the Expressionist hopes to become *wahrhaft allgemein.* Guntwar-Sorge says after his conversion:

I am such nothingness! Now more than ever a beggar! Yet I must give of my riches. . . . Oh, now I am rich enough to give, not by my own merit, but because the Living One stands by me. I must step among men to proclaim Him . . . what I know will be modest. I want to go to help carry water.[27]

This new non-Romantic humility arises at the outset of Expressionism to develop gradually toward the *Neue Sachlichkeit* (New Realism, New

---

[24] Wolfenstein, "Das Neue," *Die Erhebung,* I (1919), 4. (Italics mine.)
[25] Rubiner, "Die Anonymen," *Die Aktion,* II, 299–302.
[26] Quoted by Lewin, *Die Jagd nach dem Erlebnis.*
[27] Sorge, *Guntwar,* p. 80.

Matter-of-Factness, New Objectivity, or New Sobriety as it might be called more accurately), which was to supersede Expressionism. The counsel with which Guntwar warns his friend and disciple Mirjam against self-intoxication and headlong enthusiasm can only be termed *sachlich* (sober, objective) in the best sense of this complex and interesting term.

> But at first let us become sober, Mother! Kind and clear! Calm, awake! Let us don the armor that protects so well—let us walk with calm steps! So that it won't overwhelm us, so that we won't fly precipitously and then lie dying on dry land.[28]

Sachlichkeit is the ultimate consequence of the communionist trend in Expressionism.[29] The communionist has rediscovered a human reality, outside himself, in his fellow man. In his violent rebound from the "romantic agony"—isolation and sterility—he discovers the community, existing or potential. His style is still explosive. But the direction that his rebound takes leads in the end away from Expressionist subjectivism. After Sorge had found a firm anchoring in the Catholic Church, his style changed too. It became his ambition to write in an impersonal and objective manner. Of his three Christmas mystery plays, published under the collective title *Metanoeite*, Sorge said with a sense of accomplishment: "I think that in these works I have, for the first time, succeeded in writing objectively."[30] He had ceased to be an Expressionist.

Sachlichkeit, in the sense of humble dedication to external and particularly human life, permeates the poetry of Ernst Stadler. Stadler warns against allowing the real day to pass neglected for escapist fancy.

> When welcome dream caresses me with velvet hands,
> And daily life escapes from me,
> Strange to the world, estranged, too, from my deepest self,
> These words I hear: Acquire essence, Man![31]

---

[28] *Ibid.*, p. 81.

[29] Detlev W. Schumann points out tendencies of *Sachlichkeit* in late Expressionism, e.g., in Werfel's *Verdi*. But as Sorge's example indicates, the tendency toward *Sachlichkeit* is contained in Expressionism from its inception. Werfel's outburst against Romanticism in *Verdi* is thus to be seen not as a repudiation of Expressionism, but rather as the culmination and testament of communionist Expressionism. See Schumann, "Expressionism and Post-Expressionism in German Lyrics," *Germanic Review*, IX (1934), 56 ff., 115 ff.

[30] Quoted by Karl Muth, "Nachwort," in Susanne M. Sorge, *Reinhard Johannes Sorge*, p. 178.

[31] Stadler, "Der Spruch," in *Der Aufbruch*, p. 12.
> Wenn mich willkommner Traum mit Sammethänden streicht,
> Und Tag und Wirklichkeit von mir entweicht,
> Der Welt entfremdet, fremd dem tiefsten Ich,
> Dann steht das Wort mir auf: Mensch, werde wesentlich!

Alienation from the world amounts to alienation from the poet's "deepest self"; conversely, man can be real and essential only in active contact with "the day" and with "reality." A profound sympathy with the suffering and underprivileged of mankind inspires a number of Stadler's poems.[32] A loving interest in the small, concrete things of everyday life, under the definite influence of Walt Whitman, is beautifully evidenced in poems such as "Hier ist Einkehr," "Kleine Stadt," and "Herrad." Love of his native Alsatian landscape mingles with a mystical devotion to the commonplace and makes Stadler quite different from Expressionists such as Trakl, Heym, Lichtenstein, or Benn. Stadler, like Werfel, is not a true modernist. He is not alienated from nature and has no need to create artificial universes of expression. God is immanent in the homely details of life, and beatitude radiates from them.[33] Stadler's work more than that of any other Expressionist prefigures *Sachlichkeit*.

Max Brod, who under Martin Buber's influence overcame the sterile intellectualism of his *Nornepygge* period by embracing an expansive, missionary, and Messianic Judaism[34]—a Judaism very similar to Sorge's apostolic type of Christianity—contrasts Kafka's humility and lively interest in the progressive tendencies of his age with Stefan George's Neo-Romantic hostility to the "holy vulgarity" of everyday life.[35] According to Brod, Kafka was more than a writer. Like Sorge, he transcended the state of art and was on the way to becoming a saint. But the Expressionist saint, as Brod draws him in the image of his dead friend, is not a recluse; he is deeply interested in all efforts to build a saner and happier life on earth. Kafka was interested in theories of progressive education, followed the Czech struggle for independence with sympathy,[36] frequented Czech mass meetings and discussion groups, and drew up a plan for a workers' collective in which modern socialist and ascetic, apostolic ideas blended. The

[32] See "Abenschluss," "Judenviertel in London," "Kinder vor einem Londoner Armenspeisehaus," *ibid.*, pp. 65–68.

[33] See particularly "Herrad."

[34] Cf. Brod, "Vom neuen Irrationalismus," *Die weissen Blätter*, I/8 (April 1914), 749 ff., which states his position in 1914.

[35] Brod, *Franz Kafka*, p. 127. The expression "holy vulgarity" is used by Ludwig Rubiner to describe the direction in which the new artist should be heading. Rubiner, "Der Kampf mit dem Engel," *Die Aktion*, VII/16–17 (1917), 228.

[36] Sympathy with the oppressed Slav minorities of the Austro-Hungarian monarchy was a common characteristic of the Prague Expressionists. Werfel's preface to the German translation of the *Silesian Songs* of Petr Bezruč is an inflammatory manifesto for the cause of oppressed nationalities. See *Die schlesischen Lieder des Petr Bezruč*, tr. into German by Rudolf Fuchs. Otto Pieck made Czech authors known through his translations in *Die Aktion*. The Czech composer Janaček was greatly aided by Max Brod. See Lutz Weltmann, "Kafka's Friend Max Brod: The Work of a Mediator," *German Life and Letters*, New Series, IV/1 (October 1950), 46–50.

sainthood which, according to Brod, Kafka strove after and even embodied, implies a life lived with the most exacting sense of responsibility. The saint is not a special creature apart from all others, a superman, but merely the most advanced form of common man. Brod attributes Kafka's extreme self-criticism, his "almost supernatural modesty and reserve," to Kafka's ideal of sainthood. Religion, for this type of saint, amounts to satisfactory integration ("Einordnung") into the universe, particularly as it presents itself in the human community. Religion is a "fulfilled life . . . in the national and universal community."[37]

This "integration" of which Brod tells us is, of course, never actually realized by Kafka. Unlike Sorge, who found "the fulfilled life" in the "universal community" of the Catholic Church, and unlike Brod, who found it in Palestine, Kafka intensely yearned for but never attained such happiness. His attempt to reach "the Castle" and gain citizenship in the human community never came to fruition. Consequently, despite the style with its apparent *Sachlichkeit* and the increasing realism of his last period, the theme and tenor of Kafka's work remained Expressionistic to the end.

Objectification of subjective states characterizes, of course, the best work of the Expressionists and distinguishes it from the unvarnished subjectivism of the rhetorical Expressionists. Yet this lucid concreteness of detail, which distinguishes the work of Kafka, Barlach, Trakl, Heym, from the confused and bloodless abstractness of many lesser Expressionists, is by no means *sachlich*. It is a method of expressing subjective states more effectively; but to call the works of Kafka and Barlach—or the linguistic condensation of Kaiser and the *Sturm* poets, or the selected contrasts of Benn —*sachlich* would be as misleading as to call a dream "objective" because its images stand out in vivid clarity. All these authors abstract the full concreteness of objective reality from their subjective emphasis, their "idea" or *vision* of reality, which alone they seek to express. *Sachlichkeit*, however, is the attempt to present a "de-emphasized" objective reality, i.e., the dispassionate understanding of the external "world." It rests on a humble subordination to an external universe. The longing that informs Expressionism is to find the access to such a world. More than any other modernist group, the Expressionists are unhappy in their aesthetic subjectivism and strain to break away from it. The history of the Expressionist drama in Germany can largely be described as a movement away from its point of departure—Strindberg's dream play—to a less obscure, more readily accessible form: the parabolic or allegorical drama. A similar process can

[37] Brod, *Franz Kafka*, p. 118.

be observed in Kafka's work. The metaphoric visualizations of his early period give way to more realistic, parabolic tales in the last years of his life; "The Hunger Artist" and "Josephine" are good examples of Kafka's late parabolic form.

As Sorge's example shows, almost at the outset of the movement, many Expressionists gladly abandon the Expressionist form as soon as they reach the longed-for goal of integration in an objectively existing world and community. The enthusiastic abandonment of the subjective-Expressionist form by one of its founders will be repeated a few years later by numerous other Expressionists as they, too, find integration in an objective communal reality, in the Third International, the Zionist movement, or the Nazi "folk community." This yearning for integration in a community makes most Expressionists (except the *Sturm* poets, who were free of it) basically hostile to modernism, which, as we have seen, arises from the acceptance of a public-less isolation as the artist's natural habitat. Kant's "arbitrary freedom" of the artist, whose only purpose is to create according to his self-chosen law of creation, was by no means the goal of Sorge's Beggar-Poet. On the contrary, he longed for a theater that would be at the center of a cultic community. He yearned not for free creation but for communication. To be sure, what he strove for was not art as mimesis. Yet it was the kind of art which had given rise to and suggested Aristotle's theory of mimesis—namely the celebration of communal feasts as part of a commonly shared belief and ritual. Such an art presupposes the existence of a social center, a politico-religious community. Sorge's Beggar did not possess such a community but groped for it; and his groping assumed the form of an Expressionist drama, even as Strindberg's *To Damascus* was the form which an existential search assumed. But soon after Sorge had found this objective community in the Catholic Church, he transcended the abstract-subjective quality of his work and ceased to be an Expressionist. Expressionism in Sorge's case turned out to be the form of a search, not of a possession.

Unlike Sorge, most Expressionists believed that the cultic community for which they longed did not yet exist in any institution. Rather they conceived the task of their art to be the creation of such a community. This effort manifested itself as Messianic Expressionism, the phase which characterized the movement especially near the end of the First World War and which even today is still equated with Expressionism as a whole. Messianic Expressionism transferred the visionary quality of Expressionism to the social and political sphere. The *visualization* of subconscious or existential states became the *vision* of social renewal. Although Messianic

Expressionism gave birth to some of the worst rhetorical excesses of the movement, it offers more than mere documents of a turbulent and feverish state of mind (which in itself, of course, holds considerable social-historical interest). The combination of ethical idealism and psychological insight— partly under the direct influence of Freud and Jung, but also largely under that of Buber—presented in these dramas and narratives of inner regeneration through outer revolt, carries a fascination for the modern reader which compensates for a good deal of abstract verbiage, tastelessness, and grotesque hyperbole.

CHAPTER SEVEN

The Revolt

IN HIS "JUDGMENT UPON ZARATHUSTRA" SORGE CLAIMS THAT NIETZSCHE'S CULT of the superman is the compensation for a feeling of physical inferiority. Heinrich Mann suggests in his essay on Goethe and Voltaire that the German artist-intellectual enthroned on Olympus, high above humanity, does not trust his human status. The self-contempt of the "subman" lies hidden in the self-esteem of the superman. To become man, the artist-intellectual has to rise as well as to descend. He has to overcome his feeling of worthlessness as well as his pride.

Heinrich Mann urges the intellectual-spiritual type, the *Geistige*, to become aware that he represents a higher stage of human evolution than the practical man of action whose muscular faith in himself permits him to act spontaneously, but with results harmful and ruinous in both personal and public affairs. Even the intellectual's paralysis, which is caused by too much thought, he regards as superior to the mindless bustle of the practical man. Arnold Acton, the intellectual protagonist of Heinrich Mann's *Zwischen den Rassen* (*Without a Country*) (1907), despises the heroic as atavistic and finds the use of force revolting. History is full of barbarities because those who acted had no mind and those who had mind did not act. But once the mind decides to act, it changes the face of the world. The advances in democracy and humanitarianism have been wrested by intellectuals, physically weak and often neurotic types, from the strong men, the heroes. "It is clear," says Arnold, "that with the decrease of crude strength, cruelty also loses some of its domain. What prevents me from thinking that mind, which smashed the chambers of torture . . . will likewise smash the arsenals?"[1] The mind, according to Mann, is the hope of the world. The intellectual, in whom mind is embodied, cannot fail, if only he decides to become active, to set right what the heroes of muscle and brawn, the military and athletic "men of action," have made wrong.

[1] Heinrich Mann, *Zwischen den Rassen*, p. 186.

What the intellectual has to overcome in himself is his disastrous in-
fatuation with the strong man as an aesthetic phenomenon. Like Mario
Malvolto in Mann's "Pippo Spano," who sought to emulate a soldierly
brute of the Renaissance, Arnold cannot help admiring his antagonist, the
unscrupulous Conte Pardi who, after having taken the woman Arnold
loves from him, mistreats and humiliates her. But Arnold looks upon
Pardi as a visitor to the zoo would look upon a splendid feline beast. This
aesthetic admiration and moral impartiality hide a lack of love and manly
responsibility which stem from want of self-confidence.

The regeneration occurs when Arnold realizes that if the intellectual
is to make his humanitarian values prevail, he has to fight for them. The
Geistige must become a hero and take the hated weapon into his hand to
rescue the world and himself from those who would destroy both. When
the mind takes up arms, it is invincible. Arnold's beloved, Lola, feels the
moment in which Arnold, after years of hesitation, decides to challenge
Pardi as the moment of her own and her lover's rebirth. Arnold's action
coincides with triumphant demonstrations of the Social Democrats, whom
the reactionary Pardi considers his archenemies. Lola sees in this symbolic
coincidence the overture to a better age on earth. In the democratic and
socialist community of the future, which will be inspired by his values, the
intellectual will have found his roots and salvation.

Lola breathed more deeply in this highly charged atmosphere, charged with
the infinite goodness of democracy, its power to arouse dignity, to bring out
the humanity in man, to spread peace. She felt it like a hand extending to her,
to free her, even her. She was to become like all the people, she was to be saved.
All around her they looked at her freely and simply, without reserve, without
that polite aloofness. She was not a stranger; she was a woman like the others;
like the girls with the violets at their breasts, anyone might desire her. Then
she recalled how once, years before, Arnold in his loneliness and consuming
spirituality had rhapsodized to her of human community, of the warm and
active cooperation among human beings. . . . What he had felt, she was now
experiencing. He alone was like her. . . . (pp. 552–53)

In Alfred Wolfenstein's autobiographical *Novelle an die Zeit* (*Tale
for the Times*) resort to a violent act transforms a diffident, self-despising
intellectual into a self-respecting, nonconformist thinker. In the beginning,
the hero, a liberal and pacifist, is not sure of his right to differ from the vast
majority, who are carried along by chauvinistic enthusiasm. He suspects
that his pacifism is only a rationalization of his maladjustment. He knows
that he is weak and despises his weakness. Could it be that pacifism is the
camouflage of neurotic fear?

His mistress confirms him in his self-doubts. He is alienated from the community, she claims, and she calls him "cold and egocentric" ("mit sich selbst liegend").[2] He cannot share emotions, she says. His vaunted love of mankind is his excuse for not feeling with his compatriots. She herself has found the way back to "the others." She will leave him and join the crowds that are surging through the streets, hailing the outbreak of the First World War.

In this moment of unutterable anguish a blind fury wells up in the poet-intellectual. The raging emotions of the chauvinists impart themselves to their opponent and enable him to act. He himself "has become the war; he drags his mistress to the floor and crushes her in his . . . embrace." (p. 706)

Later he understands that his outburst has been his liberation, the answer to his self-doubts.

. . . his wish to isolate himself had been neither barrenness or cowardice nor coldness. Nothing in him had been antagonistic to mankind; only to frenzy, unconsciousness, to the darkness that reduced minds to irrational fate.

By his outburst the intellectual has proved that the human heart can beat as passionately for justice and reason as for habit and convention. The guilt feelings of the poet and intellectual are changed into a triumphant sense of justification and moral rightness. The intellectual recognizes that the present social order, which has condemned him to a peripheral place, cannot be the community to which he aspires. The insane clamor of August 1914 proves that its values are false. Conversely the despised values of the intellect, the derided opinions of the outcast, are the only true ones.

The activist ceases to despise his intellectuality and, on the contrary, asserts it as a boon to himself and the world. The parallel to Benn's shift from vitalism to abstractionism is obvious, and it is of interest to note that Benn was stylistically influenced by the activist Heinrich Mann, a fact which points to a kinship of mentalities. Both activist and abstractionist radically affirm that which has set them apart from "normality." They cease to accept the "given" in a nature and a society in which they have found themselves strangers and outcasts. There is, however, this important difference between them: whereas the abstractionist does not dream of changing anything in empirical reality, the activist rebels against the dominant type of society and, at the same time, hopes to regenerate himself. He does not merely adopt a new intellectual attitude and shift his sense of values;

[2] Wolfenstein, "Novelle an die Zeit," *Die weissen Blätter,* II/6 (June 1915), 704.

he seeks to change himself into a better, sounder, and more effective human being. Even as the Expressionist in his communionist phase or aspect seeks to cure himself by learning to love and serve others, so in his activist phase or aspect he seeks to redeem himself by transforming self-contempt into righteous indignation. In either case he relates himself to others, and this distinguishes him clearly from the abstractionist. Consequently, while communionist and activist are frequently the same person in different phases or aspects, the abstractionists of the *Sturm* circle kept, on the whole, apart from the other Expressionists, and Benn never underwent either a communionist or activist phase.

Leonhard Frank offers the best example of the Expressionist's *Wandlung* from self-abasement to human dignity through revolt, and thereby shows us the genesis of the activist attitude. Poverty and the pressures of a bigoted provincial environment weighed heavily on Frank's youth. Poverty and small physical stature engender a feeling of inferiority which undermines and destroys the autobiographical hero of Frank's first novel *Die Räuberbande* (1914). The name of Frank's protagonist Oldshatterhand comes from the hero of the Wild West adventure stories of Karl May, a nineteenth-century German author who, inspired by Cooper, wrote countless tales about an imaginary America—he himself had never visited America. In these tales a noble, manly German—Oldshatterhand—allied with noble Indians, frequently fights and gets the better of his wicked English and Anglo-American opponents. Karl May inspired several generations of German boys; he remained Adolf Hitler's favorite author throughout Hitler's life and had, next to Wagner, the most intensive influence on Hitler's imagination. Frank uses this name partly to evoke the childhood paradise of boyish games from which his protagonist can never free himself and partly to underline the ironic contrast between his weak and defeated hero and the tough, heroic idol of German boyhood. Frank's Oldshatterhand, who fights a desperate struggle to realize himself as a painter, feels that he has no right to live. He can never free himself of the fatal self-contempt which early repression and maltreatment and later the humiliation of poverty have produced in him. Even as a boy he submits to barbarous punishments with masochistic eagerness. Years later, when he is accused of a crime he never committed, he comes to believe in his guilt and performs self-execution.

The alternative to this Kafkean self-hatred and resignation is the cold pride of the Stranger, Oldshatterhand's alter ego, who scorns the bourgeois world that rejects him and, relying on his strength, leads a life of complete loneliness. But this dreary choice between despising and being despised creates an unbearable tension that contributes to Oldshatterhand's mental breakup and suicide.[3]

There is, however, a third alternative, which is merely suggested in Frank's first work but which is to be the major theme of his second. It is the effort to uncover the deep-seated cause of the feeling of unworthiness and strike back at the forces that twist and crush one's life. Oldshatterhand's crippling feeling of guilt has its roots in gruesome childhood experiences that center around the sadistic schoolteacher Mager. Mager symbolizes the oppressive social structure of provincial Germany, with its medieval anachronisms, its pious terror, and its brutal authoritarianism.

> Oldshatterhand's lips tightened to a thin line.
> "Once teacher Mager hit me in the face with his cane and didn't let go until I was flat on the floor. That was for not holding my school-friend fast on the chair when he beat him. . . ."
> ". . . Maybe the teacher is as he is, lives as he does, walks about as he does in the town because the atmosphere of the town admits of no other possibilities. . . . Catholicism, the cloisters, monks and priests, the narrow winding streets with their damp shadows, the Gothic churches, the tall gray walls from which Gothic gargoyles leap forth suddenly, all that together affects man from his childhood on. . . . Such a town produces evil men who had to confess sins even as seven-year-old children, cretins, religious lunatics, social climbers, born hunchbacks, furtive murderers, cripples, ascetics, sex criminals who rape children . . . and artists. And people like the teacher Mager. . . . Avenge yourself! Defend yourself! Hit him with the cane in the face! Until he is flat on the floor!" (pp. 239–40)

The distortion and intensity of the Expressionist form in literature is connected with that heavy atmosphere of guilt which a repressive and sadistic education creates in sensitive young people in a period when rational criticism is beginning to be applied to traditional ways. The grotesque style is, at least partially, an expression of great tensions. It is an outlet for anxiety but at the same time a means of conscious or semiconscious revolt. Significantly, the grotesquely heightened Expressionist style in Frank's first novel emerges in those passages in which Oldshatterhand is haunted by his irrational guilt.[4]

[3] In the scene with the psychiatrist, Oldshatterhand sees himself as Christ crucified. "Sometimes I know that I am the most incapable and the meanest and the lowest creature. And at other times I know that I am the greatest; the greatest in the world," *Räuberbande*, p. 278.

[4] It may be of interest to note that the cruel figure of authority, raised to a sinister and demonic power, haunts the insane hero of the Expressionist motion picture *The Cabinet of Dr. Caligari.*

If he were able to strike back at the teacher and the society he represents, Oldshatterhand would retrieve the human dignity that he lost in his childhood. But he is too weak and broken to take this course, which, however, the writer Anton Seiler pursues in Frank's next novel, *Die Ursache* (*The Cause*) (1915). The writer Seiler, a penniless, ostracized, and deeply unhappy man, develops an aggressive attitude toward society and becomes an agitator and author of revolutionary articles. While his political views deepen his isolation from all respectable people, they forge a link between him and other disinherited and desperate human beings. Seiler has friends among prostitutes; he says of a blind beggar that he "is one of us."[5]

But his radicalism fails to explain the corroding sense of inferiority and the periodic waves of self-disgust that submerge Seiler, for all his political aggressiveness. Seiler loses his argument with a well-fed and self-satisfied citizen because a strange feeling of guilt suddenly rises in him, causing him to lose his nerve and to withdraw in shameful humiliation: "As always after such experiences, it seemed impossible for him to give dignity to his life, and self-loathing put him into the penultimate state of despair." (p. 28)

It is not enough to blame society for one's personal fate. If there is any cure at all for a person like Seiler, it lies in his determining the specific events that shaped or rather deformed his character. *The Cause* is influenced by psychoanalytic theory. Seiler's regeneration is the result of a searching self-analysis. Using his dreams as his guide, Seiler discovers the cause of his failures and misfortunes in a grievous humiliation which his sadistic teacher, Mager, inflicted upon him in his childhood. This humiliation, symptomatic of many others, crippled his character and made of him a person who felt he was not entitled to happiness.

Seiler decides to cure himself by visiting his teacher, after a lapse of twenty years, and discussing the childhood incident with him. By forcing Mager to apologize, he will remove the stigma of self-contempt from his soul. Mager is to realize the injustice of his behavior and the extent of his guilt. Seiler's task is to convert Mager, as it were. Not only the victim but the culprit, too, is to become a better man.

But the sadistic teacher proves unregenerate. Seeing him maltreat a frightened little boy with the same sadistic glee which he displayed years ago, Seiler decides to kill the teacher. The murder is symbolic both of Seiler's personal regeneration—for with the murder he rids himself of his old fear-ridden self—and of a universal mission. Since in the German school system of his time no redress was possible against monsters like

---

[5] Frank, *Die Ursache*, p. 30.

Mager, the only way to save future children is to destroy the monster. In this respect Frank's novel, which on the surface has many elements of stark Naturalism, is a myth, a fairy tale, which tells how a hero sacrifices himself and slays the monster of darkness so that man may flourish on earth.[6]

After Seiler's arrest, his personal regeneration becomes a mission of social regeneration. Seiler uses his trial to make a passionate plea for a change of the social order that made possible a childhood like his with all its consequences. Because his resort to action has liberated Seiler from his self-contempt, the wretched outcast becomes the spokesman of mankind. For the duration of the trial, a community exists between the defendant and the spectators in the courtroom. He is their leader. When the presiding judge admonishes him not to waste time on generalities, Seiler replies that he has lost all interest in himself. He does not speak in his own defense, but in the defense of man.

The typically Expressionist content of Frank-Seiler's message is the universality of guilt and, therefore, the universality of innocence. Criminals are victims of emotional deformation caused by the cruelty of adults at an age when they were defenseless. No one is free to choose his character, which is the result of childhood experiences; and one's character determines one's actions. From this Freudian starting point Seiler arrives at the idea that "men become guilty without being guilty." If we regard them as the victims of their past, all criminals and evildoers are innocent. On the other hand, so-called good people may be viewed as criminals if we look at their dreams and secret thoughts, in which almost everyone commits crimes. Favorable circumstances have protected the so-called good people from being driven to that extreme of unhappiness which finds its relief in crime and violence.

But it isn't the kindly people's own merit that they are the judges and I am the murderer. . . . The reverse could very easily have been the case. . . . All souls are wounded. The whole world smells of carbolic acid. . . . We have to work to eliminate the causes of crimes, for otherwise there still will be imprisonment, beheading even, in a hundred thousand years! . . . Are men created for such a fate? (pp. 100–102)

All men, from the prosecuting attorney to the convict, are involved in

---

[6] The artificial and mythical character underlying Seiler's murder distinguishes Frank's story from the vitalist parricides of Hasenclever and Bronnen. Bronnen's Walter Fessel acts to liberate himself. His deed has no social or universal significance except as an incitement to anarchic liberty, and it involves no self-sacrifice. There is a sadistic frenzy about it which is entirely absent from Seiler's deed.

guilt. "The universal guilt merely manifests itself in the individual's guilt." Guilt is inherited from generation to generation, and will go on forever unless a drastic break is made. This sudden break must be the realization that, even as we are all guilty, we also are all victims and, therefore, innocent. In being culprits and victims alike, men possess a unifying bond. If we become fully aware of our oneness, we shall change and in changing ourselves transform our earthly hell into an earthly paradise. For even as hell is absolute isolation in guilt and victimization, paradise is absolute communion and empathy extended to every living creature.

Frank's Seiler is our first example of the artist-intellectual who seeks his salvation in openly rebelling against the social order. He follows in this the pattern of action advocated by Heinrich Mann. But whereas Mann still concentrates his attack upon the snobbishness and shortcomings of the artist, Frank's hero blasts bourgeois society and actively assumes the leadership of all the discontented elements of this society. Far from looking, like Brod's Nornepygge or Benn's Rönne, with nostalgic envy upon the emotional robustness of the Philistines, he finds too much sickness in this so-called "normal" world. His strength derives from the fact that he has ceased to consider this world normal. He sees it filled with perversity and wretchedness and views his own as merely a part of a universal maladjustment. Happiness and sanity (i.e., *Sachlichkeit,* as the objective of the artists discussed in the previous chapter) are only possible after a thorough regeneration and reconstruction of society to which he can lead the way because suffering has made him more aware than others.

The climax of the Expressionist regeneration through revolt is the revolt against war. The Expressionist views war as the natural culmination of a society that allows some human beings to live in luxury while others commit suicide because of want.[7] War is merely the extreme consequence of lack of sympathy. Furthermore, the reversal in the evaluation of the intellect leads, as we have observed in the works of Wolfenstein and Heinrich Mann, to contempt of the warrior type and exaltation of the man of reason and peace. This view is most clearly illustrated in Walter Hasenclever's drama *Der Retter (The Savior)* (1915), in which the former vitalist continues the social-humanist tendency already noticeable at the end of *The Son.*

Since the beginning of history, says the Poet in the drama, a cleavage has existed between the world of physical prowess and the world of mental

---

[7] See Kaiser's drama *Hölle Weg Erde* (1919) for a "welfare-society" attack upon this situation.

achievement. The Poet addresses the Field Marshal with these words: "We have been opponents from long ago. The caste of the sword versus that of the mind. This antagonism has never been greater than today. The victory of one of us will enslave the other."[8] Mind and force vie with each other for leadership. The Poet seeks to wrest the scepter from "the men of steel." But the bourgeois view, represented by the Minister of State, holds that the Poet is not qualified to give advice in weighty matters. He has no mental discipline and is "pleasantly ignorant" of statistics. He is advised to study economics before he adopts the "gesture of the orator."

But *Geist* is not scientific intellect. The Poet is as opposed to science as he is to militarism. Science has proven unable to devise a single creative idea with which to oppose the rule of force and violence. In fact, modern war is the child which atavism has begotten upon modern science. Science has become the instrument of the Field Marshal who even in 1915 outlines the totalitarian state soon to materialize. *Geist,* the principle of the Expressionist revolt, is connected with the poetic rather than the scienific imaginaion. *Geist* is not opposed to emotion, but crowns it. It is a religious principle, the divine element in man, the "holy spirit" or Holy Ghost (*Geist* signifies in German both spirit and ghost) and in the last analysis identical with God. The activist poet-intellectual who aspires to be the savior of a war-torn world finds his inspiration in the prophets and apostles of the Judaeo-Christian tradition. War is man's defection from God.

The image of the Old Testament prophet inspires Hasenclever's concept of the poet as the triumphant leader of nations who proclaims policies to the masses, founds a league of nations, enforces the rights of man, and announces the republic. This concept of the "political poet," in which activism culminates, leads to a new exaltation of the poet and intellectual which contrasts strangely with the communionist's humility discussed before. Since mind tames chaos and builds cosmos, the intellectual, the *Geistige,* is the natural leader of mankind. His leadership brings purpose and plan into the jumble of self-interests called history. The mobilization of the mind in the service of humane goals is the essence of activism, whose most significant slogan is Kurt Hiller's *Geist werde Herr* (*Let Mind Become Master*).

The intellectual-turned-leader must be willing to sacrifice himself for mankind and thus is akin to Prometheus and Christ. The self-sacrifice of the new type of leader is the theme of one of the most powerful dramas of Expressionist pacifism, Kaiser's *Die Bürger von Calais* (*The Burghers of*

---

[8] Hasenclever, *Der Retter: Dramatische Dichtung*, pp. 18–19.

Calais), written in the year that the First World War broke out. The French city of Calais is besieged by the king of England. The king wants to spare the city, because of its excellent harbor, if the city will surrender and, as token of defeat, deliver six citizens who will be put to death by the English. The powerful patriotic party inside the city urges a fight to the finish; they would rather see the city destroyed than surrender.

But Eustache de Saint-Pierre, "the new man," challenges this traditional patriotism with a new vision. National honor, he claims, is a destructive fiction. The supreme goal of political endeavor can only be the preservation of man and his works, not their destruction. He offers himself as hostage to the enemy, and wants to make the sacrifice of his life the foundation on which the revolutionary ideal of peace can be built. By his example he sways six other burghers to offer themselves as hostages, so that many more lives will be spared. But the typical "trick," around which Kaiser constructs his plots, occurs: only six hostages are required, while seven happen to have volunteered. Who of the seven shall survive while his comrades die? They agree to gather on the market square and walk together to the enemy camp; and he who arrives last will be released from his oath, free to live. All arrive early except Eustache himself. Finally he is carried in on a stretcher— dead. He has killed himself to show the others the way ahead and make sure that they will not regret their decision. His suicide seals their regeneration. It has cut off the return to selfish privacy and transformed them into thoroughly public or "common" men. Eustache's blind father speaks over the stretcher of his dead son: "I have seen the new man—he was born this night!"

The same night a son is born to the English king and, to celebrate the event, he sets the six hostages free. But when the king prays in the cathedral, the coffin of Eustache is raised above the altar so that the king kneels before one "greater than himself," "before his conqueror." The good man overcomes the strong man; the hero of peace conquers the hero of war. The inconsistency implied in the raising of the coffin of the humble pacifist so that he may be the "conqueror" plays an important part in the disintegration of activism, which will occupy us soon.

The "new man" is the intellectual who is able to act. But unlike the vitalist who seeks action for its own sake, the new man wants action guided by reason in the cause of love. The vitalist craves for spontaneity and impulsiveness to prove to himself that he is a feeling human being. The activist new man, on the other hand, who has attained a universal objective as his guide for action, no longer has to prove to himself that he is capable of emotional fervor. On the contrary, the importance of his task demands that he insure the seriousness and levelheadedness of his action. His sacrifice is to usher in a new world; therefore, he must act from profound conviction after severe self-questioning. The mind must weigh all reasons for and against the change of heart. Only if mind and heart concur can regeneration be real and final. This difference between "vitalist" and activist motives of behavior is the second great theme of Kaiser's drama.

Eustache and his six fellow pacifists have volunteered to tread an entirely new path of human behavior—the path of nonviolence. The question before Eustache is whether they have done so in the intoxication of the moment or whether they are really changed men, fully aware of the significance of their action. If they have acted on impulse, in heady emotionalism, their action merely constitutes the obverse of traditional heroism and is without moral value for the future of mankind. Eustache, therefore, forces by two tricks his six fellow volunteers to spend a whole night in meditation before their self-sacrifice is consummated.

Kaiser's *Burghers of Calais* is a synthesis of the abstractionist and the activist—or the aesthetic and the ethical—revolution of Expressionism. Both abstractionism and activism assert and indeed deify the intellect in opposition to nature and "the natural." In complete opposition to vitalism, both uphold the rational planning capacity of the mind and its ever-ready originality over instinct, habit, convention, and tradition. They affirm that which has been "made" against that which has "grown." Both believe in artifice.

The conflict between artifice and instinct is the central issue in Kaiser's drama. The national enemy is willing to spare the city for the sake of its great "artifice," the excellent man-made harbor. This harbor is beautiful and intelligently planned—a work of artful design. In addition, however, it is extremely useful. In this synthesis of the artful and the useful the antithesis between aesthetic idealism and ethical-humanitarian idealism is resolved. The patriots, however, would rather see the harbor destroyed than betray their country's "honor." They act from an irrational, "natural" instinct, an inherited belief. Their response is unreflective and traditional. Such behavior, so Kaiser reasons in his drama, is not only unworthy of human beings, but it also jeopardizes human life as well as human artifice. For in the patriotic fight to the finish not only the harbor but also the lives of the citizens will be destroyed. Life cannot be separated from artifice. It is not instinct, but, on the contrary, the artifice of intellect that saves and enhances life. With this complete reversal of the vitalist position Kaiser shows that there can be no conflict between vitality and intellect, even as there is no cleavage between the aesthetic and the ethical. Life to survive must foster and protect artifice; the protection of artifice is also the protection of life.

Pacifism, according to Kaiser, is, therefore, the logical culmination of a consistently aesthetic attitude. Far from contradicting each other, art and morality are complementary. For if the creative human mind is the guiding principle of human existence, as it is for the modern abstractionist, the vessel in which the mind is contained, namely the human body, must be safeguarded first of all and protected from death at all costs. Thus, an Expressionist humanism arises that in its combination of the aesthetic and the moral is not too far removed from the *Humanität* of the Weimar *Klassik*. Man is the shrine of the Expressionist religion. In man alone God emerges as *Geist*, the ordering principle that is to supersede blind nature's dance of death. Man, says Klabund's Bracke, the hero of his *Eulenspiegel* novel, is "the aristocracy of the earth"; and, he adds, "let us dethrone the eternal empress: Nature."[9] "Man is on the march" is the triumphant motif of Kaiser's essay about the "man of the future."[10] In each human being chaos is evolved into cosmos and God manifests himself. Man, Unruh said in one of his speeches, is the center and the meaning of the cosmos, and man not as an abstract concept but as any one of two billion concrete human individuals.

And if Copernicus tossed this earth out of its central position into the whirling dance of the universe among dust particles and suns: we put man back into the heart of creation. The suns are in us—in us dwells the power to move slumbering worlds.[11]

This anthropocentric humanism bridges the two views of *Geist* held by abstractionist and activist respectively. The abstractionist interprets *Geist* in the Platonic-aesthetic sense as pure form or idea which man can contemplate, comprehend, and indeed create, but which he can never actualize in life. *Geist* for him is a formal principle. It can conceal and "cover up" the horror of matter. It can invent for us the lie that beautifies, the illusion that helps us transcend matter—for a while. But *Geist* cannot be *realized* in the world. The activist interprets *Geist* in the Biblical-Messianic sense as a dynamic and divine force that transforms human nature and everyday reality. The activist's teacher is not Schopenhauer, but Martin Buber's and Tolstoy's view of the Judaeo-Christian, prophetic

[9] Henschke (pseud. Klabund), *Gesammelte Romane*, p. 314.

[10] "Dichtung und Energie (Der kommende Mensch)," in *Berliner Tageblatt*, December 25, 1923. This essay was originally entitled "Der kommende Mensch" and published in *Hannoverscher Anzeiger*, April 9, 1922. The second version contains slight changes.

[11] *Reden*, p. 29.

tradition. He is an optimist. Although he rejects and combats the world
in its existing "natural" state, he believes in its potentiality. *Geist* for him
is a fertilizer and a redeemer of matter. It can change hell into paradise.
By linking the "new man's" cause with the engineering feat of the harbor,
Kaiser links the two aspects of *Geist—Geist* as constructive mind and *Geist*
as moral innovator and redeemer.

In order to accomplish its Messianic mission, *Geist* must "dethrone the
eternal empress: Nature." Here Expressionist humanism differs essentially
from the humanism of the Weimar *Klassik*. The activist rebels against the
affirmation of and loving submission to superhuman forces—Nature, Fate,
History—which characterize traditional German culture. Following in the
footsteps of Heinrich Mann, Sternheim links Goethe's lack of political conscience to his worship of nature, which made him subservient to the *status
quo*. His "entirely banal world view" predisposed him to accept wars and
other social catastrophes as inevitable and led to *"Kadavergehorsam"* and
"Wachtparade."[12] Max Brod connects the German-Romantic idolization of
war and heroism, which he finds repulsive, with the "historical world view"
so deeply ingrained in German thinking.[13] Hugo Ball condemns the entire intellectual tradition of Germany as responsible for the First World
War.[14]

The German-Romantic tradition of submission to nature, fate, and history is associated with a certain attraction to death. Being "in love with
easeful death"—escaping into passive self-centeredness and aloneness to
evade responsibility—is the enemy which the Expressionist combats in his
country's tradition as well as in his own heart. Pacifism in the Expressionists
is the outcome of a spiritual and emotional catharsis, which transforms the
individual's deep-seated aggressive and self-destructive impulses into outgoing, life-affirming, "socialized" responses. Patriotic vitalists change into
international-minded revolutionary pacifists.[15] The most spectacular of
these conversions is Fritz von Unruh's.

Unruh, of old Prussian-Silesian nobility, son of a Prussian general and,
at one time, page at the Kaiser's court, served as an officer in the Imperial

[12] Sternheim, "Tasso oder Kunst des Juste milieu: Vorrede aus dem Jahr 1915," *Tribüne
der Kunst und Zeit*, XXV (1921), 19. "Kadavergehorsam," the "cadaverous obedience" of
lifeless automatons, is the "ideal" which Prussian militarism held in common with the Jesuit
order. "Wachtparade"—the changing and parading of the guards.
[13] Brod, "Ein menschlich-politisches Bekenntnis: Juden, Deutsche, Tschechen," *Die neue
Rundschau*, XXIX/2 (1918), 1580 ff.
[14] Ball, *Zur Kritik der deutschen Intelligenz*.
[15] Cf. Klabund's "Busspredigt," *Die weissen Blätter*, V/2 (July 1918), 106 ff. This stirring "sermon of repentance" for the author's early sin of nationalism was written in the sum-
mer of 1917.

German army until 1912, when, at the age of twenty-seven, he left the service to devote himself to writing. His first plays, *Offiziere* (*Officers*) (1911) and *Louis Ferdinand Prinz von Preussen* (1913), were hailed as memorials to the German officer caste and the spirit of Prussia, and the youthful author was acclaimed as the successor of Heinrich von Kleist. The protagonists of both these dramas are close relatives of the vitalist heroes. They yearn for the *Aufbruch,* the splendid breakthrough from the oppressive tedium of peacetime garrison life (*Officers*) or from intolerable national disgrace (*Louis Ferdinand*) into the brief splendor of war and death on the battlefield. The hero of *Officers* drinks a toast to death at the end of the first act; in both plays war is desired as liberation, and both heroes seek and find death.

One might have expected that the outbreak of actual war in 1914 would find Unruh an enthusiastic patriot. But by then Unruh had already progressed far beyond nationalism. In a semireligious moment of illumination and conversion, the action-hungry officer of 1911 had become a fighter for life against the forces of State and Church which would deny life, cripple and suppress it. The transformation of Unruh's existence is presented in the dramatic poem *Vor der Entscheidung* (*Before the Decision*), written at the front in October 1914, but because of war censorship not published until 1919. In this work, which gives the account of his *Wandlung* and revolt, Unruh evolves the Expressionist form of which there are only glimpses in the earlier plays.

His intimate experience has taught Unruh to connect nationalism with a morbid love of death. Passionate addiction to one's nation is disguised hatred of mankind. Exaltation of war is disguised fear of life. No author could exemplify this connection more forcefully than the poet whom the youthful Unruh emulated, the brilliant advocate of the House of Hohenzollern and author of a blood-curdling "catechism" of chauvinistic hate— Heinrich von Kleist, who prepared for his suicide as though for an act of love. Kleist influenced not only Unruh but also German Expressionism as a whole. Edschmid cites him with Hölderlin, Büchner, and Nietzsche as one of the prophets of the movement. Kleist's prose—calm, sober fact-reporting encasing infernal tensions—and especially his masterpiece *Michael Kohlhaas* with its juridical language, vivid lucidity of individual scenes, and perplexing mystery of the whole, is the direct forerunner of Kafka's. In his drama *Penthesilea,* the hectic abruptness and tense hyperbole of the language merge with the extreme character and drastic horror of the theme to produce a work that can be called Expressionist in every sense of the term. There are, however, other facets of Kleist which make him appear more old-fashioned and remote. The out-and-out Romanticism of his *Käthchen von Heilbronn,* the rabid Teutonic chauvinism of his *Hermannsschlacht,* the Prussian royalism and patriotism of his *Prinz von Homburg* are quite alien to the general temper of modernism. Not as the forerunner of Expressionism, of course, but as the idol of German chauvinism, Kleist became the target of Unruh's attack. Kleist appears to the Ulan, Unruh's "existential" self in *Before the Decision,* and beckons to follow him into death where alone true reality can be found. Yet he wishes he were alive in this hour of Germany's need so that he could kill the enemies of his fatherland.

> Burning with *rage* and *lust*
> I would sink my teeth
> Deep into Gallic breasts
> Trampling all love to death![16]

On the other hand, Kleist asserts that love, too, inspired his work. He hated France because he loved Germany. Man can never be universal. He is part of his native land. If he turns his back on his country and dreams of human brotherhood, he becomes "a beggar without power." But if he remains loyal to his nation and seeks to make its laws prevail, he lives in harmony with the universal law that governs the stars.

But the Ulan, who has thrown away his gun as the instrument of hell, has found a very different answer to his dreadful quest for meaning on the desolate battlefield. The spirit of Shakespeare appeared to him, and Shakespeare's humanist passion for life proves stronger than the German dramatist's passion for death. Shakespeare proclaims that art is the principle that is forever opposed to war. A poet, says Shakespeare—almost echoing the words of The First Critic in Sorge's *Beggar*—loves mankind like a mistress. He would not dispense with a single human being alive, since the variety of the human race stimulates his creativeness. But war is the most prodigal waste of art's irreplaceable raw material—the human individual. It butchers and mangles what should be treated with awe and tenderness. Whereas war brutalizes man, art deifies him. The artist cannot be a soldier. A creator cannot lend himself to the work of destruction. Thus, the spirit of Shakespeare indicated the direction in which Unruh was to travel in the future toward the communionist ideal of art as the

---

[16]   Brennend vor *Wut* und *Lust*
                         Schlüg' meine Zähne ich
                         Tief in die welsche Brust,
                         Liebe zerstampfte ich!
Vor der Entscheidung: Ein Gedicht, p. 104. (Italics mine.)

celebration, not of a particular cult, nation, or religion, but of the community of mankind.

Love can flourish only if it is undivided and universal, and if its antithesis—power—is overthrown. If love—the Ulan answers Kleist—is extended only to a particular group, as it always has been in the past, it is merely the reverse side of the lust for power. Power is the limiting principle per se. Power can have meaning only in relation to impotence. A man or a nation is powerful only if other men or other nations are powerless. Thus power is the cause of all hatred and suppression, of all cruelty and discontent. As long as power is limited—and if it is not limited it is not power—there will be unhappiness, fear, and consequently war. The new principle, which is to overthrow power, is sympathy with everything human, indeed everything alive. Universal sympathy as a revolutionary force cannot help but change the whole social structure of Europe. Thus, the new law for which the Ulan has been searching is a dynamic law. It is no longer duty molded by tradition and shaped by the past. It is found in the "sun's deepest meaning" ("der Sonne tiefster Sinn"). The sun is the creator of life, and the "sun's deepest meaning" is the creation and enhancement of life. This is the content of the new duty that "emerges from the pillar of the law." This "new law" is not man-made. It is absolute. If the traditional law of governments and courts conflicts with the absolute law of the preservation of life, as it does in war, the traditional law must be dethroned. "Outdated power" must be overthrown.

With the formulation of this revolutionary faith, the Ulan-Unruh has found his guide for action. He calls the war-weary soldiers to a last battle, not against the foe but against their own rulers who have sent them to murder and death.

The pacifist anarchism which the Expressionists developed during the First World War greatly resembles the views held by Herbert Read and Henry Miller, and partially by Dwight Macdonald's magazine *Politics* (its German and Austrian equivalents in the First World War were Franz Pfemfert's *Die Aktion* and Karl Kraus' *Die Fackel*). But a different social situation allowed the Expressionists to experience a much wider resonance than their Anglo-American successors were ever granted. The day-to-day trench warfare between two fairly similar power groups, continued month after month and year after year, appeared at once more gruesome and more senseless than the mobile, mechanized antitotalitarian crusade of the Second World War. Under the battle conditions of the First World War the voice of revolutionary pacifism had a greater chance to make itself heard. The World War seemed to be everybody's fault. But it was also everybody's punishment. It was the inferno. Men, the Expressionists believed, could not endure the losses and heartbreaks which war inflicted without changing profoundly. Exaggerating the limited echoes they did find, the Expressionists believed that the whole nation shared the experience they themselves underwent. They underestimated the persistence of traditional patterns of behavior. They had the eschatological faith in the final event, the revolution—or, as they thought of it, the conversion, the *Wandlung,* which would ring out the end of history and usher in the beginning of perfection. Any road out of hell, they thought, would have to lead to paradise.

In Leonhard Frank's *Der Mensch ist gut (Man Is Good)* the people, after suffering through the war, realize that they themselves—each one of them—bear the guilt for the orgy of dying. They had lived unthinkingly, paid their taxes for armaments, hailed their emperor and generals, bought toy guns and tin soldiers for their children. Now these children are dead, murdered, albeit unintentionally and indirectly, by none other than their own parents. The waiter in Frank's visionary story *Der Vater (The Father)*, who symbolizes the whole people, cries out his guilt to all the bereaved parents, war widows, orphans, cripples, and invalids. An awakened humanity sweeps aside its old rulers and proclaims eternal peace.

Like a confirmation of Frank's vision of the whole people repenting and changing its ways, there appeared, late in 1917, the fragments of a remarkable drama, written by an unknown ex-soldier who had once been an enthusiastic volunteer in the German army. This drama, published in its entirety only after the war, indicated in its title the fundamental Expressionist experience; it was called *Die Wandlung.* Its author, Ernst Toller, had completed it while serving a prison sentence for subversive pacifist activities.

To break out of his isolation and be accepted by "the others," the young student Toller had embraced extreme German nationalism.[17] Friedrich, in Toller's autobiographical drama, volunteers for service at the front when war breaks out. He wants to prove that he *belongs.* In war the "disgust-

---

[17] In this yearning for a community Toller follows the familiar Expressionist pattern. With some Expressionists the typical feeling of isolation and rootlessness is purely that of the introverted artist-intellectual type in a Philistine and materialistic society. With most Expressionists, however, physiological, social, national, and racial-religious factors aggravate the initial maladjustment. Kaiser suffers for many years from a debilitating disease. Frank has to fight the stigma of poverty and low birth. Heinrich Mann, Schickele, and Benn suffer from a national conflict; their fathers are German, their mothers Latin American, French, and French-Swiss respectively. A similar aggravating factor is the Jewish background of Expressionists such as Brod, Kafka, Werfel, Ehrenstein, and Toller. Toller makes it plain in his autobiography —*Eine Jugend in Deutschland,* pp. 12–13—that his earliest experience of "being different" stemmed from his neighbors' anti-Semitic discrimination against his family and himself; his bewilderment and uneasiness as a well-to-do Jewish boy in the company of a poor Christian playmate aggravated the feeling of "being different" by the addition of guilt feelings.

ing hybrid" will find community and purpose. For Toller-Friedrich, war has the chiliastic aura that the revolution against war will have later on.[18] The lonely youth frenziedly pictures war as the dawn of a paradisiacal state of national brotherhood in which all problems will be solved and isolation will cease forever. However, the actuality of war is very different from the noble dream of the patriot.

It was on the battlefield that the Expressionist idea of the oneness of all men dawned on Toller, as it had on Unruh. Toller relates, in his autobiography, harrowing experiences of trench warfare which profoundly undermined his patriotic faith. The sight of a wounded soldier hanging on the barbed wire in front of his trench for three days and nights and screaming incessantly for help that could not be administered contributed to Toller's *Wandlung* from chauvinist to pacifist. On another occasion, his spade got entangled in the intestines of a dead soldier. The shocking experience overwhelmed him.

> A—dead—man—
> And suddenly, as though darkness parted
> from light, as though the word released
> the meaning, I understood the simple
> truth, the truth which I had forgotten,
> which had lain buried and covered—
> the truth that is man—the truth that
> is the oneness and unity of all men.
> A dead man.
> Not: a dead Frenchman.
> Not: a dead German.
> A dead man.
> All these dead were men; all these
> corpses used to breathe like myself,
> all these dead ones had fathers, mothers,
> women whom they loved, pieces of land
> in which they had roots, faces that told
> their joys and sorrows, eyes that saw the
> light and the sky. In that hour I knew
> that I had been blind, blinded by myself;
> in that hour I knew at last that all these
> dead men, Frenchmen and Germans, were
> brothers, and that I was their brother![19]

[18] War fulfills a similar communal and spiritual purpose in Franz Theodor Csokor's *Der grosse Kampf: Ein Mysterienspiel in acht Bildern,* one of the few Expressionist works in which the relationship between war and pacifism is reversed. For Csokor war is the inspiration of communal feeling and altruism, while Ego, the symbol of selfishness, sponsors pacifism.

[19] *Jugend,* pp. 75–76.

After his conversion to pacifism, the hero of Toller's drama discovers that war is based upon the horrors of peace. In a series of dreamlike scenes, he experiences the misery of the proletariat. Most people, he finds, live under conditions which make military service appear an improvement over their normal lot. The Great Factory in which the majority of mankind spend their lives is indistinguishable from a prison and soon changes into one. Socialism joins pacifism to make Friedrich's *Wandlung* complete.

By the autumn of 1917, when Toller had written the larger part of *Die Wandlung,* he had already traveled far from his early nationalism. Discharged from the army because of an unexplained illness,[20] he had founded a pacifist students' league, become a disciple of the Independent Socialist leader Kurt Eisner, and plunged into the strike movement of the Munich munition workers. He distributed among the workers leaflets containing excerpts from his unfinished drama. War-weariness and impatience to end the slaughter as quickly as possible were uppermost in the minds not only of the activist intelligentsia but also of the German working class.[21] Workers struck and sailors mutinied for an immediate peace. Although the poets and intellectuals were inspired by ethical and humanitarian motives and the masses impelled by hunger rations and by resentment at gross inequality, poets and masses were, in 1917 and 1918, closer to each other than ever before or since in our century. For a brief time their aspirations seemed to merge. The isolated artist suddenly found himself carried to the crest of a wave. Suspected in his own middle class as a psychopath or a traitor,[22] he seemed at last to have found roots among the proletariat. These roots did not take hold in the soil of a country or religious group but floated, as it were, in a sea that swept toward a shore of infinite promise.

It was, however, not as a Marxist but as a spontaneous leader in the mass sentiment against the continuation of the war that Toller rose to his first position of prominence and served his first term in prison. His com-

[20] *Jugend*, p. 79. Toller is laconic about the nature of the mysterious illness that caused his discharge. But from the context it is evident that the onetime patriot was at the end of his powers of endurance, and that the "illness" may well have been of a psychological nature.

[21] Cf. Rosenberg, *Die Entstehung der deutschen Republik*, pp. 169 ff., 193–200.

[22] Toller's mother had her son committed to a sanitarium, since she could not understand why a young man of a prosperous family should get involved in radical movements (see *Jugend*, p. 121). A highly placed army doctor is quoted by Toller as saying upon reading a fine Werfel poem which he discovered in Toller's possession: "People who read such junk should not be surprised when they end up in jail," a statement which was greeted with applause by the assembled doctors, all educated men (*ibid.*, p. 114). A Jewish army doctor assigned to the inmates of the military prison in which Toller served his sentence declared that all pacifists should be shot and refused to order a second blanket for his feverish patient (*ibid.*, p. 112). In contrast to these middle-class sentiments, Toller describes the admiration of the proletarian turnkey's daughter for the young revolutionary, who appeared to her as a legendary hero to be marveled at and loved (*ibid.*, p. 115).

munity was that of the vast fraternity of the victimized at the precise
moment when it changed into a community of protest and incipient revolt.
It was only subsequently, in military prison, that Toller immersed himself
in Marxist works and made the Marxist position his own. However, he
was never to feel at ease in his Marxist home and always remained what
Mr. Willibrand called him, "the troubled, unorthodox Marxist."[23]

Like Toller, the artist Friedrich in Toller's *Wandlung* changes from a
"disgusting hybrid" into a leader of humanity marching toward a jubilant
and decidedly non-Marxist revolution. Indeed, Friedrich launches his main
attack, as Mr. Willibrand has shown, not against the feeble and tottering
representatives of the *status quo* but against the Bolshevist agitator who
incites the masses to bloodshed.

Toller-Friedrich's Expressionist revolution knows no human enemies.
Its enemies are institutions—the state, capitalism, the military system, war
—but it does not hate the men who embody these institutions or profit by
them. They, too, are victims, and the Expressionist pities them.[24] He refuses to oppress and kill the oppressors. They, too, are the victims of fear
and of the very power they wield; for power crushes the master as well
as the slave. Fear of failure and impoverishment harries the rich as fear
of hunger whips on the poor. The arrogant despise everyone because they
despise themselves.

There is an element of eighteenth-century rationalism and eudaemon-
ism hidden under the Dionysiac surface of much of Expressionism. The
Expressionist activist intensifies the Socratic faith in persuasion and reasoning until it attains a white-hot luster of ecstasy; but this ecstasy is based
on reason, this flame is the white light of reason. "There is no other Ararat
of peace than the new alliance of the mind with the throbbing heart!" says
Fritz von Unruh.[25] Though the "new man's" initial regeneration is a profound and saving inner experience, he tries to bring about the regeneration
of his fellow men by verbal and intellectual means, persuasion, speech-
making, and, in the case of Kaiser's Spazierer, highly sophistic arguments.
Spazierer's theory of penal institutions as the laboratories in which human

[23] Willibrand, *Ernst Toller and His Ideology*, in University of Iowa Humanistic Studies,
VII, 49.

[24] Cf. Becher's poem "An den Tyrannen:"
                Nein! Tyrann! Nicht würgten Barrikaden
                Dich zu end. Noch Salven Höllenflug.
                Pyramiden Liebe auf dein Haupt wir laden.
                Schmilz o schmilz vor freiester Güte Bug!
                . . . .
                Arme breiten Völker dir Tyrann!
In Becher, *Verbrüderung: Gedichte*, p. 33.

[25] *Reden*, p. 29.

brotherhood has been tested is an excellent example of sophistry and easily leads one to doubt the seriousness and sincerity of Kaiser's humanist faith. It is also worth observing, in this context, that the pacifist hero Eustache, in Kaiser's *Burghers of Calais,* assures the regeneration of his fellow men by a course whose dialectical complications border on the playful and erratic.

A second important non-Marxist aspect of the Expressionist revolution is its emphasis on the individual's spiritual rebirth, which is possible only through love; and love, as Christian *caritas,* is indeed the pivotal point of the Expressionist revolution. In their understanding of the relationship of love, destructiveness, and power, the Expressionists gain their deepest insights.

Aggression is, in Fritz von Unruh's view, self-hatred and hatred of life. This idea, already present in *Before the Decision,* receives a powerful and searching treatment in his greatest work, the abstract and proto-Existentialist drama *Ein Geschlecht (A Family)* (1916), which ranks with Kaiser's *Burghers of Calais* as one of the landmarks of the movement. The Eldest Son in Unruh's drama takes the logical step beyond nationalism. Nationalism liberates, even glorifies, individual aggressiveness when it serves the purpose of the state, but it chains and suppresses it whenever it runs counter to the state's designs. The Eldest Son, however, desires total freedom for aggressiveness. As a soldier he commits rape. By his act the Eldest Son unmasks the rule of law and order, which yet commands and wages war, as base hypocrisy. War and brutalization are linked by necessity. The law that orders violence cannot expect to be respected when it forbids violence. Rape and murder crown war. To pretend otherwise, as the national state does, is damnable two-facedness, and the Eldest Son rebels against it.

This champion of total aggressiveness, forerunner of Camus's Caligula, acts from a deep conviction of the absurdity of all life. For regardless of social and political systems, life must end in death. It is, therefore, senseless. He regrets that he was born to find out the horrible trick life plays on everyone. He abuses his mother because she is responsible for his life and, therefore, his death. The final truth for him is this:

> O Mothers, Women!
> You carry graves deep in your moisted wombs,
> And what you bear is death, nothing but death![26]

---

[26]   O Mütter, Weiber!
             Ihr tragt das Grab in Eurem feuchten Schoss,
             was Ihr gebärt, ist Tod und nichts als Tod!
Unruh, *Ein Geschlecht: Tragödie,* p. 48.

His savage, sensual energy, having surged against the law, billows back against itself. The rocks which he has smashed, his mother says, have in turn buried him. He kills himself the night before his scheduled execution.

Her son's radical nihilism serves to intensify the Mother's life-affirming faith. While he blackens all life, she finds in the ever-renewing creativeness that stirs in a woman's blood as well as in the soil a spur to hope. Her religious faith in life as an ever-triumphant, ever-emerging creativeness—this broader and deeper vitalism—enables her to transform the Eldest Son's destructive and purposeless rebellion into constructive revolution. If life is to prevail over death, creation over destruction, and joy over despair, power must pass from the patriarchal state to the mothers of the world. Only joy and pleasure, not discipline, can bring real order. She seizes the staff of power and draws the war-weary soldiers to her side. The soldiers demand that the country be given to them, the people, so that they may govern it. The militarist system, threatened as never before, has the Mother executed. But her Youngest Son will continue her work. Whereas the Eldest Son was still too close to the father to go beyond a grim, egotistical defiance, the Youngest Son is the incarnation of his mother's dream. He embraces her sacred task with fiery zeal. The revolt she inspires will become an "avalanche" that will crush the "armories of force." The mutinous soldiers lift him on their shoulders and march against the seat of power.

The pacifist revolutionary and psychoanalyst Gebhart in Werfel's novel *Barbara* (*The Pure in Heart*) (which in part is a thinly veiled account of the author's experiences during the heyday of Expressionism in Vienna) claims that love has been unknown in our world because its physical expression has been perverted into a demonstration of male power. In the sexual act man gratifies himself and proves his strength, not caring what his partner feels. Sexual love should be a mutual administration of joy. But since all our thinking is based on power and prestige, sexual joy is harnessed to the lust for power. The degradation of sexual love is institutionalized in marriage and the family. Sexual energy outside marriage is suppressed or besmirched. Taboos safeguard the dictatorship of the strong by denying enjoyment to the weak. The tyranny of man over woman leads to the tyranny of the father over the son. The servility, asceticism, envy, and self-contempt of the son and slave are as evil as the arrogance, brutality, and willfulness of the father and master. Since women sell their birthright to love in exchange for baubles and security, they too are accomplices in the universal tyranny from which all other tyrannies flow.

Once there was a golden age when women ruled and sex was the core of religion. But men had appeared who could not love. To compensate for their deficiency, they branded physical joy as sin and invented war. They easily overcame the pacific matriarchate and established the stern despotism of the fathers. With this *coup d'état* of aggressiveness against pleasure, history began. Hebrew monotheism provided the perfect religious basis for the dictatorship of the fathers.

Werfel's novel fragment *Die schwarze Messe* (*The Black Mass*), written in 1919, anticipates Gebhart's theory. In this story the creation of the world is ascribed to a *coup d'état* of Jehovah, an unstable and aggressive spirit, who overturned the aboriginal democracy of spirits and created our universe in order to rule as absolute despot. Aboriginal guilt then goes back to God Himself. God, who calls himself the "lord of hosts," has based his regime "upon the police powers of terror and grace."[27]

The opponent of militarism must strike at its deepest root, the pattern of all tyranny—the patriarchal family and the patriarchal religion based on it. The dictatorship of the male over the female and the father over the children lies at the root of social injustice, violence, and war. In the novelette *Not the Murderer*, also written in 1919, the anarchist group with which the hero collaborates wages war upon the "rule of the *father* in every sense."[28] Armies and states are fashioned in the image of the patriarchal family. Without the tyranny that prevails in the family, political and military tyranny would never arise.

The rule of the father is everything. Religion: for God is the father of man. The State: for the king or president is the father of the citizen. The penal system: for judge and warden are the fathers of those whom human society chooses to call criminals. The army: for the officer is the father of the soldier. Industry: for the boss is the father of the workers! . . . The *patria potestas*, authority, is perversity, the corrupting principle as such. It is the origin of all murders, wars, misdeeds, crimes, hate-inspired vices and corruptions, even as sonship is the root of all frustrating slave instincts, the hideous cadaver that has been buried in the foundation of all societies in history.

But we live to cleanse! (pp. 207–8)

Gebhart scorns Jesus because Jesus remained "the son."[29] He perpetuated the patriarchal dictatorship. Terrified by the father, he merely strength-

---

[27] Werfel, *Gesammelte Werke*, I, 100.

[28] Werfel, *Erzählungen aus zwei Welten*, in *Gesammelte Werke*, ed. by Adolf D. Klarmann, I, 207.

[29] The ideas expressed by the anarchist leader in *Not the Murderer*, the satanist in "The Black Mass"—both composed in 1919 at the high crest of Expressionism—and Gebhart in the later novel form a coherent whole. Gebhart must then be considered not a colorful eccentric but a spokesman for certain beliefs or, at least, for deeply disturbing ideas which enthralled Werfel in his Expressionist period, near the end of the First World War. Certain ideas about music expressed in "The Black Mass" (p. 90) anticipate *Verdi*.

ened the sexual taboos imposed by the father. The son who fears and hates sex connives with the father who forbids it. The patriarchate, based on incapacity for love, has transformed sexual desire into sadistic aggression or masochistic self-abasement. It climaxes in the World War, in which the fathers of all fatherlands send their sons to die for them.

But with this monstrous climax, the system is approaching its downfall. The economic revolution of Communism is a prelude to the sexual revolution soon to follow. All taboos will fall; the family will disappear, and the sexual act will be practiced in full freedom and equality. To hasten the coming of the nonviolent age, Gebhart and his numerous women disciples minutely analyze their sexual affairs. Each sexual experience is carefully studied and discussed in detail. Complete love—mutuality of gratification—is the goal to be attained. If inadequate love or traces of aggression and self-centeredness are discovered, Gebhart recommends immediate further sexual experiences, which are to correct previous mistakes. Complete surrender in physical love amounts to salvation.

Gebhart is an Expressionist leader against violence and unhappiness. Echoes of German Romantic philosophy—the theory of the matriarchate which was expounded by the late-Romantic writer Bachofen—also to be found in Unruh and German vitalism, combine in him with primitive Communism and pacifism to form a typically Expressionist blend. Like Frank's Seiler, he is deeply indebted to psychoanalysis. His faith in the orgasm and his juxtaposition of sexual love and the aggressive will to power anticipate the currently fashionable theories of Wilhelm Reich.

The Sick Man in Toller's *Wandlung* cannot believe in love. The best remedy for the world, he believes, would be its destruction. But when Friedrich answers him with compassion instead of abuse or scorn, the Sick Man shrieks out the cause of his sickness. He has never been loved. In the next scene Friedrich confronts the Lady, who asserts that love has nothing to do with affection. Love and kindness, the sensual and the ethical, have been mortal enemies since the beginning of time. Love is fierce and pitiless. It seeks only gratification, and it despises the weak and pursues the strong. Friedrich, the Lady says, is "a tortured fool." But the Sick Man's terrible need for affection is the answer to the Lady's glorification of ruthless sex. The Sick Man wants mass suicide and other sick men prepare wars because, never having met affection, they have come to hate themselves. Friedrich will ask the Girl Student, one of his devoted followers, to nurse the Sick Man with love. For man can be good only when he is loved. But to be loved we must first learn to love; this is what his bitter isolation has taught the Expressionist. In this core of the Expressionist world view the

Christian ideal of charity merges with the psychoanalytic ideal of the socialization and maturing of our infantile egotism.

Throughout history men have, according to Toller, let lack of love and the resultant fear twist and thwart their emotions. Out of fear they have allowed their institutions and mechanisms—their own creations—to victimize them. As a result of being victimized, men become victimizers. This vicious circle begins in earliest childhood, in the authoritarian family and school, where fear is first aroused, a fear that continues through life. Everyone leads a crippled life and is the pitiful caricature of the person he might be. Regeneration means the untwisting of our lives and the fullest development of our human potential. This is the content of Friedrich's message to the assembled people on the cathedral square.

And so you are caricatures of real man!/ You walled-in ones, you buried ones, you chained and panting ones, you joyless and embittered ones,/ For you have buried the spirit . . . / Immense machines thunder day and night/ Thousands of spades are in perpetual motion to heap ever more rubbish upon the spirit . . . / Your own hearts are stretched upon shoemaker's lasts. The hearts of your fellow men are bell-pulls for you, which you can pull for pleasure. . . .

You plant hatred in your children because you no longer know about love. You carved Jesus Christ in wood and nailed him to a wooden cross, because you yourselves did not want to walk the road to crucifixion that led him to salvation. . . . You build fortresses and appoint overlords who do not serve God or man but a phantom, a disastrous phantom.

. . . .

You, all of you, are human beings no longer, but caricatures of yourselves. And yet you might be human if you only had faith in yourselves and in man, if you were fulfilled in the spirit./ You might stride through the streets erect, but today you crawl, bent over./ Your eyes might shine with joy, but today you are half blind./ Your steps might be winged, but today you drag iron chains behind you./ O if only you were men—unconditioned free men![30]

With the same fantastic suddenness with which Friedrich's Sister had affected his own regeneration, Friedrich's speech converts the people. They repent, bury their heads in their hands or lie prostrate on the ground. Suddenly they leap up, transfigured, as "new men." All that was needed to transform the world was for men to remember their humanity. Now they are ripe for the bloodless, the truly glorious revolution.

[30] Toller, *Die Wandlung: Das Ringen eines Menschen*, in *Der dramatische Wille III*, pp. 91–93.

But in whose image is man to be reborn? What type of man is even now, before the revolution, an "untwisted" human being?

And you, soldier, imprisoned in your artificial uniform which makes all joyous life petrify: I remember your astonished look when you saw the statue of a striding youth created by an artist.—How could the artist create it?/ Because he is real, because he truly lives!

(Weil er da ist, wirklich da ist!) (p. 90)

The artist is at the opposite pole from the soldier. He is the least institutionalized, the freest, and most real man. In him *Geist,* the creative capacity which distinguishes man from beast, has not been choked. In creating, man asserts his absolute freedom and becomes godlike. *Wandlung* and revolution will change all men into artists. Liberated from fear and resentments, all men will be able to assert their innate creativeness freely and proudly, and, being fully human, become divine. The poet is merely the forerunner of all men, says Georg Kaiser.

Advances of individuals are overtaken by the collectivity. The mountain becomes a plateau on which all settle. Then energy will regulate itself, mundane and sublime. Man will have arrived![31]

Since God, in the activist-Expressionist view, is immanent in mankind, the full release of human potential amounts to the realization of God in man.[32]

The artist's plunge into political activism thus turns out to be not a betrayal of art but its elevation into the guiding star of an emerging social reality. The rank which the artist, as the embodiment of creative reason, holds in the activist thought of Kaiser, Unruh, Hasenclever, and Toller is no less exalted than the lonely eminence which we found him occupying as *poeta dolorosus.* But the loneliness is taken from him. Even as he gives vision to the revolutionary masses, they in turn provide him with a community. The sudden feeling of contact, homecoming, and belonging, which the rootless artist-intellectual experienced when he became aware of certain

[31] "Dichtung und Energie."

[32] Mr. Willibrand, in his study of Toller's ideology, says of *Die Wandlung:* "From the Christian point of view, all of this sounds rather traditional" (p. 39). Yet the activists are not Christians. They embrace some aspects of Christianity, above all the ideas of spiritual rebirth and charity, but reject others. They reject the supernatural basis of Christianity. They believe in the humanity of God or the divinity of man. Christ's double nature is for them the possession of every individual. "Lord, I am like Thee," says Kurt Heynicke ("Lieder an Gott," in *Menschheitsdämmerung,* p. 154), and in the same poem he speaks of the "Man-God." The activist Expressionists are humanists. But they galvanize humanism until it takes on the aspect of an ecstatic religion.

resemblances between his aspirations and those of the proletariat, fill him with an elation that blinds him somewhat to the inherent difficulties and contradictions of this *rapprochement*.[33] The hymnic rapture with which Schickele hails the proclamation of the German Socialist Republic on November 9, 1918, is expressed in terms of the isolated writer's homecoming to his *changed* nation.[34] In a eulogy of socialism, Holitscher remarks that the representatives of art and intellect had always been despised outlaws in the bourgeois world; it is therefore easy to understand why they plunge into the proletarian movements and make the cause of the workers their own. In the class they have adopted they find "probably for the first time in their lives the happiness and discomfort of a community."[35] Joining the proletariat, while it confronts them with some "uncomfortable" problems of adjustment, liberates the poets and intellectuals from their narcissistic isolation and brings them into healing contact with mankind. Holitscher also stresses the affinity, indeed identity, of socialism and art. The drives and instincts of the artists animate the revolutionary leader who desires to shape the future and translate vision and dream into reality. Like the artist, he creates something that has not existed before.

The activist, futhermore, believes that art, culture, and intellect, scorned or emasculated by the middle class, have their only future with the working class. At his trial for high treason, in 1919, Toller warmly praised the workers' hunger for beauty, culture, and knowledge, a hunger long unknown to the sated *bourgeoisie*.[36] The working class was seen as striving toward *Geist*. Socialism, their objective, could be viewed as a triumph of *Geist,* a social system in which, for the first time in history, the planning, ordering, and responsible mind would shape the everyday life of mankind. Since the working class, moreover, comprised more individuals than any other class, its ascent symbolized to the activist the ascent of humanity toward a spiritualized form of existence.

But during the brief span of chiliastic expectation, initiated by the Russian Revolution of October 1917 and ended by the suppression of the Bavarian Soviet Republic in May 1919, a split rent the activist camp and hastened its defeat. Some activists, such as Becher, Frank, and Rubiner,

---

[33] For the nebulous nature of activist goals, cf., for instance, Iwan Goll's ecstatic-hymnic "Prozession" (*Die Aktion,* VII [1917], 51). The poem, which starts with a Socialist or Communist mass meeting, ends in a cosmic vision of bliss.

[34] Cf. Schickele, "Der neunte November," *Tribüne der Kunst und Zeit,* VIII (1919), *passim.* Schickele actually was returning from years of exile in Switzerland and thus celebrated his physical return to Germany, too.

[35] Holitscher, "Das Religiöse im sozialen Kampf," *Die Erhebung* II (1920), 330.

[36] Toller, *Jugend,* p. 230.

thought that the *Wandlung* and salvation of mankind had already occurred—in Russia; they embraced Communism and with this decision ceased to be a part of the mental and emotional climate of Expressionism. Rubiner's anthology of 1919, *Kameraden der Menschheit* (*Comrades of Humanity*) had more the character of "proletarian" than of Expressionist poetry; and *Die Aktion*, hitherto the foremost magazine of Expressionist literature, began with Volume IX (1919) to reflect Communist party politics. Other activists, however—notably Toller, Unruh, Schickele, Brod—could not reconcile the violence and militarism of the Communists with their pacifist ideals. Thus, they were soon forced to take issue with the proletarian revolt and eventually with themselves. Their profound disillusionment is as symptomatic of Expressionism as the illusion that preceded it.

CHAPTER EIGHT

The Recoil

THE ECSTASY OF THE ACTIVIST-EXPRESSIONIST VISION LASTS FOR ONLY A MOMENT in history. Almost as soon as it it flares up, it flickers, dims, and dies out. Only one month after his outburst of enthusiasm over the proclamation of the Socialist Republic, René Schickele sees artists and intellectuals threatened as never before and suggests they soon have to flee to monasteries to escape the iron heel of victorious Communism—which will eventually crush them even there. The great disillusionment with the "God that failed," which the Occidental intelligentsia experienced in the nineteen thirties and afterwards, had been anticipated within the ranks of German Expressionism almost as soon as the "God" was born. "Then, my friends," writes Schickele in 1919, "let us go into the cloister . . . until the class-conscious pretorians of some Lenin . . . exterminate us poor church-mice of the ideal!"[1]

The most famous drama of all Expressionist literature, Kaiser's *Gas I* (1918), is the earliest of the series of Expressionist works that deal with the retreat of the Messianic hope of 1917 and 1918. The two most significant characteristics of these works are the hero's second *Wandlung,* i.e., his realization that the great conversion which made him an activist was either insufficient or wrongly directed, and the saddening discovery of a gap between himself and the masses whom he wishes to lead to regeneration and the building of a new world.

In *Gas I* the Billionaire's Son shares with his workers the profits from the enormous gas works which supply the whole world with energy. This embrace of practical socialism constitutes his first *Wandlung,* a consequence of his rebellion against the values of his father, the self-made Billionaire of *The Coral.* But although he acts from the right motive—compassion for his fellow man—the Billionaire's Son has adopted the wrong course. Socialism is not the right answer to the crisis of twentieth-century man. By

[1] Schickele, *Der neunte November,* pp. 79–80.

making the workers the partners of capitalist profit, socialism accelerates and intensifies the fragmentization and dehumanization of modern man. To increase their profits, the workers slave at their machines day and night, like robots with time out only for eating and sleep. One day an inexplicable explosion kills thousands of workers. This catastrophe causes the Billionaire's Son's second regeneration.

The Billionaire's Son now preaches the real change of man. Mechanization has caused the catastrophe; the machine, having robbed man of his soul, now demands his body as well. Salvation lies in a pre-industrial way of life. The workers are to leave the cities and build small settlements in the green fields of the countryside.

But the workers are not ripe for the leader's call. The limitations and inertia of the old mass man resist and prevail over the ardor of the Expressionist "new man." The workers fail to understand that it is the industrial system itself that has caused the explosion; instead, they look for a scapegoat. They demand the punishment of the Engineer even though he bears no guilt for the catastrophe. To force the Engineer's dismissal they call a strike. The big armament trusts fear that the interruption of the gas production will halt rearmament and reduce the war potential; therefore they join in the demands of the workers. This strange alliance convinces the Billionaire's Son that the gas must never again be produced.

The Engineer turns the tide which was beginning to run in favor of the Son. The Engineer is his supreme antagonist. While the Billionaire's Son believes in human happiness, the Engineer believes in the infinite growth of human power. Gas is both symbol and fuel for the breath-taking advance of man. The production of gas must never stop, no matter what the sacrifices in human life and happiness. To insure the resumption of work the Engineer demands his own punishment.

In the brilliant dialectics of the debate between Engineer and Billionaire's Son, two visions of human destiny clash—the technocrat's vision of limitless power through industrial specialization and the Expressionist's vision of happiness through simple spontaneous creativeness.

The Engineer's appeal to the pride of the modern proletariat prevails over the goal of the Billionaire's Son, who would lead the workers to a tranquil happiness. Scorning the vision of a pastoral paradise, the workers insist on their industrial "hell," the source of material power, even though they are too exhausted by work to enjoy the riches which they produce, and even though they know that some day another explosion may kill them. They follow the Engineer "back to work . . . from explosion to explosion." Nothing can dissuade them from their course.

The Billionaire's Son (staggering on the rostrum): Do not slay man!!—Do not make cripples!—You, brother, are more than your hand!!—You are eternal and perfect, all of you, by your origin—Do not mutilate yourselves—!! Be greater, desire—yourselves—yourselves!!!! (*The hall is empty.*)[2]

In *Gas I* the activist faith in man's goodness and wisdom suffers a resounding defeat. But the leader's optimism remains unchanged in essence. He postpones his hope but neither modifies nor abandons it. His vision is simply projected into a more propitious future. In the final scene of the drama the Billionaire's Son says to his daughter, who shares his idealism, that the reign of the new man cannot be far off.

Am I not witness for him—and for his coming . . . ?—Have I not known him in vivid vision?!—Can I still doubt!!!
Daughter (kneeling): I shall bear him! (p. 256)

All doubts are resolved and the Daughter's melodramatic announcement that she will give birth to the "new man" symbolizes the unshaken faith in the future which conquers disillusionment with the present. *Gas I* shares this postponement of hope with the other Expressionist *chefs d'œuvre* written between 1918 and 1920 which deal with the experience of disillusionment. Yet in some important respects Kaiser's drama stands apart. Despite its technical brilliance and significance as a landmark in the history of experimental drama, *Gas I* is on some accounts too superficial to be considered representative of the problem with which we shall be concerned.

In *Gas I* the activist leader does not become a problem to himself. He never questions his right to prescribe salvation to others, and when he fails the fault lies entirely with his fellow men. His vision remains unquestioned and the leader is without blame. This unregenerate conceit is unconsciously reflected by the Daughter's vow that she, in whose veins the leader's blood flows, will bear the new man. Regeneration of humanity becomes not the common task of mankind but the mysterious monopoly of a chosen family. In contrast to the heroes of later works, Kaiser's leader does not experience a genuine regeneration in the course of the drama. His *Wandlung,* if we may call it that, is not a rebirth of the heart but a change of mind, a mere switch in policy. It leaves the hero's personality and his approach to human beings precisely what it has been previously. The same fantastic faith in persuasion, the same naïve ecstatic rationalism that we discovered in the first stage of activism informs *Gas I*.

The superficiality that reduces the Billionaire's Son's *Wandlung* to a

---

[2] Kaiser, *Gesammelte Werke,* I, 240.

change of policy also mars the content of his vision. His pseudo-Rousseauan idyll is nothing but the modern faith in material progress, only in reverse. Both seek the solution to moral questions in material circumstances. Both make inner regeneration dependent on external factors. Kaiser's simple scheme of transforming industrial workers into farmers and gardeners by-passes the root problem of activist Expressionism, the emotional and spiritual renewal, the complete humanization of man. Kaiser's *Gas* fails to show how the change from industrial to agricultural production will accomplish this spiritual and psychological goal.[3] The evils of industrialism are the frequent target of Expressionist attack.[4] But to look for spiritual salvation in the abandonment of a mode of production is to grant the predominance of matter and circumstance over the spirit, which is precisely what the Expressionist, as we have seen, does not concede. The reactionary pastoralism of Kaiser's *Gas I* is by no means central to the Expressionist vision. The Expressionist-activist goal is the brotherhood of man developed to such an extent that the injury inflicted on one man will be felt as a smart by all. The socio-economic framework in which this fraternity can be realized is secondary and incidental. It is possible in a primitive village or in a modern factory. To be sure, man's inhumanity to man presents itself with particular crassness in the locale of modern industry, in the sweatshop, on the assembly line, in the factory run by efficiency experts, and on the battlefields of mechanized war. But the victory over inhumanity can be only an inner victory possible in any economic system. This is what Kaiser's *Gas* fails to make clear. Ernst Toller, in the other great drama that made Expressionism famous, *Masse-Mensch (Man and the Masses)* (1919), goes much deeper when he lets his heroine say:

> For see, this is the twentieth century;
> The case is judged, is settled.
> Machines can never be undone.

But, she adds,

> Factories must no longer be the masters
> And men the means.

[3] Cf. Fivian, *Georg Kaiser und seine Stellung im Expressionismus*, p. 88. Fivian has also pointed out (p. 258) the contradiction between Kaiser's "new man," who is a paragon of altruism and humility, and the *monomaniacal*, narcissistic characters of his dramas. *Hölle Weg Erde* is perhaps the only Kaiser drama free of this contradiction, which, as we have pointed out, plagues even the conclusion of *Die Bürger von Calais*. (Cf. p. 173 of this work.) It is a contradiction, of course, that serves as a clue to the psychological roots of Expressionism.

[4] The most savage and symptomatic example of this attack is probably found in Karl Otten's "Thronerhebung des Herzens," *Der rote Hahn*, IV (1918), 13: "Die Maschine: wie wir dieses Vieh hassen, diese kalte Eisenmordschnauze./Nieder mit der Technik, nieder mit der Maschine! . . . Fluch auf euch ihr Erfinder, ihr eitlen, kindisch mordgierigen Konstrukteure! . . ."

> Let factories be servants
> Of decent living;
> And let the soul of man
> Conquer the factories.[5]

Ernst Toller suffered the shock of collision between revolutionary dream and reality perhaps more acutely than other Expressionist, because he fought to make the dream come true. His "Soviet democracy" in Bavaria was to be the republic of love and universal brotherhood which Expressionist dramas, poems, and manifestoes had so often prophesied.[6] But immediately arose the problem of force. How could the new state assert itself against those who were preparing to destroy it by force, without resorting to force in turn?

The Expressionist belief that man could be persuaded to goodness and reason did not pass the test of reality, and as soon as that initial assumption collapsed the activist Expressionist had to end tragically, no matter what course he followed. If he tried to live up to his ideal of nonviolence, he had to allow his experiment to be wiped out; if he decided to protect it, he had to use force and thus betray his ideal. "When ethical man becomes political, what a tragic road he will have to travel!"[7] In assuming leadership of a "Red army," in order to bring about a society of peace and fraternity, Toller knew that he betrayed the essence of *his* revolution. Yet he saw no alternative.

Even after this decision Toller tried to wage civil war according to the Expressionist dream.

Authority and blind obedience ruled the Imperial army; the Red army is to be founded on free choice and understanding; we must not take over the hateful old militarism; the Red soldier must not be a machine; he has realized that he is fighting for his own cause; his revolutionary will shall create order.[8]

But the Red soldiers missed accustomed discipline, ranks, and punishments, and they grumbled; many refused to fight under such liberal conditions and went home. The worst blows to Toller's faith in the new man came from his fellow revolutionaries. These fighters and martyrs for a new way of life soon revealed by their actions that the ideal of brotherhood and love had not penetrated under their skins. They were motivated not by

---

[5] Toller, *Masses and Man*, tr. by Vera Mendel, in Toller, *Seven Plays*, tr. by Vera Mendel *et al.*, pp. 127–28. Henceforth this translation will be referred to as Toller, *Plays*.

[6] Toller, *Jugend*, p. 137.

[7] Toller, *Briefe aus dem Gefängnis*, p. 63.

[8] *Jugend*, pp. 176–77.

the dream of man's divinity but by hatred of the bourgeois. They wanted
to shoot all bourgeois hostages, whom Toller tried to save at the risk of
his life. For this humanitarianism, his Communist allies denounced him
as "petty bourgeois" and had him arrested. Recriminations among the
revolutionaries and needless sacrifices of life preceded the day of final
defeat.

These disheartening experiences formed the autobiographical basis of
Toller's play *Masse-Mensch*. The heroine is modeled on the wife of a
university professor who hanged herself in prison, but her experiences with
the Revolution are Toller's own, projected onto a symbolic and universal
plane. *"Man and the Masses* was liberation from emotional anguish, after
experiences whose impact a man can perhaps bear only once without
breaking."[9]

In this drama, the conflict between the Woman and the Nameless One,
as the Bolshevik is called, is the conflict between the Expressionist intellectual and the proletarian masses, who are not yet ripe for his vision.

The Woman has torn herself loose from her bourgeois roots and joined
the proletarian movement to realize the ideal of a brotherly world without war and exploitation. The Nameless One is part of the masses. He has
suffered the agony of the exploited in his own flesh. He cannot forgive;
desire for vengeance inspires him. The Woman and the Nameless One
propose conflicting methods of revolution. The Woman wants the bloodless general strike which would force the capitalists to put an end to the
war. The Nameless One wants a violent uprising to install the revolutionary clique in power. The two also differ in their primary objectives. The
Woman desires above all the end of the war, then raging in its sixth year.
The Nameless One desires above all punishment and extermination of the
bourgeois class. As the Woman later recognizes, the spirit of the war lives
on in him under a new guise. He would merely shift the arena of violence
from international battlefields to those of civil war. She calls him "the
bastard child of war."

The Woman's tragic guilt lies in her deification of mass man, as he is
here and now. She defers to the demands of the Nameless One, because he
is one of the toiling millions and is thus sanctified in her eyes. Consequently, she consents to the arming of the workers and the use of force.

> You are the Masses.
> You are right.[10]

[9] *Briefe*, p. 43.
[10] Toller, *Plays*, p. 132.

Soon, however, she recoils from the excesses of which her consent to force has made her guilty and returns to her original faith in absolute non-violence. She resists the Nameless One and opposes his class hatred. The use of force, she claims, always starts a vicious cycle. Yesterday's victim is to-day's victimizer, but those whom he persecutes now will find their avengers tomorrow; so it will go on in all eternity, unless a sudden break is made and retaliation changes into forgiveness. Otherwise, it will make little differ-ence whether capitalists or workers are in control. Violence does not allow a genuine revolution; it merely accomplishes *coups d'état* which pass the whip from one hand to another. The really revolutionary deed is based on sympathy. Sympathy considers the future, whereas retaliation looks to the past.

> Revenge is not the will to new and living forms,
> Revenge is not the Revolution;
> Revenge is but the axe that splits
> The crystal, glowing, angry, iron will
> To Revolution. (p. 141)

But the masses are deaf to the Woman's idealism. They listen to the Nameless One, who speaks their language and voices their desires. He arouses their class xenophobia and directs their latent suspicions against the Woman. He tells them that she protects the hostages because they are members of her own class. She is shouted down as an intellectual, accused of being a traitor and arrested by the revolutionary tribunal.

The unbridgeable gulf that opens between the intellectual and the masses distinguishes the basic mood of *Man and the Masses* from that of Toller's *Wandlung*. Friedrich, in *Die Wandlung*, influences and converts the people without difficulty; the Woman in *Man and the Masses* fails to sway them and finds herself completely alone. Thus, the original isolation of the Expressionist comes to the fore again. He is a leader without a fol-lowing. Cut off from the *bourgeoisie*, he has not been accepted by the proletariat. Once more he stands in the vacuum from which he sought to escape.[11]

The revolution is crushed. The Nameless One disappears, but the Woman is condemned to death for alleged collaboration in the murder of

---

[11] There are striking analogies between Heinrich Mann and Toller, the foremost Ex-pressionist activists. Their lack of affiliation with any definite party or program is significant. Both stand not only "zwischen den Rassen" but also "zwischen den Klassen." They remain rootless rebels who fit into neither a national nor a social community. Heinrich Mann's late Expressionist novel *Der Kopf* (1925) shows, like Toller's dramas, the failure of the intellectual idealist who tries to refashion reality according to his ideal. For Heinrich Mann, cf. Rosen-haupt, "Heinrich Mann und die Gesellschaft."

hostages. By her death she will expiate a real guilt, for indirectly she was responsible for the killing of the hostages since, seduced by the romantic glorification of mass man, she condoned the use of force.[12] She betrayed the ideal of man to the masses. When the Nameless One visits her in prison and offers her a plan of escape that would involve the killing of a guard, she rejects it.

> I have no right
> To gain my life by this man's death. (p. 149)
> Hear me: no man may kill men for a cause.
> Unholy every cause that needs to kill.
> Whoever calls for blood of men,
> Is Moloch.
> So God was Moloch,
> The State Moloch,
> And the Masses—
> Moloch. (pp. 151–52)

By her decision to die rather than take the life of another human being, the Woman has attained her second *Wandlung*. The first made her leave marriage, class, comfort, and prestige to join the revolutionary movement against war. The second *Wandlung* actually crowns the first by making nonviolence an absolute principle of conduct, even for the revolution that is to end all violence. But the high-pitched optimism of the first *Wandlung* has been toned down. The Woman still believes that the ideal community will come into being some day, when the violent bitterness of mass man will have given way to sympathy and love, but that day has been moved into a vague and distant future. It will not be here tomorrow. Infinite patience is necessary. Man as he is, mass man, is not ripe for the building of a new world.

> *The Woman*: The Masses are not holy.
> Force made the Masses;
> Injustice of possession made the Masses.
> The Masses are instinct, necessity,
> And credulous humility,
> Revenge and cruelty;
> The Masses are blind slaves
> And holy aspiration.
> The Masses are a trampled field,
> A buried people.

[12] Toller, too, considered himself responsible for the victims of the Bavarian civil war. Cf. *Jugend*, p. 271.

> *The Nameless One*: And action?
> *The Woman*: Action and more than action!
> To deliver—
> Liberate humanity in the masses,
> Transform the Masses into a community.
>
> .   .   .   .
>
> *The Nameless One*: You live too soon.
>
> .   .   .   .
>
> *The Woman*: And you lived yesterday;
> You live today;
> To-morrow you will die.
> But I—
> Turning and circling—
> I
> Come into being
> Eternally.
> I shall become
> Cleaner, more guiltless,
> I shall become
> Mankind. (pp. 150–52)

Thus, the Woman remains an optimist. True, experience has defeated the axiom "Man is good"; but it can be said that he *tries to be good*.

> Men grope for goodness.
> Even their evil doings wear the mask
> Of goodness. (p. 153)

As though to confirm her unflinch.ng optimism in the face of failure, her execution in the prison courtyard transforms the two new occupants of her cell into better human beings. The regenerating mission of the activist heroine continues in her death.

In Toller's poetry and correspondence, however, despair frequently erupts and breaks the thin crust of activist optimism. In his second imprisonment, after the failure of the Bavarian Soviet, he looked back with nostalgia to his first prison term during the war, when he still could hope for the imminent rebirth of mankind.

If I could only, as formerly, believe in rebirth, in growing purity [reineres Werden].

Mankind—always helpless, always crucified. Justice—a bitter taste is on my tongue. I believed in the saving power of socialism; that was perhaps "the illusion in my life."[18]

---

[18] *Briefe*, p. 42.

Toller recognizes that the needs of intellectuals and masses are not the same, and that the glorious joy of 1918, when they seemed to merge, has proven a cruel delusion. The poet who loves mankind must always be an unhappy lover, because in reality he and mankind have nothing in common.

> You are like our poets, O my swallows.
>
> Men make them suffer. Men they love
> With inextinguishable ardor,
> They, who are brothers to the stars and
> stones and storms
> More than to this humanity.[14]

Toller maintains only a shell of his humanist faith; beneath it there lurks the old frightful isolation of the Expressionist *poeta dolorosus*, which now, after the collapse of his activist hope, he diagnoses as universal and irremediable.

Loneliness is. No bridge leads to one's neighbor. . . . I no longer believe in *Wandlung* to a "new" humanity. . . . More deeply than ever I feel the meaning of this tragic and merciful phrase: Man becomes what he is.[15]

The isolated poet-intellectual realizes that there is no remedy and no escape for him. No matter what detours he may take, he "becomes what he is." Yet Toller always checks this pessimism by his tempered, long-range belief in socialism. The tension and counterplay between this belief and his pessimism result in his acceptance of the tragic as the basis of existence; even in the most perfect society there will always be an element of ineradicable tragedy.[16]

In contrast to Toller, Kaiser sinks into unmitigated pessimism. Tragedy for him is not a residue but the sole fate of modern man. In 1919 he wrote his glowing activist drama *From Hell to Earth;* in 1920 he arrived with *Gas II* at the final burial of hope.[17] *Gas II*, the most radical example of Expressionist style and dramatic technique, shows a dismal future in store for man. Mechanization, in this futuristic drama, has led to total war, but the two power blocs are distinguished merely by the color of their uniforms. The Blues conquer the Yellows and occupy the famous works, the scene of

---

[14] Toller, *The Swallow Book* (tr. not given), p. 11.

[15] *Briefe,* pp. 31, 85.

[16] This is beautifully shown in *Hinkemann,* the drama of the emasculated war cripple whom no social order can ever restore to human dignity and happiness.

[17] Kaiser was never to regain his social optimism of 1919. All the dramas of his late Expressionist period, following *Gas II,* are deeply pessimistic, cynical, and hopeless. Cf. particularly *Nebeneinander* (1923), in which the theme of *Hölle Weg Erde* undergoes a bitterly cynical and tragic variation, and *Gats* (1925).

Gas I. They command the vanquished to continue the production of gas for the use of the victors.

The Billionaire-Worker, who is the "new man" whom the Daughter vowed to conceive at the end of *Gas I,* warns his fellow workers against the siren song of vengeance. Their salvation lies in turning the other cheek, in meeting oppression with submission, and in transcending defeat by embracing the enemy. For "the kingdom is not of this world!" But the Great Engineer holds out another hope. He has invented a deadly weapon, a poison gas, that could wipe out the conquerors. He wins the workers. They decide to make the poison gas. In a desperate appeal the Billionaire-Worker seeks to dissuade them from the course of revenge. When he fails, he blows up the gas works, destroying himself with his fellow men. Beyond the Billionaire-Worker's mystical quietism, there emerges the goal of a literal "quietism." The quiet of the grave descends upon a world whose true salvation is annihilation.

In the "new man's" gruesome finale we can easily detect the lonely outcast-superman's bitter rejection of a humanity which has persisted in rejecting him. The *poeta dolorosus,* disguising himself as Messiah, as "new man," has failed to raise mankind to himself. Mankind, which has scorned him as an artist and genius, scorns him also as a prophet and leader. The only action left to him, if he is not to fall back into the muteness of utter isolation, is destruction. In the universal triumph of death, the "new man" achieves that union with mankind which he failed to establish by proselytizing for a new way of life. Thus, the "new man" of Expressionism turns out to be none other than the Sick Man in Toller's *Wandlung,* the man who wants to annihilate the world because he has found no love in it.[18]

Total nihilism is the end of the Messianic ecstasy only if the "new man," refusing to question himself, attributes all guilt to humanity. A very different picture presents itself if the "new man" searches for the causes of his failure in himself, his ideals, and his methods in realizing them. In that case a genuine second *Wandlung* and renewal can take place, as we have already observed in Toller's drama. The most optimistic of the poetic documents of "second conversions" is Fritz von Unruh's play *Platz (Plaza)* which continues his *A Family.*

At the very moment when the Revolution is about to be accomplished, its leader Dietrich undergoes a profound change. On the Plaza, where the monuments of age-old power look down upon him, he begins to see that

---

18 Cf. Lauckner's sequence of dramatic scenes *Schrei aus der Strasse,* in which the activist Student finally leads the human dregs of the big city to collective suicide.

revolution cannot solve the terrible problem of power. Revolution changes the personnel but not the system itself. Dietrich vizualizes himself and his comrades many years later, entrenched on the Plaza, quite as tyrannical, corrupt, and frightened as the rulers of today. Nothing will have changed in the life of the people except the names and labels of their oppressors. The experience that reveals to Dietrich the "true revolution" is love. He falls in love with Irene, the daughter of the Overlord, and his love is returned.

Before meeting Irene, Dietrich, the Messianic activist, thought he could bring love to mankind without knowing what concrete love was. In this he was typical of all communionist and activist heroes. Love for them was not eros, but agape—charity. Not the bridal couch, but (as in Johst's *Young Man*) the hospital was its proper place of consummation. This love was general and abstract, extended to everyone in like manner and intensity. It lacked the concrete transforming power of sensuous love for a single and special individual. After Dietrich meets Irene, his agape is transformed into eros. His love ceases to be a compulsion of conscience and becomes a spontaneous natural urge. It is no longer afraid of the self-indulgence of the flesh and the enticement of female beauty. Dietrich and Irene give free reins to the "selfish" happiness of the body. They delight in their youth and beauty, sport and frolic with one another, and base their relationship on shared pleasure rather than on compassion and self-sacrifice.

Unruh-Dietrich conceives of the "new love" as a monogamous union in which spirit and flesh, "heaven and earth," interpenetrate to form "freest happiness."[19] This love holds a middle position between two Expressionist extremes—vitalist promiscuity and activitist-communionist self-denial. By fusing sex and agape into eros, by combining the sensuous abandon of the vitalist with the communionist's sense of responsibility and sympathy, this "new love" reduces both extremes to an ideal normality. It corresponds to the synthesis of mind and heart, which Unruh propagates in his post-First World War speeches as the only hope for a new Europe.[20]

A complete and fulfilled love between man and woman secures a happy childhood for its progeny and therefore represents a more concrete hope for the future than do abstract schemes of universal brotherhood. As in Toller's *Man and the Masses*, hope is transferred from the present to the

---

[19] Unruh's *Wandlung* from rebellion to the "new love" is also evident in the final version of his *Stürme*, written shortly after *Platz*. There the woman who teaches the rebellious hero to love is called Iris. See also Gutkind, *Fritz von Unruh: Auseinandersetzung mit dem Werk*, p. 35.

[20] *Reden*, p. 29.

future. But whereas Toller's heroine in her lonely prison cell, deserted by husband and comrades, can cling only to a religious faith in an abstract ideal, Dietrich and Irene *live* for the future. In their love they possess not only a tomorrow but also a today. Though built on a narrower basis—marriage and the family—their hope for a paradise on earth is more substantial than that of Toller's Woman. Visible joy and happiness of two people are a more forceful argument than universal ideas held in a vacuum. By setting an inspiring example to all men and women, Dietrich's and Irene's "new love" will, in the words of Dietrich's sister, create "new men."

To his former comrades and followers, however, who believe that only violent revolution can save mankind, Dietrich's new course appears as a betrayal of their mission and a surrender to conservatism. Schleich, once his most enthusiastic disciple, becomes his bitterest foe and denounces Dietrich as sentimental and reactionary. In the context of Unruh's drama, however, it is Schleich's extremism that represents reaction. Like the Nameless One in Toller's drama, Schleich, instead of building for the future, *reacts* against the past. While Toller's Nameless One was a social proletarian, Schleich might be called a sexual proletarian; women have always scorned him, and he longs to wreak his vengeance on them. He resembles Expressionists like Ehrenstein, whose sexual maladjustment we have discussed earlier, and it is well worth noting that Ehrenstein, who suffered intensely from his feelings of sexual inadequacy, turned temporarily into a Communist activist. Schleich seizes upon the revolution as a compensation for his life-long frustrations and inadequacies. It serves him as a ladder on which he can climb to power. He frankly admits to himself that he uses pacifist slogans as a means of demagogic deception. He transforms "the battle-cry 'No more war' into a scepter of (his) rule." "Love" is "just a word" for him that if repeated often enough will make him a saint in the eyes of the people and smooth his path to power.[21]

Once at the summit, the "pacifist" revolutionary gives free rein to his fury. He orders purges and arrests and shows the women who once rejected him that he is their absolute master. Under the pretext of "socializing" the state, he tyrannizes it. Dietrich is to be executed as a counter-revolutionary. But at the end of the play, the army of the reactionary Old Man sur-

---

21   Umschaffe
den Schrei "Kein Krieg" zum Herrscherstab für mich.
Kein Krieg; das resultiert: Gefühl, Gefühl.
Ich sag! "ich liebe"—ist das schwer? Ich liebe—
Ein Wort! Lebendig Etwas, solang angewandt,
bis mir der Heiligenschein vom Schädel glotzt
. . . . Und Schleich steigt in den Sattel. . . .
Platz: Ein Spiel, p. 19

rounds the revolutionaries at the Plaza. Now Schleich, the archpacifist, dons the armor of a feudal count and leads his troops to battle, like any old-style war lord. It is immaterial whether Schleich or the Old Man will win. In either case the jails will be full and the Plaza will stay enslaved. Dietrich's sister refers to the gunfire between the Old Man's "Whites" and Schleich's "Reds" as the "ghostly battle of long-dead fantasies." What matters is that Dietrich and Irene, whom the "White" attack has liberated from the "Red" prison, are safe. In their love and its offspring lies the hope of the world.

Unruh's *Plaza* not only foreshadows the basic problem of the anti-Stalinist literature of the succeeding generation—the famous "classics of disenchantment" of Silone, Koestler, and Orwell, but it also offers us the first example of that self-condemnation with which late Expressionism questions and turns away from its own dream. For unlike Kaiser's Engineer or Toller's Nameless One, the supreme antagonist of the Expressionist hero in Unruh's play acts and speaks like an Expressionist himself. He uses the Expressionist key term "love" to establish his rule of hate, and his language imitates the telegraphic style of Sternheim's and Kaiser's drama and the extreme condensation of Sturm poetry. Schleich's radical style voices his radical ideology—his hostility to tradition, *Gemüt*, individualized love, and all other romantic values of the past that he violently opposes as the opium of the people. A good example of this union of linguistic and ideological radicalism is found in the following passage in which Schleich denounces Dietrich's conversion to love for one particular girl as a treacherous surrender to reaction.

> We've heard confession! Noble corniness!
> Leads back to law and order? Breaker of arbitrariness?
> Decomposes, de-prints, de-thinks dumb-soul of people!
> Feeling exoperates, archfoe to us negators![22]

Dietrich's language, on the other hand, with its hymnic *élan* and comparatively conservative syntax, harks back, despite colloquialisms and modernist distortions, to the traditional style of German poetic drama, particularly that of Schiller and Kleist, even as the allegorizing devices and symbols of the drama connect it with *Faust II* and the myth-inventing literature of German Romanticism, with which its gospel of salvation through romantic love perfectly conforms.

The stylistic and ideological dichotomy between Dietrich and Schleich

---

[22] Anhörten wir Bekenntnis! Edelkitsch!/ Rückführt euch an Gesetze? Willkürbrecher?/ Zersetzt, zerdruckt, zerdenkt Dummseele Volks!/ Ausoperiert Gemüt, Erzfeind uns Neinern! (p. 77)

is part of that sharp division between "true" and "false" Expressionism with which the last phase of the movement is passionately concerned. The "true" Expressionists are, on the whole, identified with moderation, idealism, and continuity of the great traditions of Western art and literature; the "false" Expressionists are identified with faddish extremism, insincerity, snob appeal, and experiment for experiment's sake. Even at the very climax of the movement, in Edschmid's programmatic definition of Expressionism, the contempt for "fellow-traveling" (Mitläufer) or "fashionable" Expressionists crystallizes into the sharpest words of rebuke: "Already that which was eruption is becoming a fashion. Already an evil spirit is sneaking in [into our movement]."[23] For Schickele the difference between true and false Expressionism is the difference between spiritual and intellectual man: "These [the spiritual] men seek to bring about the inner unity of man; those [the intellectuals] content themselves with the external change of others. They can, under no circumstances, travel together."[24]

The false Expressionist pursues the extreme for its own sake and never develops beyond it. There are "false" Expressionists of form and style, who apply themselves to shocking novelty and forced obscurity; we may conveniently classify them as abstractionists. There are other "false" Expressionists who cultivate a radical attitude in political and social affairs. They have failed to evolve beyond the simple activist stage, which the "genuine" Expressionists have outgrown or at least come to see in all its horrible complexity. Abstractionism and activism are closely linked. In abstractionism the human mind sets itself up as the creator of a kingdom of pure forms whose likeness cannot be found in nature; in activism the mind proposes a perfect social order based on absolute ideals of happiness and justice unconnected with historical reality.

Max Brod in his novel *Das grosse Wagnis* (*The Great Risk*) (1919), which he calls his document of "abjuration" of activism,[25] depicts a nightmarish society of false "new men" who live in burrows underneath a forgotten sector of the battle front of an unending European war. This underground community, called Liberia, is to be the perfect embodiment of reason and freedom, the refuge of brotherliness in a war-torn world. The Poet of that community of "absolute freedom" has evolved a radically new form of drama to do justice to the novelty of the Liberian experiment.

---

[23] *"Über den Expressionismus in der Literatur,"* p. 72. This speech was made in December 1917.

[24] Schickele, *Die Genfer Reise*, p. 157.

[25] See Brod, *Heidentum, Christentum, Judentum: Ein Bekenntnisbuch*, I, 61.

Traditional art, he has found, runs counter to the rationalistic simplicity of the utopian scheme. Traditional art shows evil mingled with good and extols the complexity of the soul. Liberia has transcended complexity and tragedy. Liberia, therefore, needed a new type of drama, entirely stylized and abstract. "The horizontal drama," which the Poet evolved, has no human content. It is "socialistic idealism" refined to a point where only exhortatory statements are left. The actors recite these in a recumbent position and with the most even, automaton-like inflections, and thus produce an incantatory effect.

> "It occurred to me [explains the Liberian Poet] that man in a recumbent position has hardly any opportunity for gesticulation. He is alive but, as it were, paralyzed. The ideal symbol for the ideal man of duty. So I invented the horizontal stage. The audience looks down from the gallery. . . . The actors are lying. . . ."
>
> "As in tombs," I insert.
>
> "Yes, you are right," he says pensively. "The whole theater resembles a cemetery."[26]

Not just the "horizontal theater" but the whole experiment of Liberia reveals itself as a graveyard of the human soul. What started with the noblest intentions, as a realization of the dream of human brotherhood, soon degenerates into a vicious totalitarianism that in most essential aspects anticipates Köstler's *Darkness at Noon* and Orwell's *1984*.[27]

The reasons for this discouraging development as explained by the artist-narrator of the novel are several, all closely related. First of all, the participants in the experiment are almost all uprooted, neurotic intellectuals, a factor from which the contemporary Central European revolutions also suffered. In the first enthusiasm of their community-consciousness, these intellectuals vied with each other for the most menial jobs. Writers, university professors, artists, and lawyers were proud to be called bootblacks, waiters, dishwashers or streetcleaners. But this enthusiasm was only theoretical. Instead of doing the work itself, they fed their democratic pride with these proletarian titles. They thought that, having embraced the theory of democratic leveling and manual work, they had taken the decisive step and that the actual labor was incidental and could wait. Thus, while they boasted of being called shoemakers and dishwashers, shoes

---

[26] Brod, *Das grosse Wagnis*, pp. 201–2.

[27] Cf., for instance, the ingenious "Dionysian ear," an invention in the art of eavesdropping that could be a feature of Orwell's nightmarish utopia. The gigantic theater is constructed as an elliptical vault whose walls carry even whispered conversations to far-away listeners. (p. 207)

were not made and dishes were not washed. The contempt for practice and detail, typical of the theoretical mentality led to chaos. Chaos led to compulsion, since the community could not survive without work being performed. Compulsion soon took on grim and horrible aspects that surpassed anything the capitalist system aboveground had ever devised.[28]

Though the Liberian intellectuals have turned from egocentrism to the building of a collective, they have not experienced this *Wandlung* in their hearts, they have not become "new men." Like Unruh's Schleich, they have not learned to love. This is the deepest reason for the failure of their experiment: "Liberia, the commonwealth of flirtation, the state without love! The name of her disease is called absence of heart." (p. 191)

Dr. Askonas, the dictator of Liberia, admits that, having never learned to be happy, he derives a sadistic pleasure from making others unhappy. He delights in crushing incipient revolts against him, instigating purges and show trials; he keeps dynamite ready to blow up his whole state. Yet this same man was once inspired by the ideal of building an earthly paradise. The sexual maladjustment of the Liberians, which in turn is a consequence of their general emotional ill-health, dooms their idealistic experiment. There cannot be a new community without a new soul; and this new soul is found, first of all, in the individual's ability to love, not mankind in the abstract, but one actual person.

"Everything goes wrong without love."—One should tell that to all statesmen, popular leaders, and public men, and ask them on their honor and conscience: ". . . What is going on in your house and (to be quite frank) in your loins? Don't you perchance drug yourself with political narcotics because your sex is crippled?"[29]

Even as Unruh's Irene teaches Dietrich the lightness and joy of love, Ruth, a gentle, mature, and tolerant woman, rescues the narrator of Brod's novel from the infernal utopia. Brod's Ruth makes the artist-narrator of his novel not only a better person but also a conscious Jew. The further concretization of universalist activism, its narrowing into a concrete national-religious community, is an important factor in late Expressionism. To be sure, Zionism played a part even in Brod's first *Wandlung*; then, however, in his unqualifiedly activist phase,[30] he stressed the social-revolutionary,

---

[28] Cf., e.g., the plight of the Waiter in Brod's novel, who lives as the embodied accusation of the disastrous gap between Liberian theory and practice. *Ibid.*, pp. 184–85; Chapter VIII, "Roulette."

[29] Brod, *Das grosse Wagnis*, pp. 266–67. Cf. also Brod, "Liebe als Diesseitswunder. Das Lied der Lieder," in *Heidentum*, II, pp. 5 ff.

[30] Cf. Brod, "Aktivismus und Rationalismus," in *Tätiger Geist: Zweites der Ziel-Jahrbücher*, ed. by Kurt Hiller, pp. 56–65. This article reveals Brod's full-fledged activism.

universal, and Messianic aspects of Judaism. He believed in a world without anguish and tragedy.[31] In this his second *Wandlung,* his recoil from activist universalism, after 1918, Zionism implies for Brod reaffirmation of spiritual and mystical elements in Judaism as well as withdrawal from an incurable Europe. It is both a restriction and an interiorization of hope.

The narrator of Brod's novel and Ruth, his "bride from Lebanon," flee a continent in which the sinister underground dictatorship of Dr. Askonas is the only alternative to permanent war. The sympathies of Brod's narrator still lie with the subterranean failure; in its intentions, at least, Liberia had been great and promising. Though Liberia failed, Palestine may succeed.[32] It will be settled by a new generation unmarred by the failure of the Expressionist generation. "*Our* generation is perhaps lost for good," says Ruth near the end of the novel; but she continues with a glowing affirmation of faith in the future.

As Brod develops from an Expressionist into a spiritual Zionist, Johst and Heynicke develop into National Socialists or fellow-travelers of National Socialism. In becoming nationalists—whether Jewish or German— the Expressionists rebounded from a universalism that proved insincere, quixotic, and oppressive. They reacted against the hothouse air of the left-wing café and returned from utopian dreams to existing communities. Even in his pacifist period, during the First World War,[33] Johst felt a certain antipathy toward the activist intellectuals and *literati.* Hans, the hero of his autobiographical novel of 1917, feels a hot anger rising in him as he overhears the pale Bohemians debating airy issues in their café corner; and he feels overjoyed when a folksy actor interrupts their abstract discussions by a rude joke or defends the German classics against their cosmopolitan irreverence. Hans is more at home with the earthy group, who drink beer, tell anecdotes, and sing patriotic songs, than with the coffee-sipping intelligentsia. As the war went on, Johst began to question the motives of his pacifism, which set him apart from the vast majority of his countrymen. Was it not a sign of his physical inferiority?

---

[31] Brod, *Heidentum,* I, 59. Brod speaks there of his "error" ("Irrweg") in mistaking Judaism for a purely secular, social-minded "religion of liberty."

[32] A similar flight from Europe is observable in other Expressionist works around 1920, an obvious reaction to the collapse of the Messianic hope of 1918. Cf. Sternheim's novel *Europe;* also, as we shall see, the conclusion of Werfel's *Nicht der Mörder.*

[33] The best example of Johst's revolutionary activism is his farce *Morgenröte: Ein Rüpelspiel (Das Aktionsbuch,* ed. by Franz Pfemfert, pp. 315–27). In *Morgenröte* Johst lampoons the patriotic anti-Semitism that he himself was later to embrace and claims that the modern poet is justified in the most acid treatment of middle-class chauvinism. He was then, as he said later, a humanist European, "ein menschheitlich orientierter Europäer." Cf. Johst, *Ich glaube!* p. 8.

Do I love people beyond our borders because I am a cripple? Does a healthy individual have boundaries? Is limitation perhaps not a duty? Is boundless humanitarianism not perhaps the stunting of hands, eyes, and heart for the sake of the brain? Was ancient man humanitarian? Was the Christian of the Crusades humanitarian? Was Luther humanitarian without limits? Is greatness not limitation . . . ?[34]

Finally impatience with the ineffectuality of German left-wing movements contributed to Johst's early conversion to Hitler.

An article written in 1919 reveals Johst's *Wandlung* from activist universalism to the national "ethos of limitation."[35] In this article he calls for the integration of the mind or *Geist* with the rest of the human organism, particularly the blood. An ideal that fails to take account of the human lifestream, the blood, is doomed. As Unruh demands the synthesis of *Geist* and heart, Johst demands the synthesis of *Geist* and blood, but with very different emphasis. While Unruh remains a universal-minded humanist and pacifist, Johst embraces the mysticism of "blood and soil" and becomes a fanatical adherent of the new barbarism. He finds in the "German awakening" of the Hitler movement the antidote to the gruesome isolation of his *poeta dolorosus.*

The German folk and German youth are the fervent hope of Kurt Heynicke. He fulminates against the "false prophets," the pale *literati* of international brotherhood, who "found clubs with the word *Geist*" and juggle the word "love" about like mountebanks exhibiting their skill before the mob. Heynicke calls upon the people, as distinguished from the mob, to rise against their false leaders, the rootless intellectuals who, ignorant of the people and their real dreams and desires, dare to make fantastic demands in the people's name.

> The people never dies!
> From it alone a new mankind is born—
> Not from the pallid masks of these days' *literati*
> Who, dated even now, are arrayed against us—against youth.[36]

While the targets of the Expressionists discussed so far—the "false prophets" of Heynicke, the "intellectuals" of Schickele, the "fellow trav-

---

[34] Johst, *Ich glaube!*, p. 15.

[35] Johst, "Resultanten," *Die neue Rundschau*, XXX/2 (February 1919), 1138.

[36] Heynicke, "Rhythmen gegn die Falschheit," *Die Erhebung*, II (1920), 1:
> Das Volk stirbt nie!
> Aus ihm allein gebiert sich neue Menschheit,
> Nicht aus den blassen Literatenfratzen dieser Tage,
> Die schon veraltet, wider uns, die Jugend stehn.

elers" of Edschmid, Brod's Liberian cave dwellers, Unruh's Schleich and
Toller's Nameless One—were either false Expressionists or mere activist
revolutionaries, Werfel's attack went to the heart of "good Expressionism"
itself. Gebhart, in Werfel's retrospective novel *Barbara* (*The Pure in
Heart*), embodies some of the basic ideals of the Expressionist revolution.
Gebhart's theory of the matriarchate and the full release of the human capacity for love as the supreme weapon against power is close to Unruh's
and Werfel's own views. Yet this herald of Expressionism's most far-
reaching rebellion turns out to be a destroyer in the guise of a savior.[37] Gebhart's destructiveness lies on a much deeper level than that of Unruh's
Schleich or Brod's Dr. Askonas. Gebhart's egocentricity is deeply hidden,
not only from himself but also from others, by layers of warm good will,
compassion, and outgoing feelings for all his fellow men, which make him
even risk his life to help a comrade in distress. But this readiness to help,
this self-sacrificing warmth and comradeliness of the Expressionist prophet,
is a subtle manifestation of a megalomaniacal will to power more vicious
than any other because of its deceptive similarity to Christlike love.

Gebhart, who talks about love incessantly, condemns his own child to
die of want of love. When the neglected infant's crying becomes unbearable, Gebhart thrusts his fingers into his ears to shut out the whines that
convict him of his "absence of heart." This underfed and disease-ridden
child of revolutionary intellectuals, whining in its dark corner while its
parents are involved in endless discussions, opens the protagonist's eyes to
the basic rottenness of Gebhart's beautiful dream of a new humanity. For
this new humanity already exists in the child whom Gebhart dooms to an
early death, because it restricts his Bohemian liberty.

Murder lurks in Gebhart's gospel of total liberation through love. His
destructiveness reveals itself not only in the relish with which he ponders
over the possibility of exploding a whole city, but it is also inherent in his
doctrine of love itself. Gebhart sets himself up as the confessor and arbiter
of the love affairs of his women disciples. He decides whether they give
enough love. In certain cases he finds an incurable lack of capacity for
love. He persuades such "impotent" girls to kill themselves and procures
the poison for them.

At the core of every missionary impulse lies, according to Werfel, the
desire to impose the self upon others. Every scheme of world salvation is a
concealed form of self-aggrandizement. Anyone who thinks he has a
mission to perform thereby implies his superiority to his fellow men. He
alone can give while they have to receive. Thus, he violates the give-and-

[37] The chapter dealing with Gebhart is called "Gebhart und die Zerstörung" (Gebhart
and Destruction). Werfel, *Barbara*, pp. 466 ff.

take between ego and nonego, which underlies the good and wholesome life.[38] There emerges, then, in the missionary Expressionist the old Nietzschean romantic against whom communionist Expressionism so violently rebelled. Werfel's activist rebel Gebhart and the aesthete-magician Wagner in his novel *Verdi* are only two manifestations of the same romantic malaise—inflation of the self at the cost of the world or, in Freudian terms, submersion of the adult "principle of reality" in infantile self-love. Below the surface, the differences between activist and romantic disappear.

Wagner, too, conceives of himself as a redeemer of mankind by dint of his *Zukunftsmusik*. He, too, has a world-wide mission to fulfill and his art breeds a sect intolerant of all genius except his own. In his life as well as in his work he seeks to subdue and convert the world to himself. The Expressionist prophet Gebhart, on the other hand, displays in his personal life the same irresponsibility, disorder, presumptuousness, physical uncleanliness, and spiritual impurity that the Senator in Werfel's *Verdi* castigates as the vices of the romantic Bohemian à la Wagner.[39] The "Shadow-Kingdom" of the Expressionist-activist circle in *Barbara,* hidden in the back room of a café where the light of day never penetrates, is as much an island of isolation as Coleridge's Romantic "pleasure dome," or Stefan George's Neo-Romantic "hanging gardens," and "totgesagter Park." That it is an ivory tower of ugliness instead of beauty does not make it less insular and fantastic. These self-styled leaders of the people do not know anything about the people. They have never lived among them, never felt with them. They are the flotsam of the European middle class, cut adrift in the Bohemian caverns of the twentieth-century cosmopolis. The bankruptcy of the old order brought on by the war gives them a brief opportunity for wreaking vengeance on all that is healthy, sane, and pious.

"In the faces of which we are speaking I can read the sign of that putrefaction, the Luciferian seal of defection, the craving to wreak vengeance for the indescribable misery called God-forsakenness. Just take a look at modern art, which is the product of those people! Its distinguishing mark is hatred without reason, hatred as such. You have misused the term salvation. Do you think those types plan for the future or love the people, the proletariat, whose name they invoke at any time? The crooks of politics are saints compared to them! They seek Revolution, as a sick man looks for a drug, to rid themselves of their own state of horror."[40]

[38] In the most inspired moments of his pacifist rebellion, Ferdinand, the hero of *Barbara,* sees himself at the head of an admiring army, as he steps forth to fling his insubordination into the faces of his officers. *Barbara,* p. 419.

[39] See Werfel, *Verdi,* p. 577.

[40] *Barbara,* p. 512. But Alfred Engländer, who condemns the activists so eloquently, finally falls himself into the activist error.

Werfel's powerful trilogy *Spiegelmensch* (*Mirror-Man*) of 1920 illustrates his deepest insight into the oneness of all self-deification, whether it appears openly as the *hybris* of the Nietzschean superman or in the guise of world-liberating altruism. Thamal, the hero of this "magic trilogy," a poet who has known success but not happiness and peace of mind, wishes to withdraw from the world and live in contemplation. But inwardly he is not ripe for it. The proof for this is his own mirror image. The man who has truly transcended himself looks out through a window upon true "higher reality";[41] but Thamal looks out upon a mirror that reflects only himself.

The abbot of the monastery in which Thamal seeks refuge from the world explains to him that there are three stages or "visions" of man. (pp. 19 ff.) In the first vision men think they see the world while they see only themselves. In the second vision they know that they see only themselves and realize the prison in which egotism keeps them shut off from reality. At that stage, man fights a desperate battle with himself. In his mirror image he recognizes his fiend, reflected self-love, which keeps him chained and blocks his yearning to love what is outside himself. But when he has defeated the "mirror-man" with whom he struggles at the bottom of his heart, he will awaken to the true vision in which the mirror changes into a window and light flows into his room. Then he is ripe for love. The third vision is actually impossible for mortal man. It is the stage of the genuine savior, Christ, who does not have to go through the struggle with his mirror-self, but is, as it were, born with a window instead of with a mirror. He sees the world instead of himself and seeing it, he redeems it. But as he redeems the world, he also redeems God, for the world in turn is God's mirror and all our inadequacy and suffering derives from God's struggle with the mirror image of His vanity, namely man.[42] The reconciliation of God to His world is the Savior's task.

Thamal mistakenly believes that he has attained the final stage of the second vision, i.e., that he has learned to see and love what is outside himself. But his mirror image troubles him as a reminder of his imperfection. He decides to shoot at the mirror and smash it. But even as for Schopen-

---

[41] Werfel, *Spiegelmensch: Magische Trilogie,* p. 222.

[42] The eschatological implications of *Spiegelmensch* become clearer if the trilogy is read in conjunction with Werfel's fragment "Die schwarze Messe," which deals with the vanity of the God-Creator in the act of creation. He created man in His image so that man is God's guilty and unhappy mirror-man. Cf. p. 186 and n. 29. Also cf. Klarmann, "Gottesidee und Erlösungsproblem beim jungen Werfel," *Germanic Review,* XIV (1939), 192. The author is indebted to Adolf Klarmann for having drawn his attention to the highly significant novel fragment of 1919, the very closely related legend "Die Erschaffung der Musik," and the fragment "Theologie," all of 1919, and now published in the first volume of the *Gesamtausgabe* of Werfel's works being undertaken by Adolf Klarmann. These three prose works may truly be called prolegomena to *Spiegelmensch.*

hauer suicide is not true liberation from the tyranny of the Will, Thamal's *tour de force,* instead of destroying the Mirror-Man, liberates him. The image leaps out of the shattered glass and assumes a spatial existence.

The Mirror-Man seduces Thamal to activism. Since Thamal has liberated the Mirror-Man from his glass prison, it will be easy for him to emancipate humanity and transform their wretched lives of "toil and trouble" into an everlasting feast.

The role of Messiah serves the egocentric man, whose egotism has become "aware of itself,"[43] as a rationalization for self-aggrandizement in the guise of altruism and self-sacrifice. Thamal persuades himself that he is acting for the sake of humanity while he only flatters and magnifies his beloved ego. In Werfel's *Mirror-Man* the two main strands of Expressionism, vitalism and activism, unite into a single whole of self-delusion and self-defeat. They are the two great temptations of spiritual man who longs to be in touch with true reality. Because activism beguiles what is noblest in man, his spirit, it is the more pernicious of the two and the fiend's last weapon. Yet at bottom vitalism and activism are, as Thamal's course shows, merely two alternating stages of man's self-deification.

After returning to the world, Thamal goes to his father to demand his inheritance. A situation typical of vitalist Expressionism arises. The son, contemptuous of everything the father represents, wants his father's money so that he can experience the world. The father refuses; Thamal kills him under the Mirror-Man's guidance, takes his money, and flees into the world. Under the Mirror-Man's applause, Thamal is enamored of the spectacle of his own attractiveness, success, and power. Intoxicated by his meteoric ascent, Thamal seduces Ampheh, the beautiful wife of his friend, holding up to her the vitalist ideal of the high life that knows no inhibitions or taboos, which are valid only for the mediocre bourgeois.

But Thamal cannot love. As soon as he has conquered Ampheh's resistance and weaned her away from husband and duty, he loses interest in her. She becomes a burden to him, and when Ampheh announces that she is with child and refuses the abortion which Thamal demands, he makes this the long-desired pretext for leaving her. Ampheh realizes, too late for her own happiness, that Thamal never loved her, but seduced her to prove his superiority over her husband.

"Selbst-und Geltungsgenuss"[44]—this mainspring of Thamal's behavior

---

[43] "Die zweite Schau ist die des um sich selbst wissenden Egoismus." Werfel, "Dramaturgie und Deutung des Zauberspiels Spiegelmensch," quoted by Klarmann, "Gottesidee und Erlösungsproblem," pp. 206 ff.

[44] "Dramaturgie und Deutung," quoted by Klarmann, *ibid.*

continues even after he changes from self-intoxicated vitalism to altruistic activism. The irony of this switch lies in the fact that it is precisely the criminal irresponsibility toward those nearest him, his mistress and unborn child, which sets Thamal free to play the role of liberator of a whole nation. In itself this altruistic deed constitutes the purest achievement of Thamal's black career, and the Mirror-Man, whom Thamal's other acts have made fat and enormous, winces and shrivels at Thamal's decision to go out, unarmed, to fight the monstrous snake-king Ananthas and free the people. But the motives of this action cancel out its positive effects. The suffering and oppression of the people are a backdrop for Thamal's self-admiration. Hardly returned from his liberating mission, he allows the Mirror-Man to proclaim him god. The priesthood is overthrown, persecution sets in, and the altruistic liberator has turned into an absolute dictator. The Mirror-Man, as Thamal's prophet, flashes the news of Thamal's deification to the newspapers of the world.

> Radiogram at once to Times and New York Herald,
> To every planet with an ear to hear us:
> "World salvation can be promptly hoped for
> God in person has arrived here at twelve-o-five."[45]

Thamal's reign as god symbolizes the heyday of Expressionism with its inner antitheses and paradoxes which Werfel satirizes in these mocking verses.

> Eucharistic and Thomistic
> Yet a little bit Marxistic
> Theosophic, Communistic
> Gothic-small-town-Cathedral-mystic,
> Activistic, arch-Buddhistic,
> Super-Eastern, Taoistic,
> Seeking in all Negro plastic
> Refuge from an age so drastic,
> Rolling words and barricades
> Making God and foxtrot mates.[46]

[45] *Spiegelmensch*, p. 138:
> Radiogramm sogleich an Times and New York Herald,
> An jedes Sternbild, das die Ohren herhält!
> "Welterlösung promptest zu erhoffen . . .
> Gott hier 12 Uhr fünf persönlich eingetroffen!"

[46] *Ibid.*, p. 130:
> Eucharistisch und thomistisch,
> Doch daneben auch marxistisch,
> Theosophisch, kommunistisch,
> Gotsch kleinstadt-dombau-mystisch,

Beneath the surface inconsistencies and paradoxes of Expressionism—its fusion of God and foxtrot, of mystic religiosity and left-wing politics—Werfel sees its basic and fatal hypocrisy in its blasphemous deification of mankind which serves as disguise for the deification of the self. Thamal, in pretending to establish Utopia and proclaiming himself god, sins not only against God but also against reality. In the blasphemous deification of man lies the archsin of Expressionism and the cause of its ruin.

Thamal's heyday, like the heyday of Expressionism, is very brief and almost immediately turns into catastrophe. Like the activist Expressionist, Thamal has not succeeded in eliminating the ancient monsters; and reaction quickly triumphs over the false and presumptuous revolution. The monstrous serpents of King Ananthas come back and ravage the country with greater fury than before. The people who hailed Thamal only a moment ago now desert him, and the kingdom of the "visible god" is at an end. Thamal's fall is swift and total. Hounded by the police for killing his father, Thamal is now forsaken by everyone, including the Mirror-Man, who, having grown robust and three-dimensional through Thamal's crimes, feels strong enough to pursue an independent career of worldly success. Activist world-salvation is no longer in fashion. Abstractionism rules in art,[47] and the old feudal-capitalist society has reasserted itself triumphantly. Thamal's brief hour of triumph, like the equally fleeting climax of activist Expressionism, is remembered only with embarrassment or derision.

The essence of both Gebhart's and Thamal's guilt lies in their relation to their children, i.e., to the visible future. Gebhart wanted to build a new world based on love and hated his own child. Thamal went out to liberate a people and did not care what happened to his child. Both wanted to renew the world, but where they had the most immediate chance to do so, namely in their own children, they failed. The glorious future of which they dreamed turned out to be malformation and death. Herein lay the fatal inconsistency between theory and practice, which we observed in Dr. Askonas' Liberian experiment and which doomed the whole activist-Expressionist dream to nothing better than a Bohemian rationalization.

Thamal's sin against the future contains and epitomizes all his other sins. His contempt for his father, which led him to parricide, foreshadowed

---

Aktivistisch, erzbuddhistisch,
Überöstlich taoistisch,
Rettung aus der Zeit-Schlamastik
Suchend in der Negerplastik,
Wort-und Barrikaden wälzend,
Gott und Foxtrott fesch verschmelzend—

[47] See the Schneemann scene, pp. 153–55.

his crime against his son. For, as his father told him, he who cannot be a son will not be able to be a father. We find here the exact reversal of Hasenclever's *Son* of 1914. Hasenclever's Son rebelled against the Father in the name of the future and for the sake of his own unborn children. In early Expressionism the rebellion against the fathers leads to a better and saner world. In Werfel's *Mirror-Man* of 1920 the culprit is not the conservative father, but the rebellious son. Late Expressionism, having become thoroughly disillusioned with rebellion, has come to realize that a ruthless severance of past and future can lead only to chaos and destruction. The future must grow organically out of the past.[48]

Thamal's willingness to die to expiate his crime against the future saves him from the Mirror-Man. After he empties the hemlock to which he has sentenced himself as the judge in his own trial, the Mirror-Man vanishes and Thamal wakes up in the cloister. Where he saw a mirror, he now beholds a window that looks out on a higher reality.

If we omit the Buddhist mysticism at the end of the trilogy, which was only an extreme and passing phase in Werfel's development, the *Mirror-Man,* like Unruh's *Plaza* and Brod's *The Great Risk,* upholds the goal of an ideal human normality. This ideal normality is expressed by the affirmation of the continuity of life as manifested by the family. But whereas Unruh's play and Brod's novel look forward to this normality as to a new and revolutionary goal of the future, Werfel's trilogy illustrates its connection with the past. The world, so runs the message of the *Mirror-Man,* can be saved only in the literal sense, i.e., *preserved* and continued from fathers to sons. This idea of the sacred continuity of the generations repudiates the activist-Expressionist goal of the kingdom of *Geist* or the traditionless paradise on earth. Werfel comes to reject this grand ideal because in its ruthless abstractness it absolves the individual of responsibility in his everyday relationships. The Expressionist theoretician and dramatist Paul Kornfeld, too, regrets that the German Revolution of 1918 did not contain a greater number of "petty" people who, instead of thinking of universal and absolute goals, would have applied themselves to a merely proper and conscientious behavior in their personal affairs.

Woe to individuals and woe to the world, if a person makes the whole world his

---

[48] Hasenclever himself stresses maturity, instead of rebellion, in his late Expressionist stage. Cf. the poem "An die Freunde," a document of great resignation, in *Verkündigung,* p. 81:

> Wir haben den Sturm der Freiheit geläutet.
> Wir waren Jünglinge. Jetzt sind wir Mann.
> Ach, die Taten des dröhnenden Mundes
> Sind vergangen. Tritt ein in die Reih! . . .

concern, not because the limited sphere of his personal life has become too con-
fining for him, but because he is ignorant of it, or scorns it, or thinks the happen-
ings in it unimportant and insignificant. . . . Whatever such a person will do,
it can only be disastrous.[49]

Kornfeld even goes so far as to welcome a certain realistic "egotism" as a
wholesome antidote to that blind and catastrophic altruism.[50]

The "ethos of limitation," as Johst calls it, which is so characteristic of
late Expressionism, seems on the surface like a reversal of all that Expressionism had striven for. Yet if we look below the surface appearances, we
find that "the ethos of limitation" crowns the fundamental aspirations of
communionist Expressionism. At the beginning of the movement stood
Werfel's phrase: "Mein einziger Wunsch ist dir, oh Mensch, verwandt zu
sein!" The longing for the integration of the isolated self with "the others,"
the not-self, the *Du*, filled Sorge and Kafka, Toller and Kaiser, Hasenclever
and Brod, Heinrich Mann and Frank. Communion with his fellow men
was the unhappy narcissist's ardent prayer and his hope for rescue from
nausea and despair. This hope inspired the activist revolt, with the reign
of sympathy as its objective. This revolt was to unite the lonely intellectual
with his fellow men and return to him the sense of reality for which he
craved. But by extending love to the whole world, the activist overshot his
mark and missed reality after all. From the vantage point of the basic
Expressionist craving, activism turned out to be a mistake. The activist had
been deluded when he assumed himself cured of his narcissism. Actually
he had only shifted his fantasies of self-glorification and superhuman status
to mankind. This was not true humility toward life. It was but a symptom
of the insanity which too great suffering produces and by no means its
cure. The basic goal of Expressionism, as we have seen, was *Sachlichkeit*—
sanity, understanding of and communion with others, and mature humility
in the face of the miracle of life. Revolution was a path by which the Expressionist sought to attain *Sachlichkeit;* he tried to cure the world in order
to cure himself. This turned out to be the wrong procedure.

This thought is mostly clearly developed in Werfel's *Not the Murderer,*
written at the same time as *Mirror-Man* and, in a certain sense, a companion
piece and supplement to it. Duschek, Jr., a would-be composer who joined
the anarchists in rebellion against his father, whose monstrous authoritarianism has made an emotional wreck of him, is on the point of killing his
father. But as he raises his arm to strike at the tyrant of his childhood and

---

[49] Kornfeld, "Gerechtigkeit: Fragment," *Die Erhebung,* II (1920), 313.
[50] *Ibid.,* p. 315.

poisoner of his life, he suddenly sees in him only a pathetic old man, cringing in the animal fear of death. A great revulsion against his own action overcomes Duschek, Jr., and he feels pity rather than hatred for his father, whom he now sees, for the first time, in his true proportions. In contrast to Frank's Seiler, Werfel's Duschek realizes the absurdity of hoping to find emotional health and human dignity through an act of murder. He can save himself only by leaving behind vindictive rebellion as well as craven submission, because the one enslaves as much as the other, and by building his life anew in a sane and realistic atmosphere. He decides to emigrate to America, marry, buy a farm, and raise a son.

I have learned one thing: Anything that fails to add to the world new blood, new life, new reality is *meaningless*. New reality is the only thing that matters.

Everything else belongs to the Devil. Above all the dreams, those dreadful vampires, to whom all weaklings and cravens submit, all those who never want to crawl out of the corner of childhood.[51]

Duschek's withdrawal from twisted and revolution-rife Europe to a fresh continent where he will be in touch with the soil, the source of all life, and learn to be a father, a procreator, and a provider, offers an analogy to Thamal's awakening to true reality. In both cases the infantile, narcissistic, fear- or pride-ridden ego matures into a purer, calmer, virginal, and authentic existence. By overcoming their childhood selves—the "boy's clothes of appearance"—Thamal and Duschek learn to see reality free of the incubus of neurotic self-obsession, which stands like a huge mirror between them and the world.

The anarchists, on the other hand, have not left "the corner of childhood." Their false relation to society corresponds to Duschek's former false relation to his father. The anarchists have not freed themselves of the neurotic hate-love characteristic of the son and slave status, which their revolution aims at overcoming. Consciously they know this and seek to emancipate their inner selves as well as external society; but the same fateful gap that we have observed elsewhere yawns between the intellectual insight of the revolutionaries and their actual lives. They look pallid and unhealthy, their meetings take place in opium dens, and Sineida, their beautiful woman leader, is wrapped in a profound, incurable melancholy. When a young girl, she was assigned to assassinate an archduke but missed her target and instead killed the archduke's small child. The memory of her terrible mistake haunts Sineida all her life, and her hopeless sadness implies that her mistake is symbolic of the greater mistake of the revolu-

---

[51] Werfel, *Erzählungen aus zwei Welten*, p. 282.

tionary dream itself. In his farewell message to Europe, Duschek obviously includes the revolutionary opposition, the romanticism of the left, in his diagnosis of the sickness of European civilization.

> Who can say what creativeness is? But whatever it is, it can arise only from an untwisted, unbroken soul! Therefore beware of the dreams of the crooked, the crushed, the contorted, the witty, the vindictive, if they offer their dreams as creative acts! . . .
> We left the earth. She has avenged herself by taking all reality from us and giving us a thousand delusions and nightmares in exchange.
> But I want to wed my stock to the earth again, to a boundless unfettered earth, so that she may cleanse us of all the murders, vanities, sadisms, and putrescences of congested living. (p. 283)

The America to which Duschek emigrates is not the continent of unlimited possibilities for "rising," which lures the hero of Edschmid's early Expressionist tale *The Lazo*. It is the country to which, one hundred years earlier, Goethe's Wilhelm Meister went to find a sane and balanced way of life, free of the "thousand delusions and nightmares" of too rich a past.

The comparison of the late-Expressionist "ethos of limitation" observed in Johst, Werfel, Kornfeld, Unruh, Brod, and earlier in Sorge and Stadler, with the practical and socially conscious "ethos of renunciation" of the old Goethe enables us to place the antisubjective, antiromantic tendency of late Expressionism as firmly into a German tradition as its subjective, vitalist-romantic counterpart. For there is a tradition of *Sachlichkeit* in German life and literature just as there is one of idealistic and romantic subjectivism, and it has been variously designated as *Aufklärung, Klassik,* "poetic realism," *Neue Sachlichkeit;* but its basic tendency may be best defined by Hölderlin's two words "heilig-nüchtern," holy and sober. Piety and sobriety, loving embrace of the cosmos and meticulous cultivation of fact—this was what science meant for Goethe; and it is in the contrast between Goethe's loving submission to the cosmos and Kant's radical negation of a cosmos that the dichotomy between objectivity and subjectivism in German literature and thought appears at its clearest. The Frankfurt patrician and Weimar courtier guarded himself against the subjectivist radicalism inherent in the lonely East Prussian professor's thought. Goethe insisted that the artist was not only the lord but also the slave of nature. He asserted that nature and art corresponded everywhere and that the Greek artists were the greatest because their works perfectly revealed the laws of nature. Goethe, who called the Romantic taste for Gothic art sickness, could have had nothing but the severest condemnation for the distortions practiced by Cubists, Expressionists, and Surrealists. Basically Expressionism, as we have seen, sided with Kant against Goethe; but in the late Expressionism of Werfel, Johst, Kornfeld, Unruh, Brod, the return to the Goethean strain of conservative objectivity became more and more marked.

In late Expressionism a revolt arose not only against activist content but also against the "revolutionary form" which had been the essence of Expressionism. This counter-revolution led the Expressionists back to the great tradition of German and Western literature and re-established the link with the conservative idealism of German middle-class culture. As early as 1919 Johst declared that he was aiming, in his art, not at the new but at the necessary. A genuine work of art, according to Johst, is never entirely original; and he was completely at one with Goethe in stating that art was nothing but the "pure undistorted total expression of a personality."[52] He demanded that art return from modernistic excesses to the great tradition. He reproached the Expressionists for their intellectuality and abstractness: they forgot that spirit is immanent in nature and not an exclusively human property. He upheld Novalis as an example of the poet who "from the most profound feeling for nature became prophet of the extrasensory, the absolutely spiritual." Johst thus returned to the German romantic tradition, which, following in the footsteps of Goethe and Schelling, views nature as a manifestation of the world spirit, as the "living garment of divinity"; consequently, he de-emphasized both the humanism of the activist who saw God only in mankind and nature as an alien chaos to be subdued and humanized and the formalism of the abstractionist who refused to recognize external nature as possessing any bearing upon his art.

Even in the heyday of Expressionism the conservative sympathies of its late phase were already apparent. The most important programmatic pronouncements of the movement also placed the strongest emphasis on the continuity between past and present. Edschmid was eager to assert, in his famous manifesto of the movement, that Expressionism was by no means a new phenomenon. It had existed, under different names, in all great periods of the human spirit. It was almost identical with the creative impulse itself. It was the false Expressionists, the fashionable and faddist "fellow travelers," who created the impression that the movement was altogether new and monstrously perverse. Kornfeld in his programmatic essay "Souled and Psychological Man" attacked modernist extremism with greater polemical sharpness than Edschmid. According to Kornfeld, it is a mistake to believe that the modernistic experiments have superseded Naturalism. The same old Naturalistic assumptions live on in the

---

[52] "Resultanten," *Die neue Rundschau*, XXX/2 (February 1919), 1138.

disguise of experiment, abstraction, and distortion. Even as social revolution is only a reaction to the *status quo* and not its transcendence, so the
experimental movement in art is only a reaction to, but not a transcendence
of, Naturalism. The Naturalists give a portrait of surface reality; the experi-
mentalists give a caricature of the same surface. They go as little beneath
it as do the Naturalists. Distortion is not transcendence. Erroneous reportage is not superior to faithful reportage; if anything, it is worse. The
modernist distorters and experimenters are incompetents, who hide their
lack of talent under the pose of daring innovation.

Their lack of talent for the bourgeois professions does not, as they think, prove
their talent for art. They cannot find their way in real life, and so they believe
that they have left reality behind them and acquired the right to escape to Art,
that asylum for all incompetence. . . . They think that they are revolutionaries,
because they make a lot of noise, whereas they are merely—*bourgeois manqués*.[53]

The antimodernist attitude of late Expressionism finds its climax in the
work with which the movement closes—Werfel's *Verdi* (1923). In this
"novel of the opera" Werfel attacks Wagner, to whom modernism in
music, literature, and art owes an enormous debt, and espouses the popular
musical style and the "simple" personality of Verdi as the ideal of art and
the artist. Werfel equates experimental form with sickness of the soul and
sees Wagner as a rootless and pathological adventurer, a neurotic and
megalomaniac. He contrasts the twisted and thoroughly diseased character
of Wagner with the humane normality and sanity of Verdi and opposes
the humble "objectivity" or *"Sachlichkeit"* of Verdi's music to the pioneering subjectivism of Wagner's style.

Verdi's fame comes from the direct appeal of his melodies. His arias
are sung in the streets after their first night performance; they are immediate "hits." He himself is a vessel, an instrument, a divining rod employed
by God to reveal treasures of music to mankind.

In truth man is not given the power to create but merely the power to discover.
. . . Melodies exist. They cannot be produced but merely discovered. . . .
Genius is the faculty of man to become, at certain moments, a divining rod. He
is nothing more. (p. 483)

Genius is a *gift* in the literal sense of the word. It was *given* to the artist
in trust, for him to develop and perfect for the pleasure and benefit of his
fellow men. He must never forget that he is only an intermediary (and

<hr>

[53] Kornfeld, "Der beseelte und der psychologische Mensch," *Das junge Deutschland:
Monatsschrift für Theater und Literatur*, I (1918), 9–10.

even that only in inspired moments) and not God. Flying in the face of the whole modernist tradition, first originated in the aesthetics of Kant, which assumes the godlike and complete automony of genius, Werfel demands that the artist employ his gifts not for unbridled experiment but for the exhilaration of the people, a view which Werfel himself was to follow in practice until it carried him to the world-wide triumph of *The Song of Bernadette,* which was as far from modernist spirit and Expressionist form as anything could be.

Wagner's art, within the content of Werfel's "novel of the opera," is a frantic attempt to save himself through self-expression. Its roots are neurotic. The effect of his work on others is entirely subordinated to his own need to free himself of his anguish and to unburden his soul. "At bottom Wagner never engaged in a real battle for humanity. . . . *For in the actual process* of creation he made no effort to write for a real people." (p. 123) Wagner's art is Wagner's salvation. In this lies his *Unsachlichkeit.* His work appeals to those who suffer from a neurotic disposition similar to that of the artist, to the hypercivilized and overrefined. But it does not cure them and make them better human beings. It drugs or intoxicates them and excites neurosis to hysteria. When Italo, a young Wagnerian in the novel, plays the scores of his adored master on the piano, he undergoes an experience quite similar to that of amorous intercourse; afterwards he feels the same effeteness and exhaustion as after a "night of love." Like a great cocotte, a *femme fatale,* the modernist artist (descendent of the Romantic), as personified by Wagner, consumes all the emotional (and material) wealth the world can offer and produces in return sensations, raptures, and "all forms of *unhappy* love." He works incessantly, he is feverishly active, but only to be passive—saved, loved, deified—in the end. The "sinfulness" of romantic-modernist art, as Werfel understands it, lies in the selfish passivity of its aim. It is not ethical but narcotic.

In Werfel's "novel of the opera" the contrast between the ethical and the egocentric-romantic-modernist artist is a contrast between Latin and German civilization. Werfel recognizes very well that, as our analysis has shown at the outset of this work, the modernist aesthetics is closely linked to the social and existential crisis of the creative man which, at first apparent in Germany, spread in the course of the nineteenth century to the rest of Europe, especially to France. "Wagner was a German. And to be German means: 'You are allowed everything because no form, no past, no *relationship* binds you.' A charter of magnificence and peril." (p. 123) The German artist as portrayed by Werfel is an innovator because he lives and creates in isolation. Since he does not write for a public with definite tastes and con-

ventions, there is no need to abide by traditional forms. To prove himself
worthy of attention, in a land of lonely individuals, he has to be original,
break tradition, and rise above everything that existed before him. He must
be all alone, monstrous, rising from the depths of obscurity, a gigantic
shadow that is to blot out everything else and envelop the world. Lacking
a genuine community, which can afford tolerance and variety within the
unifying boundaries of a broad tradition, the Teutons can show their
creativeness only in the violent eruptions of rebellious and dictatorial individuals who smash the work of their predecessors, astonish the world with
iconoclastic forms, and succumb, after describing their meteoric course, to
new rebels, even more original and even less connected with a universal
tradition. Such a creativeness is like the "creativeness" of a volcano which
offers a wonderful spectacle but devastates the countryside. Verdi, the
heir to centuries of Mediterranean civilization, views such a destructive
creativeness with deep misgivings and even hatred.

So what can they do, those Germans? Destroy!!
A sudden wave of hatred swept through the Maestro. The same hatred that
he had felt after the Battle of Sedan. It was the hatred of the Roman for the
barbarians. . . . This hatred ignited the spark of a profound insight: "The
idealism of these Goths and their destructive fury are one and the same." (p.
181)

The modernist artist, who strives for originality in order to compel the
world to take notice of him, is forced by the same token, to restrict his
appeal to an ever-smaller audience. Finally a point is reached where un-
conventionality becomes obscurity and communication ceases. In Werfel's
novel, Fischboeck, an utterly obscure, starving German expatriate, takes
this next step beyond Wagnerianism. A precursor of Schoenberg, he puts
an end to harmony. Fischboeck shares the extreme modernist position of
Mann's Leverkühn. "I do not write for this age!" says Fischboeck. Nor
does he write for posterity. "I simply realize," he says, "in my compositions
the essence of music as a tree realizes the essence of nature by its growth.
After all, my hair and nails also grow without purpose and public. My
music grows the same way. What the world does, or fails to do, with it, does
not concern me." (pp. 329–30) Fischboeck's extremism appears "monstrous" to Verdi. He cannot imagine that a true artist could give up his
natural desire for an audience. As Verdi sees it, Fischboeck's renunciation
of public appeal is not true humility. It is resentment, it is vanity thwarted
and turned inward. Thus, it is the ultimate consequence of the Wagnerian *hybris,* which makes the artist's subjective ego a law of life and beauty.

Verdi's plebeian background and Italian nationality preserve him from this extreme fate of the modern artist. He is rooted in a firm and popular tradition. On an infinitely higher level he still represents the simple fiddler, the wandering musician who goes from village to village and plays for the peasants at their weddings and country fairs. Musical convention, which his contemporaries felt inclined to smash "with an athlete's gesture" because they had been gorged with it to satiation, filled Verdi with wonder as something new and glorious. He did not have to break the old vessels; he could fill them with new wine.

Verdi's audience is neither Society nor Bohemia but the people, the whole community. In such an artist Werfel draws the ideal for which he strives. It is typical, however, that this ideal artist is not a German but an Italian. In Verdi's Italy, the late Expressionist author sees art still functioning as a part of life, a daily necessity for vinegrowers, butchers, and notaries, at least as important to them as their taverns and card games. The disastrous split between art and people has not yet occurred or has already been overcome. Verdi, the Italian artist, feels at home in his country; the German Expressionist does not feel at home in Germany. An artist who feels at home among people has no need to think of startling theories of "absolute art" and *Zukunftsmusik*. He creates like the painters of the Renaissance or of seventeenth-century Holland, "who did not paint in order to solve problems of light or form but because the pious needed pictures. . . . In a like manner, Verdi wrote for people, not for excited intellects, for very definite people who crowded the theaters of Italy." (pp. 123–24) Art for Werfel's Verdi is functional within a human context; i.e., it fulfills very concrete human needs. Its problems are not abstract but arise from specific demands and tastes which the artist tries to meet without having to deny his temperament or outlook.

For the youthful Verdi . . . who had to . . . write for season and company, the word "Art" . . . did not have that romantic connotation of the special, of garret idealism, mission, standing above men, all that stilted meaning which was to prove so disastrous to it. (p. 123)

Werfel's novel shows the artist's integration in the community, the dream that had motivated activist Expressionism from its beginning, not as a utopian goal attainable only through a revolutionary upheaval and the regeneration of mankind, but as a commonplace reality, the result of fortuitous geographical, historical, and psychological circumstances. These circumstances had always been lacking in Germany and were becoming ever rarer in the whole modern world; but neither a collective revolution nor a spectacular personal regeneration could produce them. One could humbly search for them, reverently discern them wherever they did exist, or patiently wait for their coming; but one could not hope to force them or manufacture them by either personal of collective means. With this realization the recoil from the activist euphoria had gone as far as it was possible to go. It had advanced beyond the point where the fundamental qualities and devices of Expressionism—the tense urgency, the extremism and violence, the need for the outcry, for the breathless condensation, the hectic hyperbole, the metaphoric visualization—were still appropriate. For Werfel and the great majority of Expressionists, Expressionism had lost its *raison d'être*.

Epilogue:
The Parting of the Ways

WERFEL'S ATTACK ON WAGNER REVEALED THE FUNDAMENTAL CONTRADICTION lurking in German Expressionism from its beginning. German Expressionism sought to be two things in one: a revolution of poetic form and vision, and a reformation of human life. These two aims were hardly compatible. As a part of the stylistic revolution of modernism, Expressionism was too difficult and recherché to serve its didactic and proselytizing ambitions; as a Messianic revolt it had to be too preachy to form a genuine part of modernism. The ideal of "the new man" clashed with the ideal of "the new form," and each interfered with and diluted the other. Only the haze of Messianic enthusiasm which enveloped the movement for a brief span of time was able to conceal the basic contradiction. The moral idealism of activism and the aesthetic idealism of modernism were capable of being confused and seen as one during a few years of intoxication. Both scorned existing reality as the subject matter of art and both strove to create a new reality through abstraction. But no true symbiosis could ensue; and the rapid collapse of the chiliastic illusions brought the underlying incompatibility of the two idealisms quickly to the fore. Shortly after 1920 the two goals of Expressionism—attachment to an objective reality and free creation of a surreality—appeared distinct and irreconcilable. The ethical and the aesthetic wings of Expressionism divorced and this divorce spelled the end of the movement. Henceforth the former Expressionists were to travel on widely separate and diverging routes. Among the international best-sellers and potential Hollywood scripts of Werfel, the Communist clichés of Becher, the Nazi clichés of Johst, and the esoteric abstractions of Benn, there existed no common denominator. Nothing was left to indicate that four so radically different authors had once united in a common movement.

Yet the movement had contained the seeds of all four developments.

Werfel, Becher, Johst, and many other Expressionists, had decided to attach themselves to an objective external reality. They eschewed experimental form and returned to the most conventional and "popular" forms of writing. Werfel's spiritual anchorage became a happy and profitable blend of commercialism and Judaeo-Christian sentiments. Becher and Johst found a spiritual and material haven in the totalitarian movements. Despite the vast differences between them, these three authors (and many others like them) had found solutions to the serious writer's crisis that were alike in one fundamental respect: they decisively accepted an objective communal reality which, while it caused them to repudiate and utterly forsake formal experiment, brought them in return a spiritual shelter, a vast public, and material or social success. Millions of shopgirls from Zurich to California wept and rejoiced over Werfel's *Song of Bernadette*, while a few years later millions of East German school children learned Becher's accolades to Stalin and the proletariat by heart. The world-famous resident of Hollywood and the Communist commissar of East German literature—both former Expressionists—had moved from modernism and the experimental phase of their youth as far as it was possible to move; and in return they had succeeded in different contexts and by different means in becoming truly "popular" authors. Their abandonment of the Expressionist form, however, did not imply a complete reversal of all the tendencies that had inspired them as Expressionists; on the contrary, it constituted the fulfillment of the most basic yearnings of their Expressionist phase. Formal experiment had not been essential to their Expressionism; ethical conviction and moral faith had, and these were fully and consistently developed only in their post-Expressionist period.

Werfel's *Song of Bernadette* was the most triumphant exemplification of the view, expressed in his *Verdi*, that man achieves the truth of his existence when he lives and acts as a vessel of God. By writing a novel in a style as simple, naïve, and conventional as that of *Bernadette*, and utilizing a theme made for capturing the imagination of millions of readers, Werfel successfully emulated his ideal of the artist set forth in *Verdi*. Ironically enough, the actual composer Verdi failed to conform to the ideal of his Austrian admirer. Unlike Werfel's image of him and unlike Werfel himself, Giuseppe Verdi traveled not toward greater and greater simplicity but, on the contrary, toward ever more pronounced sophistication and complexity. *Otello* and *Falstaff*, if not close to modernism, are at any rate far removed from the facile popular style of Verdi's earlier works; they were not the kind of music to be whistled and sung by the masses in the streets.

Werfel's image of Verdi (which must be carefully distinguished from the historical reality of Verdi) had been the ideal of his entire Expressionist period. It arose from his craving to be "related to man." The same ideal guided the planned "theater of the masses" of which Sorge's Beggar had dreamed at the outset of Expressionism. For Sorge, as for Werfel, the goal of "the new art" lay in a direction opposite to that in which the main development of modernism had taken place. The goal was the artist's liberation from his ivory tower and his communion with mankind. The kind of art capable of redeeming him from his isolation would also be a soothing solace of the unfortunate, an exhilarating uplift for the underprivileged and oppressed. Not to the connoisseurs but to the masses did these (and most) Expressionists hope to appeal. There can be little doubt that *The Song of Bernadette* achieved this Expressionist goal better than any work written in the Expressionist period. Since its aim was to stir the masses rather than to stimulate aesthetes and connoisseurs, it cannot be denied that the facile best-seller and the Hollywood movie were more suitable for communionism than the esoteric Strindbergian form in which it had originally appeared.

Those Expressionists who joined the totalitarian movements and rose in them to heights of power did not essentially betray their Expressionist past either. Not the experimental form but the ecstatic spirit of revolt had been most remarkable about Johst's Expressionist "scenario" *The Young Man*. Nazism promised a perpetuation of this ecstatic state on a nationwide and eventually universal scale. In contrast to the low-pressure bourgeois world, Nazism raised life to a feverish intensity and endowed the commonplace with a strident pitch. It eradicated the privacy of the person which Expressionism, too, had hated and despised; and it drowned isolation in an orgy of communal festivals. At the same time, it confirmed the insight of late Expressionism which had realized that the Utopianism of the activist phase had to be wedded to an existing objective reality if it was not to perish or degenerate. This context of reality was the national, racial, and linguistic community of Greater Germany which Nazism began to postulate around the same period. The confluence of late Expressionism and Nazism was consequently neither a chance happening nor a reversal of the Expressionist current but a natural denouement of basic Expressionist tendencies.

The consistent continuity between activist Expressionism and Communism is even more marked than that between late Expressionism and Nazism. Whereas Nazism was closely related to the second *Wandlung* or recoil of the Expressionists, Communism was reached by numerous Expressionists in a straight line from their first *Wandlung*. Rebellion against his nationalist-bourgeois family and background which propelled Becher to his activist Utopianism soon afterward led him to Communism; and when he joined the Communist movement in the flush of his activist period, Becher was convinced that he continued to travel toward the same goal— the universal brotherhood of the World Commune. After his decision he merely had to adhere to it inflexibly and ignore whatever discrepancies arose between activist dream and Communist reality. His road from lonely outcast and dissenter in bourgeois Germany to boss of culture in Communist East Germany appeared to Becher as a straight and logical course. The powerful rhetorics of his youthful Expressionism had to be jettisoned and changed into the hollow rhetorics of "Socialist Realism," and in this process his poetry lost whatever vigor and strength it had once possessed. But the ideology, the politico-moral content of his Expressionist poetry, which for Becher as for most Expressionists had been of far more vital relevance than the Expressionist form, had in his view simply matured; it had been freed of youthful naïveté, filled with "concrete content," tempered in "the furnace of social reality," wedded to "the truth of the class struggle." Communist actuality fulfilled Expressionist potentiality. Like Werfel, Becher could feel that he had never betrayed his Expressionist beginnings; and his final dignity and power as Communist commissar of culture probably appeared to him as the well-deserved reward of unswerving loyalty to youthful ideals and lifelong convictions. In contemplating Becher's career one wonders whether one should respect his dogged perseverance, despise his blind inflexibility, or admire his skill in self-deception.

Werfel, Johst, and Becher eliminated all traces of Expressionist form from their mature works; but they retained something of the ethical aspirations that, even in their Expressionist period, had mattered more to them than style. However, the totalitarians among them compromised the ideals they retained with the exigencies of reality until only soothing self-deception could claim these ideals as essentially unchanged. What all of them gained was success in personal terms, a mass audience, the triumph of personal integration and power in the world. What they lost was success in aesthetic terms—the permanence and long-range effectiveness of their works. None of them, not even Werfel, whose literary power far surpasses that of the rest, has achieved the rank of a classic.

Those Expressionists who refused to compromise the ideal of "the new man" achieved neither personal nor aesthetic success. In 1939, when Hitler's avalanche began to engulf all of Europe, Toller committed suicide in New York. Long before that he had been a thoroughly defeated and disillusioned man. As early as 1919, he had seen his cause kill itself at the moment of its illusory triumph. Soon afterward his creative energy was exhausted. After he had given voice to his doubts, self-defeat, disillusionment, and despair in *Man and the Masses, Hinkemann,* and *Hoppla, We Live!,* only pale ghosts of his former dramatic vitality issued from his pen.

Even more acutely than Toller, Unruh experienced premature decline from work to work. Unruh never compromised the symbiosis of ethical idealism and experimental form which had been the most salient feature of Expressionism. He refused to make concessions to the facile formulae of commercialism, or the crippling distortions of the ideal perpetuated by totalitarianism. Loyal to the symbiosis, he remained an Expressionist to the end. But his end was inglorious and pathetic. The symbiosis proved to lack the breath of life. It failed to produce viable works of art. The cancer of high-flown and nebulous oratory that had plagued Expressionism from the beginning devoured in Unruh's later works whatever substance there had been in the works of his youth. While Toller in the act of suicide acknowledged personal defeat and historical disaster in one gesture, Unruh suffered a worse tragedy by failing to acknowledge his tragedy. He survived his own significance without comprehending his fate. Unrecognized in his American exile and forgotten in his homeland, he continued to produce in all seriousness works that could no longer be taken seriously. Since he continued to combine the ethical idealism and the aesthetic-formal experimentalism of the movement, Unruh symbolized better than any of his former comrades the ultimate failure of Expressionism. The continued combination of "the new man" with "the new form" had led to oblivion— commercial failure and aesthetic bankruptcy in one.

Utter failure or at best ephemeral success was the fate of former Expressionists who placed the ethical ideal, the gospel of moral regeneration, in the foreground. A very different kind of success came to those Expressionists who had never concerned themselves with hope for "the new man," but had developed new forms in which to express their despair. The poetry of Heym, Trakl, Stramm, and Benn, and the prose of Kafka, form that aspect of Expressionism which is alive and relevant today.[1]

---

[1] As Wolfgang Paulsen in a brilliant article has shown, Georg Kaiser's post-Expressionist drama could be included here. See Paulsen, "Georg Kaiser im expressionistischen Raum: Zum Problem einer Neudeutung seines Werkes," *Monatshefte,* L(1958), 289–303. There is no doubt that Kaiser in his Swiss exile exerted an important influence on the interesting group of young Swiss-German experimental dramatists who have become prominent in Europe since the Second World War—Fritz Hochwälder (a native Austrian who matured in Switzerland), Max Frisch, and Friedrich Dürrenmatt.

Bibliography

Aktion, Die: Zeitschrift für freiheitliche Politik und Literatur (later title: *Wochenschrift für Politik, Literatur und Kunst*). Vols. I–IX (1911–1919), ed. by Franz Pfemfert.

Aktionsbuch, Das. Ed. by Franz Pfemfert. Berlin-Wilmersdorf, Verlag der Wochenschrift *Die Aktion,* 1917.

Anders, Günther. *Kafka: Pro und Contra.* Munich, C. H. Beck'sche Verlagsbuchhandlung, 1951.

Arendt, Hannah. *The Origins of Totalitarianism.* New York, Harcourt Brace, 1951.

Auerbach, Erich. *Mimesis: The Representation of Reality in Western Literature.* Princeton, Princeton University Press, 1953.

Bab, Julius. *Die Chronik des deutschen Dramas.* Vier Teile. Berlin, Oesterheld & Co., 1922.

—— *Neue Wege Zum Drama.* Berlin, Oesterheld & Co., 1911.

—— *Der Wille zum Drama: Neue Folge der Wege zum Drama, deutsches Dramenjahr 1911–1918.* Berlin, Oesterheld & Co., 1919.

Bahr, Hermann. *Expressionismus.* Munich, Delphin-Verlag, 1920 (1st ed., 1916).

Ball, Hugo. *Hermann Hesse: Sein Leben und sein Werk.* Mit einem Anhang von Anni Carlsson. Berlin, S. Fischer, 1927.

—— *Zur Kritik der deutschen Intelligenz.* Bern, Der freie Verlag, 1919.

Barlach, Ernst. *Der arme Vetter.* Drama. Berlin, Paul Cassirer, 1918.

—— *Ernst Barlach: Leben und Werk in seinen Briefen.* Ed. by Friedrich Dross. Munich, R. Piper, 1952.

—— *Ein selbsterzähltes Leben.* Munich, R. Piper, 1948.

—— *Der tote Tag.* Drama in fünf Akten. Berlin, Paul Cassirer, 1919 (1st ed., 1912).

Becher, Johannes Robert. *An Europa: Neue Gedichte.* Leipzig, Kurt Wolff, 1916.

—— *Ein Mensch unserer Zeit: Gesammelte Gedichte.* Berlin, Universum-Bücherei für Alle, 1930.

—— *Verbrüderung: Gedichte.* Leipzig, Kurt Wolff, 1916.

Benn, Gottfried. *Doppelleben: Zwei Selbstdarstellungen.* Wiesbaden, Limes Verlag, 1950.

—— *Essays.* Wiesbaden, Limes Verlag, 1951.

—— "Gehirne," *Die weissen Blätter,* II/2 (1915), 210 ff.

Despite his temporary flirtation with Nazism in 1933, Benn never abandoned the experimental form of his poetry; on the contrary, he developed and matured it to ever greater perfection. After the silence imposed on him by the Nazis, he emerged in the late 1940's as the most representative poet of the Expressionist generation, the only one who had remained both a great artist and faithful to himself. He became an inspiring example for the post-Hitlerite generation of German poets and very few escaped his influence. Closely related to that of Pound and Eliot, his style was helped to fashionable prestige by the decisive influence which Anglo-American literature, and especially T. S. Eliot, acquired in defeated Germany. Benn formed the powerful living link in Germany between the new Anglo-American modernism and the long-forgotten Expressionist modernism once indigenous to Germany, and he did not tire of stressing his kinship with the movement from which he had sprung. His ever-continuing and maturing productivity in post-Hitlerite Germany brought about a revival of interest in the roots of this poetry. Editions of Heym, Trakl, and Stramm appeared, and Fritz Martini's scholarly and critical study of the great poets of early Expressionism (1948) formed a milestone in the rediscovery of the movement by the country which had sought to extirpate its memory.

The most successful of all Expressionists, however, was the one least successful in his life—Franz Kafka, whose work had grown from the same soil as that of the early Expressionists Strindberg, Trakl, and Heym, and whose death in 1924 coincided with the death of the movement. Unlike Benn's, Kafka's art is not at one with the form modernism has taken in other countries. It constitutes the most distinctive gift of German Expressionism to the world. Like most Expressionist dramas, Kafka's novels and late tales are parabolic formulations of existential questions. But what distinguishes Kafka from the contemporary dramatists and constitutes his unique significance is his refusal to go beyond the formulation of questions. Kafka's parables show that nothing can be shown. They convey, not ethical doctrine and moral imperative, but fragmentariness, indeterminacy, and ambiguity as last (not ultimate) meanings to be obtained. Thereby they express the innermost truth of an age which has learned that the nature of answers is the posing of questions.

Benn, Gottfried. *Gesammelte Gedichte.* Wiesbaden, Limes Verlag, 1956.

———— "Die Insel," *Die weissen Blätter,* III/1 (1915), 241 ff.

———— *Nach dem Nihilismus.* Berlin, Kiepenheuer, 1932.

———— *Der neue Staat und die Intellektuellen.* Stuttgart, Deutsche Verlagsanstalt, 1933.

———— *Probleme der Lyrik.* Wiesbaden, Limes Verlag, 1954 (1st ed., 1951).

———— *Der Ptolemäer.* Wiesbaden, Limes Verlag, 1949.

———— "Die Reise," *Die weissen Blätter,* III/3 (1916), 244 ff.

Benn, Gottfried, ed. *Lyrik des expressionistischen Jahrzehnts von den Wegbereitern bis zum Dada.* Wiesbaden, Limes Verlag, 1955.

Blei, Franz. "Reichtum und Literatur," *Die Aktion,* VII/49–50 (1917), 666 ff.

———— *Über Wedekind, Sternheim und das Theater.* Leipzig, Kurt Wolff, 1915.

Brod, Max, "Aktivismus und Rationalismus," in Kurt Hiller, ed., *Tätiger Geist,* 56 ff.

———— "Commentary on Extracts from Franz Kafka's Letter to My Father," translated by Sophie Prombaum, in *A Franz Kafka Miscellany: Pre-fascist Exile,* rev. enl. 2d ed., by Harry Slochower *et al.* New York, Twice A Year Press, 1946.

———— *Die Einsamen.* Munich, Kurt Wolff, 1919.

———— *Franz Kafka: Eine Biographie (Erinnerungen und Dokumente).* Prague, Heinrich Mercy & Sohn, 1937.

———— *Das grosse Wagnis.* Leipzig, Kurt Wolff, 1919.

———— *Heidentum, Christentum, Judentum: Ein Bekenntnisbuch.* 2 vols. Munich, Kurt Wolff, 1921.

———— "Ein menschlich-politisches Bekenntnis: Juden, Deutsche, Tschechen," *Die neue Rundschau,* XXIX/2 (1918), 1580 ff.

———— *Schloss Nornepygge: Der Roman des Indifferenten.* Leipzig, Kurt Wolff, 1918 (1st ed., 1908).

———— "Vom neuen Irrationalismus," *Die weissen Blätter,* I/4 (1914), 749 ff.

———— *Zauberreich der Liebe.* Berlin, Vienna, and Leipzig, Paul Zsolnay, 1928.

Bronnen, Arnolt. "Die Geburt der Jugend," *Die Erhebung,* II (1920), 218 ff.

———— "Vatermord," *Die Erhebung,* II (1920), 155 ff.

Bruggen, Max Ferdinand Eugen van. *Im Schatten des Nihilismus: Die expressionistische Lyrik im Rahmen und als Ausdruck der geistigen Situation Deutschlands.* Dissertation, Amsterdam, 1946.

Buber, Martin. *Daniel: Gespräche von der Verwirklichung,* 2nd ed. Leipzig, Insel Verlag, 1919.

———— *Ekstatische Konfessionen.* Jena, E. Diederichs, 1909.

Camus, Albert. *L'Homme révolté.* Paris, Librairie Gallimard, 1951.

———— *Le Malentendu.* Pièce en trois actes. 15th ed. Paris, Gallimard, 1944.

Carls, Karl D. *Ernst Barlach: Das plastische, graphische und dichterische Werk.* Berlin, Rembrandt Verlag, 1931.

Corrinth, Curt. *Potsdamer Platz oder die Nächte des neuen Messias: Ekstatische Visionen.* Munich, Georg Müller, 1919.

Csokor, Franz Theodor. *Der grosse Kampf: Ein Mysterienspiel in acht Bildern.* Berlin, S. Fischer, 1915.

Cysarz, Herbert. *Zur Geistesgeschichte des Weltkrieges*. Halle, Max Niemeyer, 1931.

Dahlström, Carl Enoch Wm. Leonard. *Strindberg's Dramatic Expressionism*. Dissertation, Michigan, 1930.

Däubler, Theodor. *Wir wollen nicht verweilen: Autobiographische Fragmente*. Dresden-Hellerau and Leipzig, Insel-Verlag, 1915.

Deri, Max. "Naturalismus, Idealismus, Expressionismus," in Max Deri *et al., Einführung in die Kunst der Gegenwart*. Leipzig, E. A. Seemann, 1919.

Diebold, Bernhard, *Anarchie im Drama*. Frankfurt am Main, Frankfurter Verlags-Anstalt, 1921.

—— *Der Denkspieler Georg Kaiser*. Frankfurt am Main, Frankfurter Verlags-Anstalt, 1924.

Edschmid, Kasimir. *Die sechs Mündungen*. Novellen. Leipzig, Kurt Wolff, 1917 (1st ed., 1915).

—— *Timur*. Novellen. Leipzig, Kurt Wolff, 1916.

—— *Über den Expressionismus in der Literatur und die neue Dichtung*. Berlin, Erich Reiss, 1919. *Tribüne der Kunst und Zeit*, No. I.

Ehrenstein, Albert. *Die Gedichte*. Leipzig and Vienna, Ed. Strache, 1920.

—— *Der Mensch schreit*. Leipzig, Kurt Wolff, 1916.

—— *Der Selbstmord eines Katers*. Munich, Georg Müller, 1912.

—— *Tubutsch*. Translated by Eric Posselt and Era Zistel. New York, Ben Abramson–The Profile Press, 1946 (1st ed., 1911).

Eliot, Thomas Stearns. *Collected Poems, 1909–1935*. New York, Harcourt Brace, 1934 and 1936.

—— *The Three Voices of Poetry*. New York, Cambridge University Press, 1954.

Emrich, Wilhelm. "Die Literaturrevolution und die moderne Gesellschaft," *Akzente*, III (1956), 173 ff.

—— "Die poetische Wirklichkeitskritik Franz Kafkas," *Orbis Litterarum*, XI (1956), 215 ff.

—— "Zur *Aesthetik der modernen Dichtung*," *Akzente*, I (1954), 371.

Erhebung, Die: Jahrbuch für neue Dichtung und Wertung. Ed. by Alfred Wolfenstein. 2 vols. Berlin, S. Fischer, 1919–1920.

Expressionistische Dichtungen vom Weltkrieg bis zur Gegenwart. Ed. by Herwarth Walden and Peter A. Silbermann. Berlin, C. Heyman, 1932.

Fivian, Eric A. *Georg Kaiser und seine Stellung im Expressionismus*. Munich, Kurt Desch, 1946.

Fowlie, Wallace. *The Age of Surrealism*. New York, The Swallow Press & William Morrow & Co., 1950.

Frank, Leonhard. *Bruder und Schwester*. Leipzig, Insel-Verlag, 1929.

—— *Der Mensch ist gut*. Potsdam, Kiepenheuer, 1919 (1st ed., 1918).

—— *Die Räuberbande*. Leipzig, Insel-Verlag, 1920 (1st ed., 1914).

—— *Die Ursache*. Erzählung. Munich, Georg Müller, 1916 (1st ed., 1915).

Friedmann, Hermann, and Otto Mann, eds. *Expressionismus: Gestalten einer literarischen Bewegung*. Heidelberg, Wolfgang Rothe Verlag, 1956.

Gilbert, Stuart. *James Joyce's Ulysses: A Study*. 2d rev. ed. New York, Alfred Knopf, 1952.

Goethe, Johann Wolfgang. "Maximen und Reflektionen über Kunst," in Weimarer Ausgabe, I. Abtg., Vol. 48.

Goethes Märchen, mit Einführung und Anhang. Ed. by Johannes Hoffmeister. Iserlohn, Silva Verlag, 1948.

Goll, Iwan. *Dithyramben*. Leipzig, Kurt Wolff, 1918.

———— *Der neue Orpheus: Eine Dithyrambe*. Berlin-Wilmersdorf, Verlag der Wochenschrift die Aktion, 1918. "Der rote Hahn," No. V.

———— "Die Prozession: Dithyrambe," *Die Aktion*, VII/51–52 (1917), 684.

Greulich, Helmut. *Georg Heym (1887–1912): Leben und Werk: Ein Beitrag zur Frühgeschichte des deutschen Expressionismus*. Berlin, E. Ebering, 1931. "Germanische Studien," No. VIII.

Gronicka, André von. "Thomas Mann's Doctor Faustus," *Germanic Review*, XXIII/3 (1948), 206 ff.

Gutkind, Curt Sigmar. "Fritz von Unruh," in C. S. Gutkind *et al., Fritz von Unruh: Auseinandersetzung mit dem Werk*. Frankfurt am Main, Frankfurter Societäts-Druckerei, 1927.

Haftmann, Werner, Alfred Hentzen, and William S. Lieberman, *German Art of the Twentieth Century*. Andrew Carnduff Ritchie, ed. New York, Museum of Modern Art, 1957.

Hain, Mathilde. *Studien über das Wesen des frühexpressionistischen Dramas*. Frankfurt am Main, Moritz Diesterweg, 1933.

Hasenclever, Walter. *Dramen*. Berlin, Die Schmiede, 1924.

———— "Der politische Dichter," in Kurt Pinthus, ed., *Menschheitsdämmerung*, 64 ff.

———— *Der Retter*. Dramatische Dichtung. Berlin, E. Rowohlt, 1919.

———— *Der Sohn*. Leipzig, Kurt Wolff, 1917 (1st ed., 1914).

Heidegger, Martin. *Sein und Zeit*. 7th ed. Tübingen, Niemeyer, 1953.

Henschke, Alfred (pseud. Klabund). "Busspredigt," *Die weissen Blätter*, V/2 (1918), 106 ff.

———— *Gesammelte Romane*. Vienna, Phaidon Verlag, 1929.

———— *Gesammelte Werke in Einzelausgaben*. Vol. III: *Romane der Sehnsucht*; Vol. IV: *Erzählungen und Grotesken*; Vol. V: *Gesammelte Gedichte: Lyrik, Balladen, Chansons*. Vienna, Phaidon-Verlag, 1930.

———— *Kunterbuntergang des Abendlandes: Grotesken von Klabund*. Munich, Roland-Verlag, 1922.

Hentzen, Alfred. See Haftmann.

Heym, Georg. *Gesammelte Gedichte*. Ed. by Carl Seelig. Zurich, Verlag der Arche, 1947.

Heynicke, Kurt. "Lieder an Gott," in Kurt Pinthus, ed., *Menschheitsdämmerung*, p. 154.

———— "Rhythmen gegen die Falschheit," *Die Erhebung*, II (1920), 1 ff.

Hiller, Kurt. *Geist werde Herr! Kundgebungen eines Aktivisten vor, in und nach dem Kriege*. Berlin, Erich Reiss, 1920. *Tribüne der Kunst und Zeit*, Nos. XVI, XVII.

Hoffmeister, Johannes. *Die Heimkehr des Geistes: Studien zur Dichtung und Philosophie der Goethezeit*. Hamelin, Seifert, 1946.

Hoffmeister, Johannes, ed. See *Goethes Märchen*.

Horney, Karen. *Neurosis and Human Growth: The Struggle toward Self-Realization*. New York, Norton, 1950.

Horwitz, Kurt. See Trakl.

Huelsenbeck, Richard. "Die dadaistische Bewegung: Eine Selbstbiographie," *Die neue Rundschau*, XXXI/2 (1920), 972 ff.

Humfeld, Maria Seraphica. *Reinhard Johannes Sorge: Ein Gralsucher unserer Tage*. Paderborn, Ferdinand Schöninger Verlag, 1929.

Johst, Hanns. *Der Anfang*. Roman. Munich, Delphin-Verlag, 1917.

——— *Der Einsame: Ein Menschenuntergang*. Munich, Albert Langen, 1925 (1st ed., 1917).

——— *Ich glaube!* Munich, Albert Langen, Georg Müller, 1928.

——— *Der junge Mensch: Ein ekstatisches Szenarium*. Munich, Albert Langen, 1924 (1st ed., 1916).

——— "Morgenröte: Ein Rüpelspiel," in *Das Aktionsbuch*, pp. 315 ff.

——— *Mutter*. Gedichte. Munich, Albert Langen, 1921.

——— "Resultanten," *Die neue Rundschau*, XXX/2 (1919), 1138.

Joyce, James. *Ulysses in Nighttown*. New York, Modern Library Paperback, 1958.

Junge Deutschland, Das: Monatsschrift für Theater und Literatur, herausgegeben vom Deutschen Theater. Vols. I–II (1918–19). Ed. by Arthur Kahane and Heinz Herald.

Kafka, Franz. "Brief an den Vater," *Die neue Rundschau*, LXIII/2 (1952), 191 ff.

——— *Briefe an Milena*. Ed. by Willy Haas. New York, Schocken Books, 1952.

——— *Dearest Father: Stories and Other Writings*. Translated by Ernst Kaiser and Eithne Wilkins. New York, Schocken Books, 1954.

——— *Gesammelte Schriften*. Ed. by Max Brod. New York, Schocken Books, 1946 (1st ed., 1935).

——— *Hochzeitsvorbereitungen auf dem Lande und andere Prosa aus dem Nachlass*. New York, Schocken Books, 1953.

——— *The Diaries of Franz Kafka, 1910–1913*. Ed. by Max Brod. Translated by Joseph Kresh. New York, Schocken Books, 1948.

——— *The Diaries of Franz Kafka, 1914–1923*. Ed. by Max Brod. Translated by Martin Greenberg, with the co-operation of Hannah Arendt. New York, Schocken Books, 1949.

Kaiser, Georg. *Die Bürger von Calais*. Berlin, Kiepenheuer, 1931 (1st ed., 1914).

——— "Dichtung und Energie (Der kommende Mensch)," *Berliner Tageblatt*, December 25, 1923.

——— *Es ist genug*. Berlin, Transmare Verlag, 1932

——— *Die Flucht nach Venedig*. Berlin, Die Schmiede, 1923 (1st ed., 1922).

——— *Der Geist der Antike*. Komödie in vier Akten. Potsdam, Kiepenheuer, 1923.

——— *Der gerettete Alkibiades*. Stück in drei Teilen. Potsdam, Kiepenheuer, 1920.

——— *Gesammelte Werke*. 2 vols. Potsdam, Kiepenheuer, 1928.

——— "Historientreue," *Berliner Tageblatt*, September 4, 1923.

Kaiser, Georg. *Hölle Weg Erde.* Stück in drei Teilen. Potsdam, Kiepenheuer, 1919. "Der dramatische Wille," No. II.

—— *Die jüdische Witwe.* Bühnenspiel in fünf Akten. Berlin, S. Fischer, 1911.

—— *König Hahnrei.* Berlin, S. Fischer, 1913.

—— *Konstantin Strobel (Der Zentaur).* Lustspiel in fünf Aufzügen. Potsdam, Kiepenheuer, 1920 (first published as *Der Zentaur*, Berlin, S. Fischer, 1916).

—— *Nebeneinander: Volksstück 1923 in fünf Akten.* Potsdam, Kiepenheuer, 1923.

—— *Noli me tangere.* Stück in zwei Teilen. Potsdam, Kiepenheuer, 1922.

—— *Der Protagonist.* Ein Akt Oper von Georg Kaiser. Musik von Kurt Weill. Vienna, Universal-Edition A. G., 1925 (appeared as stage manuscript 1920).

—— *Rektor Kleist.* Berlin, S. Fischer, 1918.

—— "Vision und Figur," *Das junge Deutschland*, I (1918), 314.

Kaiser, Hellmuth. *Franz Kafkas Inferno: Eine psychologische Deutung seiner Strafphantasie.* Vienna, Internationaler Psychoanalytischer Verlag, 1931.

Kameraden der Menschheit: Dichtungen zur Weltrevolution. Ed. by Ludwig Rubiner. Potsdam, Kiepenheuer, 1919.

Kandinsky, Wassily. *Über das Geistige in der Kunst.* Bern, Benteli-Verlag, 1956 (1st ed., 1912).

Kant, Immanuel, *Critique of Aesthetic Judgment.* Translated by James Creed Meredith. Oxford, Clarendon Press, 1911.

—— *Die drei Kritiken: In ihrem Zusammenhang mit dem Gesamtwerk.* Ed. by Raymund Schmidt. Stuttgart, Alfred Kröner Verlag, 1952.

—— *Träume eines Geistersehers, erläutert durch Träume der Metaphysik.* Ed. by Karl Kehrbach. Leipzig, Reclam, 1880.

Kaufmann, Walter. *Nietzsche: Philosopher Psychologist Antichrist.* Princeton, Princeton University Press, 1950.

Kayser, Rudolf, ed. See under *Verkündigung.*

Kayser, Wolfgang. *Das Groteske, seine Gestaltung in Malerei und Dichtung.* Oldenburg, G. Stalling, 1957.

Klabund: See under Henschke, Alfred.

Klages, Ludwig. *Der Geist als Widersacher der Seele.* Leipzig, Barth, 1929.

Klarmann, Adolf D. "Franz Werfel's Eschatology and Cosmogony," *Modern Language Quarterly*, VII/4 (1946), 385 ff.

—— "Gottesidee und Erlösungsproblem beim jungen Werfel," *Germanic Review*, XIV (1939), 192 ff.

Klee, Wolfhart Gotthold. *Die charakteristischen Motive der expressionistischen Erzählungsliteratur.* Dissertation, Leipzig, 1933 (printed Berlin, 1934).

Klemm, Wilhelm. *Ergriffenheit.* Munich, Kurt Wolff, n.d.

—— *Verse und Bilder.* Berlin-Wilmersdorf, Verlag der Wochenschrift *Die Aktion*, 1916.

Koch, Thilo. *Gottfried Benn.* Munich, Albert Langen-Georg Müller, 1957.

Koenigsgarten, Hugo F. *Georg Kaiser. Mit einer Bibliographie von Alfred Löwenberg.* Berlin-Potsdam, Kiepenheuer, 1928.

Kondor, Der. Poems by Ernst Blass *et al.* Ed. by Kurt Hiller. Heidelberg, R. Weissbach, 1912.

Kornfeld, Paul. "Der beseelte und der psychologische Mensch," *Das junge Deutschland*, I (1918), 1 ff.

—— "Himmel und Hölle. Eine Tragödie in fünf Akten und einem Epilog," *Die Erhebung*, I (1919), 93 ff.

—— *Die Verführung.* Eine Tragödie. Berlin, S. Fischer, 1916.

Krieger, Murray. *The New Apologists for Poetry.* Minneapolis, University of Minnesota Press, 1956.

Kutscher, Artur. *Frank Wedekind.* 3 vols. Munich, Georg Müller, 1922–1931.

Landauer, Gustav. *Der werdende Mensch: Aufsätze über Leben und Schrifttum.* Ed. by Martin Buber. Potsdam, Kiepenheuer, 1921.

Lasker-Schüler, Else. *Die gesammelten Gedichte.* Munich, Kurt Wolff, 1920.

—— *Gesichte: Essays und andere Geschichten.* Berlin, Paul Cassirer, 1920 (1st ed., 1913).

—— *Mein Herz: Ein Liebesroman mit Bildern und wirklich lebenden Menschen.* Munich-Berlin, Heinrich F. S. Bachmair, 1912.

—— *Die Nächte der Tino von Bagdad.* Berlin, Paul Cassirer, 1919 (1st ed., 1907).

—— *Der Prinz von Theben.* Leipzig, Verlag der weissen Bücher, 1914.

Lauckner, Rolf. *Schrei aus der Strasse.* Berlin, Erich Reiss, 1922.

Law-Robertson, Harry. *Walt Whitman in Deutschland.* Giessen, 1935. "Giessener Beiträge zur deutschen Philologie," XLII.

Lehmann, A. G. *The Symbolist Aesthetics in France, 1885–1895.* Oxford, Basil Blackwell, 1950.

Lewin, Ludwig. *Die Jagd nach dem Erlebnis: Ein Buch über Georg Kaiser.* Berlin, Die Schmiede, 1926.

Liebermann, William S. See Haftmann.

Lindenberger, Herbert. "Georg Trakl and Rimbaud: A Study in Influence and Development," *Comparative Literature*, X (1958), 21 ff.

Lohner, Edgar, "Die Lyrik des Expressionismus," in Hermann Friedmann and Otto Mann, eds., *Expressionismus*, pp. 57 ff.

—— "Gottfried Benn und T. S. Eliot," *Neue deutsche Hefte*, XXVI (1956), 100 ff.

Lotz, Ernst Wilhelm. *Wolkenüberflaggt.* Leipzig, Kurt Wolff, 1916.

Mallarmé, Stéphane. *Divagations.* Paris, Fasquelle, 1897.

Mann, Heinrich. *Die kleine Stadt.* Roman. Berlin, Vienna, and Leipzig, Paul Zsolnay, 1925 (1st ed., 1910).

—— *Der Kopf.* Roman. Berlin, Vienna, and Leipzig, Paul Zsolnay, 1925.

—— *Madame Legros.* Drama in drei Akten. Leipzig, Kurt Wolff, 1913.

—— *Macht und Mensch.* Munich, Kurt Wolff, 1919.

—— *Die Novellen.* Leipzig, Kurt Wolff, n.d. "Gesammelte Romane und Novellen," No. IX.

—— *Professor Unrat oder das Ende eines Tyrannen.* Roman. Leipzig, Kurt Wolff, 1905.

—— *Zwischen den Rassen.* Roman. Berlin, Vienna, and Leipzig, Paul Zsolnay, 1925 (1st ed., 1907).

Mann, Otto. See Friedmann.

Mann, Thomas, *Doktor Faustus: Das Leben des deutschen Tonsetzers Adrian Leverkühn, erzählt von einem Freunde.* Stockholm, Bermann-Fischer Verlag, 1948.

—— *Doctor Faustus* . . . . Translated by H. T. Lowe-Porter. New York, Knopf, 1948.

Martini, Fritz. *Das Wagnis der Sprache.* Stuttgart, Ernst Klatt, 1956.

—— *Was war Expressionismus?* Urach, Port Verlag, 1948.

Meidner, Ludwig. *Septemberschrei: Hymnen-Gebete-Lästerungen.* Berlin, Paul Cassirer, 1920.

Menschheitsdämmerung: Eine Symphonie jüngster Dichtung. Ed. by Kurt Pinthus. Berlin, E. Rowohlt, 1920.

Myers, Bernard S. *The German Expressionists.* New York, Frederick A. Praeger, 1956.

Nerval, Gérard de. *Selected Writings.* Translated with a Critical Introduction and Notes by Geoffrey Wagner. New York, Grove Press, 1957.

Nietzsche, Friedrich. "The Use and Abuse of History," in *Thoughts Out of Season*, Part 2. 2d ed. Translated by Adrian Collins in *The Complete Works of Nietzsche* (ed. by Oscar Levy), Vol. V. New York, Macmillan, 1911.

—— "Vom Nutzen und Nachteil der Historie für das Leben," *Unzeitgemässe Betrachtungen.* Stuttgart, Alfred Kröner Verlag, 1955.

Otten, Karl. *Die Thronerhebung des Herzens.* Berlin-Wilmersdorf, Verlag der Wochenschrift *Die Aktion*, 1918. "Der rote Hahn," No. IV.

Paulsen, Wolfgang. *Aktivismus und Expressionismus: Eine typologische Untersuchung.* Bern-Leipzig, Gotthelf, 1935.

—— "Carl Sternheim: Das Ende des Immoralismus," *Akzente*, III (1956), 273 ff.

—— "Georg Kaiser im expressionistischen Raum: Zum Problem einer Neudeutung seines Werkes," *Monatshefte*, L (1958), 289 ff.

Picard, Max. "Expressionismus," *Die Erhebung*, I (1919), 329 ff.

Pinthus, Kurt. "Rede für die Zukunft," *Die Erhebung*, I (1919), 398 ff.

—— "Zur jüngsten Dichtung," *Die weissen Blätter*, III/1 (1915), 1502 ff.

Pinthus, Kurt, ed. See *Menschheitsdämmerung*.

Raymond, Marcel. *De Baudelaire au surréalisme.* Paris, Editions R.-A. Corréa, 1933.

Rehm, Walter. "Der Dichter und die neue Einsamkeit," *Zeitschrift für Deutschkunde*, XLV (1931), 545 ff.

Rockenbach, Martin. *Reinhard Johannes Sorge: Auswahl und Einführung.* München-Gladbach, Führer Verlag, 1924.

Rosenberg, Artur. *Die Entstehung der deutschen Republik, 1871–1918.* Berlin, E. Rowohlt, 1928.

Rosenhaupt, Hans Wilhelm. *Der deutsche Dichter um die Jahrhundertwende und seine Abgelöstheit von der Gesellschaft.* Bern-Leipzig, Paul Haupt, 1939.

—— "Heinrich Mann und die Gesellschaft," *Germanic Review*, XII (1937), 267 ff.

Rubiner, Ludwig. "Die Anonymen," *Die Aktion*, II (1912), 299 ff.

———— "Aus der Einleitung zu Tolstois Tagebuch," *Die Aktion*, VIII/1 (1918), 1 ff.

———— "Dichter der Unwirklichkeit," *Der Sturm*, I (1910), 14 ff.

———— "Der Dichter greift in die Politik," *Die Aktion*, II (1912), 646 ff.

———— "Der Kampf mit dem Engel," *Die Aktion*, VII/16–17 (1917), 211 ff.

Rubiner, Ludwig, ed. See *Kameraden der Menschheit*.

Sack, Gustav. *Gesammelte Werke in zwei Bänden*. Ed. by Paula Sack. Berlin, S. Fischer, 1920.

———— *Ein verbummelter Student*. Berlin, S. Fischer, 1917.

Samuel, Richard, and R. Hinton Thomas. *Expressionism in German Life, Literature and the Theatre (1910–1924)*. Cambridge, England, W. Heffer and Sons, Ltd., 1939.

Schering, Arnold. "Die expressionistische Bewegung in der Musik," in Max Deri *et al.*, *Einführung in die Kunst der Gegenwart*, pp. 139 ff.

Schickele, René. *Benkal, der Frauentröster*. Roman. Leipzig, Verlag der weissen Bücher, 1914 (1st ed., 1913).

———— *Der Fremde*. Roman. Berlin, Paul Cassirer, 1913 (1st ed., 1909).

———— *Die Genfer Reise*. Berlin, Paul Cassirer, 1919 (1st ed., 1918).

———— *Hans im Schnakenloch*. Schauspiel in vier Aufzügen. Leipzig, Verlag der weissen Bücher, 1915.

———— *Der neunte November*. Berlin, Erich Reiss, 1919. *Tribüne der Kunst und Zeit*, No. VIII.

Schiller, Johann Christoph Friedrich. *The Aesthetic Letters, Essays, and the Philosophical Letters*. Translated by J. Weiss. Boston, Little and Brown, 1845.

———— "Über die ästhetische Erziehung des Menschen in einer Reihe von Briefen," in Vol. XII of *Sämtliche Werke, Säkularausgabe*, ed. by Oskar Walzel *et al.* Stuttgart, Cotta, 1904–1905.

Schneditz, Wolfgang. See Trakl.

Schneider, Ferdinand Josef. *Der expressive Mensch und die deutsche Lyrik der Gegenwart*. Stuttgart, J. B. Metzler'sche Buchhandlung, 1927.

Schneider, Karl Ludwig. *Der bildhafte Ausdruck in den Dichtungen Georg Heyms, Georg Trakls und Ernst Stadlers*. Heidelberg, 1954.

Schöeffler, Herbert. *Protestantismus und Literatur: Neue Wege zur englischen Literatur des 18. Jahrhunderts*. Leipzig, Täubner, 1922.

Schumann, Detlev W. "Expressionism and Post-Expressionism in German Lyrics," *Germanic Review*, IX (1934), 54 ff., 115 ff.

Seelig, Carl. See Heym.

Simon, Klaus. *Traum und Orpheus: Eine Studie zu Georg Trakls Dichtungen*. Salzburg, Otto Müller, 1955.

Slochower, Harry. See Brod, *A Franz Kafka Miscellany* . . . .

Smith, Grover Cleveland. *T. S. Eliot's Poetry and Plays: A Study in Sources and Meanings*. Chicago, University of Chicago Press, 1956.

Soergel, Albert. *Dichtung und Dichter der Zeit: Eine Schilderung der deutschen Literatur der letzten Jahrzehnte. Neue Folge: Im Banne des Expressionismus*. Leipzig, R. Voigtländer, 1925.

Sorge, Reinhard. *Der Bettler: Eine dramatische Sendung.* Berlin, S. Fischer, 1928 (1st ed., 1912).

————— *Gericht über Zarathustra: Vision.* Munich and Kempten, Verlag Josef Kösel und Friedrich Pustet, 1921.

————— *Guntwar: Die Schule eines Propheten.* Munich and Kempten, Verlag der Josef Kösel'schen Buchhandlung, 1914.

Sorge, Susanne M. *Reinhard Johannes Sorge: Unser Weg.* Munich, Josef Kösel and Friedrich Pustet, 1927.

Spoerri, Theodor. *Georg Trakl: Strukturen in Persönlichkeit und Werk: Eine psychiatrisch-anthropographische Untersuchung.* Bern, Francke, 1954.

Stadler, Ernst. *Der Aufbruch.* Gedichte. Leipzig, Verlag der weissen Bücher, 1914.

Starkie, Enid. *Arthur Rimbaud.* London, Faber and Faber, 1938.

Sternheim, Carl. *Europa.* Roman. 2 vols. Munich, Musarion, 1919–1920.

————— *Die Hose: Ein bürgerliches Lustspiel.* Berlin, Paul Cassirer, 1911.

————— *1913.* Schauspiel in drei Aufzügen. Leipzig, Kurt Wolff, 1915.

————— *Prosa.* Berlin-Wilmersdorf, Verlag der Wochenschrift *Die Aktion,* 1919. "Der rote Hahn," No. XII.

————— *Der Snob.* Komödie. Munich, Kurt Wolff, 1920 (1st ed., 1913).

————— *Tasso oder Kunst des Juste milieu.* Berlin, Erich Reiss, 1921. *Tribüne der Kunst und Zeit,* No. XXV.

Strich, Fritz. See Wedekind.

Strindberg, August. *Plays.* Trans. by Edwin Björkman. New York, Charles Scribner's Sons, 1913.

Sturm, Der: Wochenschrift für Kultur und die Künste. Vols. I–VII (1910–1917). Ed. by Herwarth Walden.

Stuyver, Wilhelmina. *Expressionistische Dichtung im Lichte der Philosophie der Gegenwart.* Dissertation, Amsterdam, 1939.

Tätiger Geist: Zweites der Ziel-Jahrbücher. Ed. by Kurt Hiller. Munich, Kurt Wolff, 1918.

Thomas, R. Hinton. See Samuel, Richard.

Toller, Ernst. "Bemerkungen zu meinem Drama 'Die Wandlung,' " in *Schöpferische Konfession.* Berlin, Erich Reiss, 1920. Pp. 46 ff. *Tribüne der Kunst und Zeit,* XIII.

————— *Briefe aus dem Gefängnis.* Amsterdam, Querido Verlag, 1935.

————— *Hinkemann.* Eine Tragödie. Potsdam, Kiepenheuer, 1925 (1st ed., 1922).

————— *Eine Jugend in Deutschland.* Amsterdam, Querido Verlag, 1933.

————— *Masse-Mensch: Ein Stück aus der sozialen Revolution des zwangzigsten Jahrhunderts.* Berlin, Kiepenheuer, 1930 (1st ed., 1920).

————— *Seven Plays.* Translated by Vera Mendel *et al.* New York, Liveright, n.d.

————— *The Swallow-Book.* Translator not given. Printed in England, at the Oxford University Press, n.d.

————— *Die Wandlung: Das Ringen eines Menschen.* Potsdam, Kiepenheuer, 1925. "Der dramatische Wille," No. III. (1st ed., 1920; fragments of the drama were printed in leaflet form 1917).

Trakl, Georg. *Die Dichtungen: Gesamtausgabe*. Ed. by Kurt Horwitz. Zurich, Verlag der Arche, 1946.

—— *Gesammelte Werke*. Vol. I (1953): *Die Dichtungen*. Vol. II (1953): *Aus goldenem Kelch: Die Jugenddichtungen* Vol. III (1949): *Nachlass und Biographie: Gedichte, Briefe, Bilder, Essays*; ed. by Wolfgang Schneditz. Salzburg, O. Müller, 1949–1953.

Trilling, Lionel. *The Liberal Imagination: Essays on Literature and Society*. New York, Viking, 1950.

Unruh, Fritz von. *Flügel der Nike: Buch einer Reise*. Frankfurt am Main, Frankfurter Societäts-Druckerei, 1925.

—— *Ein Geschlecht*. Tragödie. Munich, Kurt Wolff, 1922 (1st ed., 1917).

—— *Louis Ferdinand Prinz von Preussen*. Ein Drama. Frankfurt am Main, Frankfurter Societäts-Druckerei, 1925 (1st ed., 1913).

—— *Offiziere*. Ein Drama. Frankfurt am Main, Frankfurter Societäts-Druckerei, 1925 (1st ed., 1912).

—— *Platz*. Ein Spiel. Munich, Kurt Wolff, 1920.

—— *Reden*. Frankfurt am Main, Frankfurter Societäts-Druckerei, 1924.

—— *Stürme*. Ein Schauspiel. Munich, Kurt Wolff, 1922.

—— *Vor der Entscheidung*. Ein Gedicht. Berlin, Erich Reiss, 1919.

Valéry, Paul. *Poésies*. Paris, Gallimard, 1950.

—— *Variété*. 14th ed. Paris, Gallimard, 1924.

Verkündigung: Anthologie junger Lyrik. Ed. by Rudolf Kayser. Munich, Roland-Verlag, 1921.

Walzel, Oskar. "Eindruckskunst und Ausdruckskunst in der Dichtung," in Max Deri *et al.*, *Einführung in die Kunst der Gegenwart*, pp. 26 ff.

Wassermann, Jakob. *Caspar Hauser oder die Trägheit des Herzens*. Roman. Berlin, S. Fischer, 1924 (1st ed., 1908).

—— *Das Gänsemännchen*. Roman. Berlin, S. Fischer, 1920 (1st ed., 1915).

—— "Offener Brief," *Die neue Rundschau*, XXI/3 (1910), 999.

Wedekind, Frank. *Gesammelte Briefe*. Ed. by Fritz Strich. Munich, Georg Müller, 1924.

—— *Gesammelte Werke*. Munich and Leipzig, Georg Müller, 1913.

Weissen Blätter, Die: Eine Monatsschrift. Vols. I–V (1913–1918).

Wellek, René. *A History of Modern Criticism*. Vols. I and II. New Haven, Yale University Press, 1955.

Weltmann, Lutz. "Kafka's Friend, Max Brod: The Work of a Mediator," *German Life and Letters, New Series*, IV/1 (1951), 46 ff.

Werfel, Franz. *Barbara oder die Frömmigkeit*. Berlin, Vienna, and Leipzig, Paul Zsolnay, 1933 (1st ed., 1929).

—— "Brief an Georg Davidsohn," *Die Aktion*, VII/11–12 (1917), 152 ff.

—— *Einander: Oden, Lieder, Gestalten*. Munich, Kurt Wolff, 1920 (1st ed., 1915).

—— *Erzählungen aus zwei Welten*. Vols. I–III of *Gesammelte Werke*, ed. by Adolf D. Klarmann. Stockholm, Bermann-Fischer, 1948–1954.

—— *Die Mittagsgöttin*. Munich, Kurt Wolff, 1923 (1st ed., 1919).

—— *Nicht der Mörder, der Ermordete ist schuldig*. Munich, Kurt Wolff, 1920.

Werfel, Franz. *Spiegelmensch: Magische Trilogie.* Munich, Kurt Wolff, 1920.
———— "Substantiv und Verbum: Notiz zu einer Poetik," *Die Aktion,* VII/1–2 (1917), 4 ff.
———— *Verdi: Roman der Oper.* Berlin, Vienna, and Leipzig, Paul Zsolnay, 1930 (1st ed., 1924).
———— *Die Versuchung: Ein Gespräch des Dichters mit dem Erzengel und Luzifer.* Leipzig, Kurt Wolff, 1913.
———— "Vorwort," to *Die schlesischen Lieder des Petr Bezruč, verdeutscht von Rudolf Fuchs.* Leipzig, Kurt Wolff, 1916.
———— *Der Weltfreund.* Erste Gedichte. Leipzig, Kurt Wolff, 1918 (1st ed., 1911).
———— *Wir sind.* Neue Gedichte. Leipzig, Kurt Wolff, 1917 (1st ed., 1913).
Willibrand, William Anthony. *Ernst Toller and His Ideology.* University of Iowa, Humanistic Studies, VII. Iowa City, Iowa, 1945.
Wolfenstein, Alfred. *Jüdisches Wesen und neue Dichtung.* Berlin, Erich Reiss, 1922. *Tribüne der Kunst und Zeit,* No. XXIX.
———— *Mörder und Träumer.* Drei szenische Dichtungen. Berlin, Verlag Die Schmiede, 1923.
———— *Die Nackten.* Eine Dichtung. Leipzig, Kurt Wolff, n.d.
———— "Das Neue," *Die Erhebung,* I (1919), 1 ff.
———— "Novelle an die Zeit," *Die weissen Blätter,* II/3 (1915), 701 ff.
Worringer, Wilhelm. *Abstraktion und Einfühlung: Ein Beitrag zur Stilpsychologie.* Munich, R. Piper, 1948 (1st ed., 1908).
Zech, Paul. *Die eiserne Brücke.* Neue Gedichte. Leipzig, Verlag der weissen Bücher, 1914.
———— *Das trunkene Schiff: Eine szenische Ballade.* Leipzig, Schauspiel-Verlag, n.d.
Das Ziel: Aufrufe zu tätigem Geist. Ed. by Kurt Hiller. Munich, Kurt Wolff, 1916.

Index